ELIZABETHAN LIFE
IN TOWN AND COUNTRY

QUEEN ELIZABETH
(*From Camden's " Annals "*)

ELIZABETHAN LIFE
IN TOWN AND COUNTRY

M. ST. CLARE BYRNE, M.A.

ALAN SUTTON
1987

ALAN SUTTON PUBLISHING
BRUNSWICK ROAD · GLOUCESTER

First published in 1925
by Methuen and Co. Ltd

British Library Cataloguing in Publication Data

Byrne, Muriel St. Clare
Elizabethan life in town and country.
1. England—Social life and customs—
16th century
I. Title
942.05′5   DA320

ISBN 0-86299-323-7

Printed in Great Britain by
The Guernsey Press Company Limited
Guernsey, Channel Islands

PREFACE

FOR its author this book has taken on something of the nature of a serial " to be continued in our next," acquiring in the course of seven editions an extra introductory chapter, new material, revised and up-to-date select reading lists, some revised or rewritten appendices and additional chapter-notes. Personal friends, therefore, to whom for thirty years the original preface has offered my warmest thanks for their help, will I hope forgive me if now I use this space to record two other debts of gratitude which have been running over-long without acknowledgment—the first to readers from various parts of the world who write either asking or giving further Elizabethan information, and the second to my publishers who have not merely suffered this progressive expansion but have positively encouraged it, even to the extent of allowing me extra paper when the war-time shortage was acute. It was a book which I enjoyed writing, which was reward in itself. That it should still meet with this live response, while new books on the age multiply steadily, is reward beyond anything that the young writer of 1925 could have dared to hope. Any pleasure, moreover, that it may have given its readers has been fully repaid by this encouragement to keep in touch with the progress of modern Elizabethan studies when my own research interests moved back to the earlier half of the century.

When this book was being written, interest in things Elizabethan, in literary and scholarly circles, was at a low ebb. One's friends were more interested in medieval or modern history, and in seventeenth or eighteenth century literature. In the introductory chapter added ten years later I tried to convey the feeling of that earlier mood of disinherited Victorianism. Ten years later again, revising another edition in the summer months of 1944, it was obvious that Elizabethan scholarship had more than come back into its own, and, in particular, that readers and writers alike had become profoundly interested in the picture of society and the understanding of its structure and modes and habits of thought. What happened to me, in the process of writing this book (cf. p. 11), was in fact significant of a change in attitude which was presumably affecting all serious Elizabethan students, had already borne fruit in Elizabethan bibliographical and historical studies of a highly specialized kind, and was to come to a climax in major works and general surveys by the nineteen-forties. I fell in love with the documents—with inventories and bills and household accounts, letters and diaries, houses and furniture, with the ordinariness of life, which gave my book its theme and consequently its use during the ensuing years and its modest place among its betters. For by 1944 everybody had fallen in love with social history.

One of the very real satisfactions this book has brought me is the knowledge that it has led many readers to the full-length authoritative studies of the subjects briefly touched on in these chapters. To keep still within the range of the restricted outlay possible to those for whom it was originally planned—the general reader, the university student, the sixth-former—it must remain a general introduction to the age : a thumb-nail sketch, comparatively speaking. But I shall think this new edition most happily justified if it directs its readers in particular to Mr. A. L. Rowse's magnificent full-length " portrait of the age " in *The England of Elizabeth*, for the completion of which we are all eagerly waiting. In it, and in the recent additions to Elizabethan scholarship of which I have tried to give some indication in notes and lists, there lies a wealth of interest which will amply repay exploration. Incidentally, it has been reassuring to find, among all these diverse studies and varying opinions, much support at the highest level for the belief I set down in my original preface, to which I still hold—that the hero is Everyman and the presiding deity Elizabeth the Queen.

MURIEL ST. CLARE BYRNE

LONDON
May 1954

CONTENTS

INTRODUCTION

THE nineteenth century sang and shouted with enthusiasm when it stumbled upon the treasure trove of the Elizabethans and their literature. Critics and historians united to lavish approval upon these progenitors after their own hearts. The echoes were still reverberating in the early nineteen hundreds. Even twenty years ago, Symonds, who in the eighties had so completely included and exemplified the view of the ultra-romantics, was still entirely acceptable. His brilliant colours were habitually borrowed to splash most canvases. The age was picturesque—" one of those rare periods when the past and the future are both coloured by imagination, and both shed a glory on the present. The medieval order was in dissolution : the modern order was in process of formation. Men stood, as it were, between two dreams— a dream of the past, thronged with sinister and splendid reminiscences : a dream of the future, bright with unlimited aspirations and indefinite hopes. Neither the retreating forces of the Middle Ages, nor the advancing forces of the modern era pressed upon them with the iron weight of actuality."[1]

Nous avons changé tout cela. The First World War made a difference to our temper. When our tercentenary homage to Shakespeare had been well and truly paid, Elizabethan enthusiasm cooled down somewhat. Scholarly and literary interests focussed themselves on the seventeenth and eighteenth centuries ; Elizabethan dramatists were at a discount, except as material for bibliographical research ; and veracious and scandalous narratives unearthed in the Public Record Office began to give the impression that Hobbes's description of the natural state of man was an accurate summary of Elizabethan life—" poor, nasty brutish, and short." By 1925 Mr. E. M. Forster was

[1] J. A. Symonds : *Shakespeare and his Predecessors.* 1884.

expressing what many had thought, but few had the courage to say : " Do you wish you had lived in the days of Queen Elizabeth ? I am thankful to have escaped them. The noise, the hopefulness, the vitality, the cant about chastity —I should have found them hard to bear, nor would a Reformed Religion have consoled. Gone was the dear Pope, overseas, underground ; gone the traditions that echoed out of the past and whispered of future unity, and in their place, closing every vista, stood a portentous figure shaped like a dinner-bell. The hard reverberations of this creature filled the air, her feet twinkled in a septuagenarian dance, she made progresses and rude metallic jokes, she exploited a temper naturally violent, she was a public virgin—and all she did she did for the honour of England." It is the counterblast comprehensive to Symonds, and its final word is that the Elizabethans " were at once too violent and too hazy to contribute much towards the development of the human mind." [1]

It was inevitable that Symonds's fancy picture should be roughly handled. His " past and future coloured by imagination " and both " shedding a glory on the present " was sheer nonsense. Elizabeth's grandfather won the Battle of Bosworth in 1485. The past that people still remembered as the experience of their grandfathers—far too near to be splendid or glamorous or anything but a terrible memory—was the Wars of the Roses. Civil war, cutting—so far as the nationally-minded Elizabethan could see—at the very roots of England's existence, impoverishing her, destroying her princes and nobles—that was the past which gave fearful point to Shakespeare's frequent utterances on the subject of national unity. Nor was the immediate past any more favourable to glorified reminiscence. " Sinister," indeed, it was, with the blazing fires of Smithfield as the background against which was silhouetted for the whole of Mary's reign the vision of an England doomed to become a mere appanage of Spain. There was little glory or satisfaction in retrospect for either religious party—little but bitterness and hatred. The old

[1] E. M. Forster : *Peeping at Elizabeth. Nation and Athenæum.* August 8, 1925.

order of life had been left stricken by the intensity and vigour of Henry's attack upon it : the new had as yet no roots. Calais was lost, and with it the last of our military credit abroad. The Treasury was empty; the coinage debased, the country impoverished—and, on all sides powerful and potentially hostile nations were waiting to see what they could get out of England under the rule of a young woman of twenty-five. And as for the " dream of the future, bright with unlimited aspirations and indefinite hopes "—it is even more sentimental and hopelessly opposed to the actuality. For monarch and ministers it is doubtful if the foreign sky has ever looked much gloomier. For the Protestant party there was trouble brewing from the very beginning of the reign, as soon as they realized that a compromise, based on national expediency, and not a wholesale reformation based upon religious principles, was to govern the Queen's policy towards the Church throughout. On the other side, never, assuredly, has there been a more unhappy position than that of the honest Catholic patriot in Elizabeth's reign—forced, in the end, to choose between his country and his religion.

We can dismiss more quickly the nasty and brutish anecdotage. Police-court news was no more the real clue to an age, nor its brief epitome, then, than it is now. It can never sum up a civilization. Mr. Forster is more elusive. It is more difficult to demonstrate one's conviction that his neo-Georgian imagery and idiom are only a little nearer the truth than Symonds's Victorian equivalent. But his final joke—entertaining though it may be—is double-edged, and dangerous. To call Elizabeth " a public virgin " is to say the thing well enough to make us think ; and that is fatal—to the joke. For as soon as we begin to think we begin to realize the tremendous implications of the phrase. *It is true* : what, therefore, does it mean ? It means that while Elizabeth calculated to a nicety the practical and political uses of her perpetual virginity, it had, in itself, an infinitely greater and quite incalculable " metaphysical " value. We need not seek to understand the worship accorded to virginity from earliest times, nor even the later romantic devotion to spotless maidenhood which was such a large part of the chivalric ideal. It is enough to recognize that when the Roman Catholic Church directed this stream of feeling throughout the Middle Ages into the especial cult of Our Lady it was canalizing and harnessing something amazingly powerful, something instinctive, and deeply rooted in the more emotional and imaginative side of the religion of simple people. For energy of this kind a channel must always be found, and it is by no means fanciful, therefore, to suggest that when the Reformation left this tremendous force undirected and unorganized, it found in the Virgin Queen of England a not altogether unsatisfactory substitute for the Virgin Queen of Heaven, as a focus of devotion. It is difficult otherwise to account for the emotional response amounting almost to worship which the name and idea of Elizabeth inspired in the men of her time. Henry VIII might commandeer legislation to establish the supremacy of State over Church : but the hearts of men are not altered by act of parliament. Elizabeth of England, virgin queen, earthly divinity, set star-like in the midst of the somewhat austere intellectualities of the reformed theology, met the psychological need of her people as no Tudor prince could ever have done, and thus lured their hearts to that new devotion which made possible the triumphs of her reign.

The modern mood, in certain of its manifestations, may be expected to find Elizabeth and the Elizabethans altogether too hearty. Wit, at their expense, however, will only appeal to the few. For most people romance still touches their figures with a legendary brightness ; and the pronouncement which has carried most weight, and has been most frequently quoted of recent years, is that of the late Lytton Strachey, in the first chapter of his " Elizabeth and Essex." He speaks of our desire to " reach to an imaginative comprehension of those beings of three centuries ago," but concludes that " the path seems closed to us." He finds the Elizabethans strangers : " The more clearly we perceive it, the more remote that singular universe becomes. With very few exceptions possibly with the single exception of Shakespeare—the creatures in it meet us without intimacy." " It is, above all," he continues, " the contradictions of the age that baffle our imagination and perplex our intelligence. Human beings, no doubt, would cease to be human beings unless they were inconsistent; but the inconsistency of the Elizabethans exceeds the limits permitted to man. . . . How is it possible to give a coherent account of their subtlety and their *naïvete*, their delicacy and their brutality, their piety, and their lust ? . . . How is it conceivable that the puritans were the brothers of the dramatists ? What kind of mental fabric could that have been which had for its warp the habits of filth and savagery of sixteenth-century London, and for its woof an impassioned familiarity with the splendour of "Tamburlaine" and the exquisiteness of "Venus and Adonis "? Who can reconstruct those iron-nerved beings who passed with rapture from some divine madrigal sung to a lute by a bewitching boy in a tavern to the spectacle of mauled dogs tearing a bear to pieces ? "

It is a passage seriously written, and for rhetorical appeal and force is worthy to be put beside Symonds'; but the view of the age which it presents is, I believe, as fundamentally false. Boiled down, or stripped of its glitter, that paragraph means that the contrasts and contradictions with which the age presents us are too great to allow us to accept the Elizabethans as credible human beings. It is as profitable to ask whether we can believe that the " Midsummer Night's Dream " and " Troilus and Cressida " are the work of the same artist, as to ask if it is credible that the puritans were the brothers of the dramatists. The " filth and savagery of sixteenth-century London " make an admirable background to "Tamburlaine," which is certainly a splendid thing, but neither a delicate nor a subtle one, and with a good share of savagery. The " exquisiteness " of "Venus and Adonis " might be alien to the filthy alleys and gutters of Elizabethan London, but it was certainly at home in the lovely London gardens which were just as much a part of the city scene. And as for the purely rhetorical juxtaposition of the madrigal and the bear-baiting—it is the type of contrast which can be found in any age. Our own contemporaries can enjoy the exquisite delicacy of a book like " The Bridge of San Luis Rey," and pass on to the spectacle of a stag-hunt, or of an otter being torn to pieces by terriers. Contrast and contradiction we must allow, but not therefore Mr. Strachey's denial of intimacy. We might as well deny our intimacy with our own age, on the ground that the inconsistencies between the pictures of our civilization presented by James Joyce and Mrs. Virginia Woolf " exceed the limits permitted to man." To accept Mr. Strachey's argument is equivalent to allowing that the contrast between the vulgarity, the crudeness and the immensity of life in " Ulysses," and the exquisiteness, the delicacy, the sensitiveness and the seclusion of spirit in " Mrs. Dalloway " and " To the Light-house " ' baffle our imagination.'

The modern novel and modern drama should by now have taught us something of the selection and use of signifi-cant detail for the purpose of characterization. The settings described in a novel like Wells's " Marriage," or in the stage directions of Granville-Barker's " Voysey Inheritance " or " The Madras House " should give us the clue for the method of our own approach to another age. As the significant detail accumulates so it should lead us towards intimacy—not, indeed, a particular intimacy with the individual, but that general intimacy with the average man and his ordinary ways of thought, which is the first step if we are to go on to an understanding of a Francis Bacon or any other remarkable personality. We know exactly what to think of the rectory family in " Marriage " when we discover that their black and gold piano is " sur-mounted by a Benares brass jar, enveloping a scarlet geranium in a pot." The literature, and even more particu-larly the records of the Elizabethan age are rich in just this kind of detail. The effigy of the Elizabethan ancestor looks a forbidding object—distorted by buckram and busks of steel, swollen by puffs and padding, deformed by peascod-bellied doublets, telescoped by enormous ruffs and farthin-gales. But strip it of these lendings, and it becomes the poor forked radish who liked a fire in his bedroom and flowers about his house, and who wanted his shirt and his sheets properly aired. He went sightseeing, and delighted to scribble or carve his name upon ancient monuments ; he thrust and jostled for glimpses of royalty ; and he had second-best tablecloths to lay over his best table-carpets for ordinary occasions. He gave, or expected tips, according to his social standing—" a shilling to drink " is the phrase provided by the conversation manuals for the guidance of the foreigner. And being an Englishman he had already begun to cook his cabbage as abominably as he still does, so that a Frenchman was driven to remark of this national dish, " They say commonly in England that God sendeth us meat and the Devil cooks ! " Surely it is the height of pedantry to deny our intimacy with him.

Schoolboys disliked early rising, little girls slouched over their lesson-books, or else lost them, great ladies bought their silk stockings by the half-dozen, and in Sir John Harington's household the stairs were " done " regularly every Friday. Could we ask for a more illuminating comment upon both the life and character of their owner, and upon the age, when the Kenilworth Castle inventory reveals the fact that in his gallery the Earl of Leicester kept the portraits of Counts Egmont and Horn, and, also, the portrait of Alva of the unspeakable atrocities?[1] Fitting mementoes for a Protestant nobleman, leader of the English troops in the Low Countries, who had also managed skilfully to weather the Catholic storm of Mary's reign, and had at one time been willing to intrigue with Philip of Spain, in return for the promise of that monarch's support of his wild scheme for marriage with Elizabeth ! Even when the Elizabethan manner of life appears to show the

---

[1] Counts Egmont and Horn were Flemish patriots during the period of Philip of Spain's dominion in the Netherlands. With William the Silent they had refused to be instrumental in enforcing upon the Protestant Netherlands the Catholic edict of the Council of Trent. In consequence, as soon as opportunity offered, they were judicially murdered by Alva, Philip's general, as part of his régime of terrorism. They were arrested for treason ; and although as Knights of the Golden Fleece they could only be condemned by their peers of that order, they were executed without trial in 1568.

widest divergence from ours a solitary phrase will often take us straight to the core of their thought. The Elizabethan use of the word " housekeeping " has to be explained for us, if we are to realize that it meant the keeping of open house, the offering of hospitality to any stranger at the gate who claimed it. Read, however, an Elizabethan nobleman's instructions to his domestics for dealing with the departure of such guests : " See the chambers to be well and handsomely dressed up, *and that nothing be missing.*" Their ways may be strange, but their behaviour, we realize from the last five words, was as our own would have to be, if we lived as they did. Is it possible to deny consanguinity and intimacy with the minds and characters that lie behind and are revealed by such details ?

Admittedly there are stumbling blocks—the filth and brutality, for example, that perplexed Mr. Strachey and which it would be absurd to attempt to deny. It is unsound, however, to over-emphasize this aspect of Elizabethan life. Such things are always relative, and it is doubtful if we shall fare much better ourselves, at the hands of the impressionist writer in the twenty-third century. Emphatic assertion of the filth and squalor of another age makes the picture generally accepted because it is vigorous and definite. In consequence, the evidence for filth has been given *in extenso* and too much stress laid upon the unpleasant habits of our Elizabethan ancestors by those in search of the picturesque. Here again, however, if we are on the look-out for instructive detail we shall realize that the truth lies in some more modified description, such as we ourselves might give if attempting to handle modern conditions. As an example—in Chapter II of this book reference is inevitably made to the Elizabethan custom of strewing the floor with rushes ; and, as usual, Erasmus's unflattering description of the appalling filth that was allowed to accumulate in them and to be left lying for years is also cited. Every schoolboy knows Erasmus and the rushes : the description is lurid, and not easily forgotten ; whereas the abundant evidence, given by household accounts, to show that fresh rushes were continually supplied, and that rooms were cleaned and swept, is not in the least picturesque. We can, however, give Erasmus picture for picture—not to cancel, but to balance. In his " English Romayne Lyfe " (1582) Anthony Munday has occasion to comment upon the cleanliness of a flight of steps in the church of St. John Lateran in Rome. He describes how the worshippers go up and down these stairs on their knees, and then, looking round for an image to drive home vigorously his own acute sense of their appearance, and realizing instinctively that the homely and familiar is the best image to make vivid something remote and strange, he writes, " with the number that creep up and down these stairs daily *they are kept as clean as the fine houses in London, where you may see your face in the boards.*"

Symonds and Mr. Strachey gave us their own imaginative reactions to the general atmosphere of the Elizabethan age, which is a very different thing from the background of daily life against which we want to place the Elizabethans and their literature. A superb gesture like the defeat of the Armada, or the trumpet-blast that we call *Tamburlaine*, are not, in the real and contemporary sense, part of the background. Background, to the Elizabethan, was an affair of " shoes and ships and sealing wax, of cabbages and kings "—a mixture, like the conversational efforts of the Walrus, but a familiar mixture, and definitely comprehensible, within our imaginative grasp. It is difficult to approach the Elizabethan mind by way of anything so perfectly of its period as " The Faerie Queen " : it is easy to approach by way of the Elizabethan abundance of significant detail. Shoes and sealing wax . . . Roger, Lord North, losing hundreds of pounds to the Queen " at play," and sending his shoes to be resoled at a shilling a pair . . . the typical school seal of the period—in idea, a mixture of benevolence and violence, symbolized by some such design as an elderly gentleman, accompanied by an open book and several small children, flanked by a birch-rod of superhuman dimensions . . . In things like these the trend and range of the contemporary imagination express themselves in the simplest terms.

And if we follow up the Walrus's catalogue it will bring us to an aspect of the Elizabethan background of which little mention can be made in the following pages, owing to the natural limitations of the book, which is concerned not with the speculation of the Elizabethan mind but with the detail of daily life. Midway between these two realms, however, partaking of the nature of both, compact at once of factual and imaginative value, lies Drake's world-encompassing " Golden Hind." Before the time of the Tudor dynasty the larger background of life was the cosmos as limited when seen through the distorting glass of authority and the medieval church. After the Tudors it becomes much more the microcosmos of the individual soul. But the Elizabethan, in his life and literature, bestrides the *theatrum orbis terrarum*, literally and imaginatively. It is significant that his literature contains not one but two epics of his seven-leagued boots—Hakluyt and Purchas. His great historical enterprise is nothing less than a "History of the World " : even in prison nothing short of the world will satisfy a Raleigh for his subject matter. The mind of a Bacon cannot be content with less than an *Instauratio Magna*, or scientific process for the acquisition of all knowledge. Symonds describes the age as free from the iron weight of actuality, but as a matter of fact the actuality of life was terrific. When Drake circumnavigates the globe in the " Golden Hind " human endeavour and adventure have caught up on the human spirit, and go hand in hand with it. The reach of man no longer exceeds his grasp. He is master of his circumstance. His world is spanned—set in the scheme of things as something comprehended by his mind. It is the beginning of the actuality in which we have lived ever since, and it gives us yet another bearing upon the Elizabethan imagination.

So by way of those immortal English cabbages, badly cooked, we should come to the climax—kings. To realize that, from the Elizabethan point of view, it is the real climax, is quite essential to an understanding of the age.

It is the fashion, nowadays, in the biographies of great individuals of the past to insist upon their private lives ; and to aim at depicting first and foremost a credible human being. It is a method which provides good reading, but is often of singularly little use if we happen to wish to re-capture something of the contemporary impression. In the present instance argument and conjecture as to the amiability of Elizabeth's character are of no help : what matters is the apprehension and acceptance not of a human being of genius, but of that image of a queen which she herself created of herself for the adoration of her people.

In the following chapters no attempt is made to chronicle the achievements of the age. They are concerned entirely with the ordinary things. They aim at substituting for the highly coloured and rhetorical descriptions of the Elizabethans and their manner of life something more nearly related to contemporary fact. The romantics have given us, each in his own way, an imaginative synthesis, evolved too exclusively from the literature of the age. It gives us something, but at a distance of more than three hundred years not nearly enough. The brutal anecdotists suggest what should be added, sending us whenever possible to all the books that are not literature—letters, diaries, state papers, accounts, documents, legal records. We read in the records of the Privy Council notes of annual payments of £10 to one Jones for keeping the Council Room clean and supplied with flowers : we realize, from his laundry bills, that a country gentleman staying in London sent half a dozen shirts and six or eight handkerchiefs to the wash each week ; and we soon find ourselves echoing Dr. G. B. Harrison : " Even in Elizabethan England the majority of men were reasonably honest and genuinely charitable. They paid their debts, they were faithful to their wives, fond of their children, and they died in their beds as peacefully as the physician would allow them." The idea of the Elizabethan background which can be built up in this way from significant detail will not compare for picturesqueness with the impressionist versions. It will be too homely and unsensational. Background is not a thing to be conveyed to other people in terms of one's own perception of effective and dramatic contrasts. We need to make up our minds as to what was normal to the Elizabethans, before allowing the imagination to play over the surface and isolate the telling moments. For any real understanding we must first perceive the normal pattern of human thought and activity.

January 1934

POSTSCRIPT IN 1944

It was significant of the lack of illuminating specialist comment that in 1934 one turned for expression of the modern attitude to writers such as Strachey and E. M. Forster—eminent as critics, but neither of them fundamentally in sympathy with the essential qualities of the Elizabethan age. It is the sign of a healthier state of affairs that in these ten intervening years scholarship has again begun to tackle its own business. I quoted Strachey's rhetorical question in order to protest against the uncritical acceptance of the answer which its form implied and encouraged ; but also because its real core—that is, " What kind of mental fabric . . . ? "—was a key question. The basic material for a reasoned answer had been assembled before he wrote : notably in Henry Osborn Taylor's *Thought and Expression in the Sixteenth Century* (1920) and Lewis Einstein's *Tudor Ideals* (1921), which gave simple objective accounts of the characteristics of renaissance culture and of the carry-over of the ideas of the Middle Ages into the Tudor period. But with the honourable exception of Hardin Craig's *The Enchanted Glass* (1936)—still, I think, the foremost as well as the first of its kind—literary studies were slow to follow the historian's lead ; and not until recently was it obvious that investigation of the background of thought and of the commonly accepted ideas of the age had become the focal point of enquiry. It is disconcerting, however, to find the " meddling intellect " in danger of manufacturing difficulties which for the ordinary man do not and need not exist ; and to find, still, a tendency to echo Strachey

and emphasize the strangeness, the queerness, the other-
ness of the age. Unless this challenge is met more com-
prehensively than is possible here, we shall find ourselves
burdened with a conception that is a positive hindrance both
to literary appreciation and to historical understanding.

It seems ungracious to quarrel with so lucid an exposition
of the thought of the age as Dr. Tillyard's recent *Elizabethan World Picture*; but when he concludes with the
verdict that to us it is " a very queer age ", and the substance of his book " a very queer affair ", it would be dis-
honest for a writer concerned to show Elizabethan life as
on the whole a very normal affair to ignore his opinion.
It is true that we have examined different sets of facts ;
but ultimately we are dealing with the same thing—the
Elizabethans and their age. If he is concerned with their
idea of cosmic order, I am concerned with their idea of
order as displayed in their methods of running their state,
their institutions, their households. And if a particular way
of thinking is rightly to be described as queer, then its
reflexion in matter and action which we call ' the life of
the time ' must be queer too. We cannot both be right
in our opposed conclusions ; and when he re-affirms
Strachey's view by attributing to Elizabethan England
" standards of hygiene, decency and humanitarianism
which would make a modern sick " it is time to ask,
" Which modern ? " " Which standards ? " and finally,
" Why ? " Unless we are equally sickened by the material
and spiritual standards of twentieth century England
revealed in such documents as *Our Towns*, *Branch Street*,
Working Class Wives, *The Road to Wigan Pier*, *Brighton
Rock*, *None but the Lonely Heart*, and others too numerous
to mention, it is unreasonable to stress the alien quality
and the ' other-ness ' of the Elizabethan mentality which
tolerated such standards until this ' modern ' England
has set its own house in order. For dirt, squalor and
" man's inhumanity to man " there is not a ha'porth to
choose between them.

" To see ourselves again we need not wait for Plato's
year " : and of this, I think, Dr. Tillyard is as fully con-

vinced as I am. But to insist on the differences without balancing them with the kinship is to get the picture out of focus, and also to confess ourselves out of touch with the comprehensive reality of our own time. In seeking to understand the Elizabethan mind it is just as necessary to notice the carry-over of metaphor as the discarding of so-called facts—more necessary, indeed, if we are not to underestimate continuity and tradition and their absolute importance in literary and historical criticism, for to-day's fact is to-morrow's discarded theory, but the metaphor tends to persist, in life as in literature. The sun does not rise and set, but the metaphor remains valid as description of experience : it is not merely fossilized fact. We cannot very well quarrel with the Elizabethans' idea that the plague was God's punishment for their sins, when among many sections of the community to-day we find the same metaphor in use, and this present war felt and described and understood as God's punishment for our sins. A generation which has taken astrology sufficiently seriously to make it one of the most paying features of popular journalism is ill-qualified to regard Elizabethan ideas as curious. Our secular superstitions may differ, but in their quality they imply a similar level of credulity in large masses of the population ; and that they do not necessarily differ even in kind is suggested by the following extract from a recent letter in one of our most popular dailies, (offered for comparison with p. 249) : " This is not so old-fashioned. A friend of mine, with a child 3 years old, is at present giving the mite stewed mice for bladder trouble—and is curing her. Of course, she buys clean healthy mice from a pets' store."

To stress an affinity in social standards and the ways of daily life and thought, however, will not meet the other part of Dr. Tillyard's contention, that the Elizabethan way of thinking about the nature of the universe and of the social organism was ' queer '. And there is, I think, a real danger in this insistence : the danger not only of encouraging in the tyro the attitude of " 'ere's a stranger— 'eave 'arf a brick at 'im ! ", but of leaving out of count for oneself the very basis and procedure of poetry. A single example must serve—the statement that it is a measure of this Elizabethan queerness that " it should really *matter* to Spenser that he should insert Platonic ideas into the order of Heaven ". One does not have to be a Spenser nor born into the Rennaissance to know the moment of illumination when the idea of the Platonic Ideas is first grasped and known as something of infinite worth. Allowing that great literature is concerned with fundamental truths, and that serious thought is concerned with the problem of including all such truths in the current scheme of belief, the only thing I find impossible is that it should *not* have mattered to Spenser to make such truth fit into the contemporary scheme of heavenly order. If this is ' queer ', then it is equally queer that it should really matter to Tennyson to find some way of including in his picture of world order the idea of evolution as well as the idea of personal immortality, and equally queer that we should seek to reconcile the truths of religion and science.

It is unwise to overlook the pictorial or essentially picturesque quality of the Elizabethan world picture. It was not a record of fact, but of imaginative response to sensation and perception, expressed almost entirely by image, analogy and metaphor. And because it was embodied in the great literature of the age it is still very largely our picture. Balance the affinities in outlook and metaphor against changed notions of the material universe brought about by the progress of scientific enquiry, and although the sum will be different from ours it will not be any queerer. In a sense the shoe is on the other foot. The average half-educated modern, reared on what Dr. Joad has called " the petrified science of fifty years ago ", and lagging well behind the physicists in his belief that only the material world is real, accepts the idea that his world is as insignificant in relation to the universal scheme of things as a grain of sand is to this great globe, and that he himself, far from being the central point of creation, is a mere accident or by-product. This he ' knows ' as his world picture ; yet he still feels and behaves as if " the last utterance of doom " is nothing, and " the bearing of man facing it is all ". Which was reasonable for his Elizabethan brothers-in-arms at Flores or Arnhem, but is surely very queer—or Elizabethan—of the man who fights such immortal actions as the *Jervis Bay* or the bridge at Arnhem, at a time when the human race has so successfully convinced us by practical demonstration of its power and will to wipe itself off this purposeless planet.

Of significant differences in the pattern of ordinary life I am as convinced as Dr. Tillyard—notably the supreme importance of religion and the fundamental seriousness of life : differences which I stressed in 1925 as I would still (see pp. 155, 257, etc.).   But ' queerness ' is another matter —a matter of opinion, which must, I believe, be challenged. To give a clear account of the notions reflected in the Elizabethan picture he has presented them as so many facts, as annotations of the Elizabethan text : insisting, rightly, that the Elizabethans took these notions seriously. Seriously, yes ; but also much more pictorially than we take our facts to-day, and more as Sir Thomas Browne took them : "The severe Schools shall never laugh me out of the Philosophy of *Hermes*, that this visible World is but a picture of the Invisible, wherein as in a Pourtraict, things are not truely, but in equivocal shapes." It is not the facts themselves that give us real insight into the Elizabethan mind, but the way the poet handles them, the use to which literature puts the facts then available in order to give us a reading of life that can still be understood and admired, can still satisfy. That is the ultimate standard of measurement. In the historical sense, the Elizabethan comment is not queer : it is not alien to our feeling and our understanding, not unaccountable as a development, not a pocket in human continuity. I would rather hazard a guess that future historians may find us a good deal queerer.

CHAPTER I

ENGLAND'S ELIZABETH AND ELIZABETH'S ENGLAND

IT is no mere literalism to say that without Elizabeth there would have been no Elizabethan age. The Tudors all had powerful and interesting personalities, but it is significant that only the last of them has given her name to an epoch. With all the faults of her remarkable race, all its admitted kinks and perversions, she yet created in a whole people a passionate loyalty, half personal, half national, wholly English, which was the one thing necessary if the promise of the destiny of Tudor England was to be fulfilled. It is perhaps most simply explained by saying that she possessed that touch of genius for kingship which had been denied to her calculating grandfather and lost by her undisciplined father. It is difficult to form a sober estimate of her character. It has been blackened by many : and it has obviously baffled many an otherwise competent historian. Vain she may have been, fickle, unreasonable, hard, vacillating, contradictory : the list of her unpleasant traits is familiar to every one. Burghley may have saved her from disaster time after time ; it is Froude's now somewhat discredited thesis that his was the real directing brain. As speculation it is most of it beside the point ; take away " England's Elizabeth," put in her place some docile figure-head of a monarch, and not all the statesmanship of two Burghleys could have piloted the age to its splendid destiny. It was no grey-bearded minister who elicited that amazing efflorescence of national enthusiasm which bound together high and low, Catholic and Protestant, into one people, so that the nation was enabled to resist the aggression of Spain at that most crucial period in its history. It was a young woman of twenty-five, beautiful then, whatever havoc the years may afterwards have made ; a princess, who by her sufferings and persecution had already won the sympathies of all classes ; a Tudor, with all the mental vigour and dominating qualities of that family—it was, finally, a naturally gifted and extremely well-educated young woman, with all her father's charm of personality, who had been schooled and disciplined for over ten years by some of the most bitter experience that has probably ever fallen to the lot of young royalty. Burghley may be responsible for much, but he is not so fundamental to our understanding of the age as the fact of the queenship of Elizabeth.

Opinions may well differ as to whether or not her character was an estimable one, but here again argument tends to obscure the essential fact ; estimable or not, her character was the right one for the situation—it made her alive to the needs of the moment, and it made her sensitive to the feeling of the nation as none of her predecessors had ever been. Whatever she may have lacked she was at one with her people in their national ardour and their hatred of Spanish aggression. Hence she became to them almost the incarnation of their own nationalism, as well as its focus and its directive genius. When we venture farther we tend to find ourselves on slippery ground ; all her life Elizabeth managed to disappoint and mislead conjecture, and we to-day fare little better than those ambassadors and others who in committing their opinions to paper have left us due warning of the difficulty of fathoming her motives and her methods. Tudor, queen, and woman ; through that threefold obscurity of statecraft, officialdom, and femininity what documentary searchlight can really hope to penetrate ? Only Elizabeth herself, perhaps, could have plucked out the heart of her mystery ; the secret does not lie open in any archives.

It is not difficult, however, to know what the people she ruled thought about her. Elizabeth herself may escape us, but the impression she made is fully recorded, and somehow a great many essentials seem to have crept in. One thing, for example, which is always being repeated, not only in the avowed panegyrics, but as a commonplace, is the statement that she gave her country peace. It sounds curious, when we think of such facts as the Spanish Armada, of expeditions to the Netherlands, of the unceasing Irish troubles, of conspiracies and Jesuit alarms at home. Nevertheless it is substantially the truth ; what her people instinctively recognized was that, under Elizabeth, strong and stable government, concentrating solely on the good of the country, had replaced politicians with axes of their own to grind, and had out of civil chaos evolved order and " the Queen's Peace." The court might be the haunt of speculators, and the scene of a greedy scramble for wealth and position ; favourites might come and go, and the mere courtier who was up one moment might be down the next : but Burghley stood firm. Troubles might arise, but they would not involve the ordinary individual in disaster, because there was a strong central authority to deal with them. An Essex might bring his rash head to the block, but there was no great dramatic ministerial fall throughout the whole reign. At the centre of things there was a feeling of stability which the country had not known since Henry VII's time or the early years of his son's reign. Restoration of the coinage, rigid national economy, compromise on difficult problems such as religion, cautious avoidance of collision with foreign powers—the whole policy of the early part of the reign gave a materially exhausted but spiritually vigorous nation the opportunity to recuperate after the troublous years of Edward VI and Mary.

Naunton's assertion that " she ruled much by faction and parties, which she herself both made, upheld and weakened " [1] is also very revealing. The cautious Burghley might be her minister, and able, according to Leicester

[1] "Fragmenta Regalia," 1641.

to " do more with her in an hour than others in seven years," but Leicester the favourite was also of her Council, and leader of a more progressive and belligerent section. One faction balanced the other, and neither was all-powerful ; both sides of a question might be fully thrashed out in a Council meeting, but while there was a forward party and a conservative party there could be no doubt at all that the final and deciding factor was the Queen. No one was permitted to encroach upon the royal prerogative ; the nation realized this, and expressed its realization, quite naïvely, partly in its amazement that a woman could do what she did :

> She rul'd this Nation by her selfe,
>   And was beholden to no man ;
> O she bore the sway and of all affairs,
>   And yet she was but a woman.

So runs one of the popular ballads that laments her death.[1] Her people were certainly not under the impression that Burghley was the Queen ; Essex may have persuaded himself that he could twist her round his little finger, but both Burghley and Leicester knew far too well the real state of affairs ; it is not from their correspondence that a puppet queen can be pieced together.

Two other verses of this same funeral ballad show us again some of the traits upon which the nation had seized :

> A wiser Queen never was to be seen
>   For a woman, or yet a stouter ;
> For if anything vext her, with that which came next her,
>   O how she would lay about her !

> And her scholarship I may not let slip,
>   For there she did so excel
> That amongst the rout, without all doubt,
>   Queen Bess she bore the bell.

Elizabeth chose wise ministers, but she chose them to carry out her will for her people. In pursuit of England's welfare she was absolutely single-minded and stout-hearted

---

[1] Ashmole MS. 36, 37 ; fol. 296r and v.

all her days, and this England realized, so that even her imperious temper becomes matter for elegiac praise. The temper which could deal out to a foolishly presuming courtier a box on the ear was also the temper which showed a fearless front to any personal danger, and which spoke unhesitatingly for herself and her people when she reviewed the troops before the Armada : " We have been persuaded by some that are careful of our safety to take heed how we commit ourselves to armed multitudes for fear of treachery, but I do assure you I do not desire to live to distrust my faithful and loving people. Let tyrants fear : I have always so behaved myself that under God I have placed my chiefest strength and safeguard in the loyal hearts and good will of my subjects. . . . I know I have the body of a weak feeble woman, but I have the heart and stomach of a King—and of a King of England too, and think foul scorn that Parma or Spain or any prince of Europe should dare to invade the borders of my realm." Whether, as an utterance, this is literal and authentic is beside the point ; some willing historian, anxious to record the address, may have been driven to compose it himself, but if so then it illustrates even more forcibly the thing about Elizabeth which really matters—the fact that this was the kind of utterance she had been able to make people imagine would be hers.[1]

That her people fully believed in Elizabeth's devotion to her country was perhaps never more strikingly evinced than in the long-winded preamble to the grant of taxes passed by the Commons in 1601. Elizabeth and her Commons might—and did—clash, for Elizabeth's peace was rapidly educating a vigorous and self-assertive nation, anxious to think and manage for itself ; nevertheless, each realized their interdependence and the unanimity of their

[1] The earliest known version of this speech is to be found in *Cabala*, an anonymous collection of letters of the great, published in 1651. It forms part of a letter from Dr. Leonel Sharp, at one time chaplain to Queen Elizabeth and also to the Earl of Essex. His statement is :—" The Queen made an excellent oration to her army, which the next day after her departure I was commanded to redeliver to all the army together." (See *History* : N.S., Vol. X, pp. 226–7, 1925.)

aim. Stripped as far as possible of its verbiage this preamble is a magnificent testimony to the affection and understanding which existed between ruler and subjects :

" Forasmuch as . . . we have sufficiently perceived how great and inestimable charges your Majesty hath sustained many years in seeking . . . to hinder all such foreign attempts as . . . might long since have proved perilous to the whole estate of this commonwealth ; and where it is apparent to all the world that if your Majesty had not exhausted the greatest portion of your private treasures . . . we should long before this day have been exposed to the danger of many sudden and dangerous attempts of our enemies, and failed in all those happy successes which have accompanied your royal actions taken in hand for the defence of this estate ; . . . for as much as we do seriously consider that your Majesty and we your faithful and obedient subjects are but one body politic . . . and that no good or felicity, peril or adversity can come to the one but the other shall partake thereof . . . being fully resolved to leave both lands, goods, and whatsoever else that is dearest unto us, yea and this mortal life, rather than we would suffer your royal estate to be in any part diminished, or the imperial crown of this realm deprived of any honour, title, right or interest thereunto belonging . . . we have thought meet not only to make it one of our first works to consult of that matter, which in other sessions of parliament hath usually succeeded many other acts and consultations, but so to enlarge and improve the measure of this oblation which we shall offer to your royal person, as it may give your Majesty an assured testimony of our internal zeals and duties . . . in a manner far exceeding any former precedent, *because no age either hath or can produce the like precedent of so much happiness under any prince's reign, nor of so continual gracious care for our preservation as your Majesty hath shewed in all your actions, having never stuck to hazard, or rather neglect for our preservation any part of those worldly blessings wherewith Almighty God hath so plentifully endowed you in this time of your most happy government:* and therefore we do with all duty and humble affections that heart can conceive or tongue can utter, present to your sacred Majesty four entire subsidies, and eight fifteenths and tenths toward your Highness' great charges for our defence." [1]

It is a documentary tribute that cannot be explained away, or alienated to the great Burghley in his three years' grave. It is said that the men of the English navy were half starved and unpaid at the moment when the Armada was threatening our shores, and many historians have attributed this simply and solely to Elizabeth's parsimony, condemning her in no half-hearted terms. It may be true : her grandfather was reputed a mean man, and Elizabeth undoubtedly cut down court expenses ruthlessly : but what the long tax-preamble makes clear to posterity is that the national imagination conceived of its queen as a ruler ready to sacrifice her personal wealth for the national good, even as the people themselves were ready. One may prove irrefutably that it was extremely unreasonable of the national imagination to behave in this way, and that the nation would have been much better employed in investigating this scandalous treatment of itself as an underfed seaman. One may quote with disapproval Sir Christopher Hatton's saying that " the Queen did fish for men's souls, and had so sweet a bait that no one could escape her network." [2] The fact remains that Elizabeth and the national imagination between them made a success of the nation's affairs—a most unreasonable success, because, as Pope Sixtus V pointed out at the time, Elizabeth and her England were braving the two greatest kings of Europe both by land and sea.

The passionate, personal loyalty which Elizabeth deliberately fostered in every possible way for the sake of her country was largely cultivated by her policy of showing herself to her people, especially on important occasions. All their devotion and every chivalric sentiment was kept

[1] See " Statutes of the Realm, 43 & 44 Eliz. cap. XVIII." A slightly longer excerpt than this given above is given in Prothero, "Select Statutes," p. 106, 1913.
[2] See Harington, " Nugæ Antiquæ," II, 136 ; 1779.

vivid and alive by her constant progresses and visits throughout the kingdom, and by such things as the *beau geste* of her appearance at the head of her troops at Tilbury on the eve of the Armada. As a supplement to the usual anecdote about John Stubbes who, when his right hand was cut off for writing against the French marriage, seized his hat in his left hand and cried " God save the Queen ! " it may be allowed to cite here a less known but equally suggestive story. In an Oxford college library there is preserved an Elizabethan schoolboy's " Cæsar," in which, after the manner of his kind in all ages, he has scribbled freely. There is his own name and a date : " John Slie his book 1589 " : and from the fact that he has scribbled on most of the blank pages, and the margins of no less than thirty-one others we may infer that he was not conspicuously virtuous. Nevertheless, on the empty pages what he has scribbled most often is the name " Elizabeth," and when he takes to versifying—which he does prettily enough—it is in the vein and even the words of the schoolboy of to-day, except for his last line :

> John Slye—is my name
> And with my penn—I writ the same.
> God that made both—sea and land
> Give me grace—to mende my hand ;
>
> .   .   .   .
>
> The rose is redd—the leves—are grene
> God save—Elizabeth—our noble—Quene.[1]

How many a schoolboy since has tagged out " The rose is red, the violet's blue " with " Sugar's sweet and so are you " : but what sprang naturally to John Sly's tongue was " God save Elizabeth our noble Queen." She was something ever present and potent in the hearts and minds of her people. She sustained to perfection that most exacting and effective of royal parts, that of the approachable divinity. The Gloriana of the poets, the Queen who was served and attended with the most elaborate and stately ceremonial, was also the friendly monarch of

[1] " An Elizabethan Schoolboy and his Book," A. M. Bell ; reprinted from " The Antiquary " in " Gleanings after Time," ed. G. L. Apperson.

popular approval who enjoyed such incidents as that of the good man who came to salute her when on progress in Huntingdonshire, and who, walking up to her coachman, said, " Stay thy cart, good fellow, stay thy cart, that I may speak to the Queen."[1] The " fair vestal throned by the west," whom her greatest poets delighted to celebrate, was also the theme of the Westminster school-boy's jingle. Therein lay her strength, and no one has proclaimed it more often than Elizabeth herself : " My mortal foe," she wrote to Stafford, one of her ambassadors in France, " can no ways wish me a greater harm than England's hate ; neither should death be less welcome unto me than such a mishap betide me."

Dekker in his " Wonderfull Year " (1603) describes the dead queen whom he is lamenting as " having brought up (even under her wing) a nation that was almost begotten and born under her." It was no mere exuberance of speech, it was the literal truth. Her strict control had nursed her people through perilous years into a strong nation. She had kept order for them until they were fully able to manage their own affairs. By the time her task was over England was ready to embark upon the adventure of governing herself. Opportunist as she was, serving always the need of the immediate present, it was yet given to her to serve also the whole future of her race.

Alike in town and country the process of the transition from the medieval to the modern state was at its height in Elizabeth's reign. The growth of London and the development of trade, the complete change in the very nature of our entire rural economy, our interests in the New World, our importance in the European situation committed us fully to the new order, and made any going-back impossible. And although it had not come to pass in her time, Elizabeth had prepared the way for the most radical change of all—the change from Tudor absolutism to parliamentary government. 1641 cast long shadows before : all through Elizabeth's reign the House of Commons had been trying its strength and learning its powers,

---

[1] See Puttenham, " Arte of English Poetry," III, 22.

and the Queen, though she might be peremptory with
these critics of her actions, took no firm steps to undermine
their position. The practical supremacy was still hers,
and that sufficed her practical mind which looked to the
immediate present and the matter in hand. But the
Stuart dynasty never had a chance from the beginning ;
Elizabeth had served her country's need so effectually,
given it peace in which to develop and grow, that by the
time her long reign was over she had enabled her people
to outgrow the need of her and her kind.

From the preceding pages, then, something may be
gathered of the impression Elizabeth made upon her
people. Whether or not we can feel that this gives us
the truth about her character, it was at least her effective
simulacrum, the idea that she had been able to create in
men's minds. It was by the projection into their imaginations of a personality of this kind, whether real or assumed,
that she was able to achieve her ends for England. The
legends, the scandals, the private character, all sink into
insignificance beside the inspiration that was the Queen.

Of the character of the England that she ruled it is
much less easy to speak briefly. In the fascination which
it possesses both for the student and for the general reader
no epoch of English history has ever rivalled the Elizabethan. No age is more intensely national in its feeling,
none captures more easily our assent to its mood.
Elizabeth's was the reign which finally and definitely
raised England to the position of a first-class power in
Europe ; it was the reign which saw English literature
develop into the peer and rival of the best that France or
Italy could produce ; it was in these years that the full
quickening effect of the Renaissance was felt in this
country. With these facts embedded as it were in our
national consciousness it is not surprising that most people
approach the age predisposed to yield their minds to its
multifarious attraction.

As the result, the popular imagination has seized upon
Elizabeth's " spacious times " as its rightful province ;
here it locates a " merrie England " that never was, which

it peoples with chivalrous and splendid figures. In the nursery we assimilate the Elizabethan legend and form our associations, Raleigh and the cloak, Drake with his game of bowls and the treasures of the Spaniard, Leicester balanced precariously between the sinister suggestions of Amy Robsart's death and the "princely pleasures" of Kenilworth. If we embark upon serious study, however, modern scholarship leading us in a painful pursuit of the truth does its best to disillusion us at all points. It dismisses the picturesque anecdotes as apocryphal, it assures us that Elizabethan society was corrupt through and through, it reveals only too clearly the plagiarisms and the dullnesses of certain sections of Elizabethan literature. By the studied moderation of its terms and its abnegation of enthusiasm it tends, most unfortunately, to alienate the interest of all but the avowed specialist.

This is not only unfortunate, it is surely unnecessary, for the modern scholar has under his hand something much more romantic than the anecdotist has ever been able to provide. Documents by themselves may be dry reading to those not skilled in their interpretation, and literature by itself has for many a tinge of unreality ; but working together in friendly alliance, illuminating and reinforcing each other, they reveal that most fascinating of all secrets —the ordinary way of life of other people. By the time these two have revealed to us all that they can, they will, if kept to this working alliance, bring us back to our starting point with our apprehensions enlarged, and our enthusiasm undiminished. Alone, either may give us an undue bias : together they can reconcile the contradictions of instinct and knowledge. Together they will give us instead of our "Merrie England," Elizabeth's England, and however accurate and unillusioned our new conception may be it can never be devoid of the old splendour provided always we keep in touch with literature.

We may take the Court as a definite example of the necessity for this alliance. The documents, as Mr. Hubert Hall has shown, reveal the Elizabethan courtier as "greedy and remorseless " [1]; this, however, is no more the whole truth than the opposite idea that the courtier was a magnificent and heroic figure. If we try to picture the Court of Elizabeth we find, on the one hand, that it was quite as corrupt and unpleasant a place as the gloomiest democrat could wish, but, on the other, that it was also something rather magnificent in its own way. It was overrun with place-seekers, all scrambling for perquisites, offices, money, favour ; but it was also undeniably the focus ot the national life. It drew to it the clever mountebanks, but also the real vigour and talent. It captured and stimulated men's imaginations, even if, eventually, it disheartened and disgusted them. A pretty figure of a man might attract the Queen's passing regard, but it took something more to win substantial advancement. It took Sir Christopher Hatton twenty-three years' use of an able brain as well as a nimble toe to dance his way to the Lord Chancellorship. Raleigh may have attracted attention in the first instance by his six feet of " handsome and well compacted person," his dark hair, his splendid clothing, and his " bold and plausible tongue," but the favour that came his way was not un-worthily bestowed upon one of the most enterprising and original minds of the age.

For literary men like Spenser and Lyly the Court was a place of disappointment and hope deferred : " a thousand hopes, but all nothing ; a hundred promises, but yet nothing," [2] is the cry of the latter, and the sum of more than twenty years of vain expectation. Waiting for the post that never materialized he writes : " After ten years' tempest I must at the Court suffer shipwreck of my times, my hopes and my wits " ; he implores the Queen for " some plank or rafter to waft me into a country where in my sad and settled devotion I may in every corner of a thatched cottage write prayers instead of plays, prayers for your long and prosperous life, and a repentance that I have played the fool so long " [2]—" so pitiful a thing is

[1] " Society in the Elizabethan Age," Chap. VII.
[2] See Harleian MS., 1323, ff. 249-50, printed in Bond's edition of Lyly's " Works."

suitor's state," as Spenser commented on his own somewhat similar experience.

Spenser eased his heart of its chagrin in his poetry: " each man's work is measured by his weed," he cries in scorn ; " a good bold face " and big words are the would-be courtier's best qualification ; and the Court itself is a place

> Where each one seeks in malice and with strife
> To thrust down other into foul disgrace,
> Himself to raise.

But having spoken freely he can then remind us that there was another and finer aspect of Court life, that among the place-seekers and the adventurers there moved

> Full many persons of right worthy parts,
> Both for report of spotless honesty
> And for profession of all learned arts.

In the brightest jewel of that Court, in that "noble and matchless gentleman " Sir Philip Sidney the poet found the living counterpart of his ideal courtier :

> . . . all his mind on honour fixed is,
> To which he levels all his purposes,
> And in his Prince's service spends his days,
> Not so much for to gain or for to raise
> Himself to high degree, as for his grace,
> And in his liking to win worthy place . .
> For he is fit to use in all assays,
> Whether for arms and warlike amenaunce,
> Or else for wise and civil governaunce,
> For he is practised well in policy,
> And thereto doth his courting most apply . . .
> Such is the rightful Courtier in his kind.

In this and in his other tributes to Sidney, Spenser brings us as near as possible to an explanation of the paradox of Elizabeth's Court. It lies in the new conception of the courtier, which became possible under the Tudor monarchs : at their courts men took their places as the counsellors of princes not by inheritance merely, but by fitness and education as well. Apart from the fact that the policy of all the Tudor reigns was to curb the power and the erstwhile semi-royal importance of the older nobility, these monarchs, being extremely well-educated themselves, prized culture and fitness in their servants. They all had due regard to birth and breeding—it is worth while investigating the antecedents and connections of some of the prominent figures of Elizabeth's Court before laying undue stress upon their purely "upstart" quality. But the way lay open for men other than the scions of a few great families : it lay open to all who could conceive the new ideal of the courtier—the man liberally educated, trained for all affairs of State, fashioned into a gentleman or "noble person by virtuous and gentle discipline," the man ready to develop every power and capacity he possessed to fit himself for the service of his prince and his country.

That was the ideal that the Elizabethan age set before itself ; its imagination bodied forth the perfect Court and the perfect courtier, and it saw its brave imaginings realized sufficiently often in the lives of such as Sidney to avoid disillusionment. It was not so much what Elizabeth was, but what men conceived her to be, that mattered ; it was not the Court of the sycophants and the place-grabbers that mattered, but the Court and the courtier that the nation's imagination could conceive that was the potent thing, focusing men's actions and desires. Its "valuable reference" is not the squalid documentary records of monopolies, bribery, and favouritism, but Spenser's "Faerie Queene" and Raleigh's Virginian voyage. The Court of Gloriana existed, not in any point of time or space, but in the minds of men. And this paradoxical duality that was true of queen and Court was also true of the nation at large : the journalism of the age is of a lively character, and the impression we receive is not edifying : the documents are apt to be depressing if not actually scandalous ; but however much journalism and documents may perplex our minds it is easy enough to realize that other values existed when we turn to the real literature of the age. The former give us the material aspect of life, invaluable in its place and of the highest interest; but the spiritual index is to be found in a Shakespeare and a Spenser. It is posterity's privilege to take cognizance of intention and ideal, as well as of the actuality.

It is not given to a nation in every age to see visions ; but in Elizabeth's time we were in the youth of our realization of ourselves as a nation, and able to imagine its future on the grand scale. It is in its imagination that we find the real clue to the age and its tremendous activity. In its capacity to conceive greatly of the end and aim of life for the individual, in the unanimity with which the individual was able to identify his personal aim with the national aim, and in the combination, with these fused and identified aims, of a sufficient scope and opportunity for the desire of service to materialize in action, lies the secret of the Elizabethan strength. In the following pages it will not often be possible to recur to this aspect of life ; they will be concerned with the material values, and the concrete items which form the essential substratum of fact. But because fact alone cannot always tell us the truth, may even definitely mislead, it is necessary here to emphasize the point that the journalism and the documents from which any such account as this must largely be written cannot, by themselves, explain what every one has at some time or other felt (and rightly felt)—that overwhelming appeal to our imaginations which starts us off with a predisposition to find in this particular period of our history an interest which no other ever quite manages to rival.

Of the character of the Elizabethan people there is no need to speak here. The aim of the rest of this book is to present this character as it appears in contemporary literature and records, and to attempt to give, mainly from the same sources, an account of the Elizabethan way of life. It is safer to approach the subject by this method, for to generalize is to risk submersion by the contradictions, or in the end to be committed to a thesis. It is much wiser not to try to prove anything about the Elizabethan character or the Elizabethan age ; there is more to be gained in the long run simply by observing both. When it comes to a comparison with the present day any resultant generalization usually boils down to the old stale: " Human nature does not alter very much." Taken separately, however, the details of life reveal just those slight differences which give a fascination to such exploring. It is the " portrait of an ancestor " that we are examining, and the features are familiar, but the ruff and doublet and the novel background against which he has taken his stand invite our curiosity by their strangeness.

Note.—For more detailed accounts of Court life and ceremonial, and of what the Elizabethans understood by " service ", reference can be made to E. K. Chambers' " Elizabethan Stage " (Vol. i, Bk. I, Chaps. 1–3), and to the present writer's chapter on " The Social Background " in " A Companion to Shakespeare Studies " (ed. Barker and Harrison). For a recent estimate of the Queen's character see Rowse's *The England of Elizabeth*, Chap. VII, The Government of the Realm. For a hitherto unpublished contemporary account, see *Certain Observations concerning the Life and Reign of Queen Elizabeth by John Clapham*, ed. E. P. and Conyers Read (1951). For selections from her official speeches see *The Public Speaking of Queen Elizabeth*, ed. G. P. Rice (1951). For her letters see *The Letters of Queen Elizabeth*, ed. G. B. Harrison (1935) ; and *Letters of Queen Elizabeth and King James VI of Scotland*, ed. J. Bruce, Camden Soc. (1849). For a vivid picture of Elizabeth and her Court see *De Maisse : A Journal . . . 1597*, translated and edited by G. B. Harrison and R. A. Jones (1931) ; and for a brilliant succinct account of patronage, place-seeking, faction and power at Court see J. E. Neale's *The Elizabethan Political Scene* (British Academy Raleigh Lecture on History, 1948).

CHAPTER II

THE ELIZABETHAN AT HOME

IT is the private antiquities of a bygone age which always appeal most to the ordinary man and woman. For one who will appreciate the sonnets of a Sidney there are, at a safe estimate, many hundreds who can appreciate the beauty of his Penshurst home. The houses Elizabethan folk lived in, the beds the Queen slept in, the clothes men and women wore and the food they ate have an immediate and direct interest for us all. Inessential in themselves as such things may be, they yet serve to bring us extraordinarily close to the men and women and the life of the time. Domesticities, provided they are sufficiently remote, have a charm of their own, and a real use : they help to give us our orientation in a strange land. We feel reassured and more at our ease when an Elizabethan hostess offers us oysters with salt and pepper and vinegar and brown bread as a *hors d'œuvre*. We know where we are when we find a Frenchman complaining about our badly cooked cabbage.[1]

Almost inevitably, therefore, one begins by exploring the Elizabethan house, appraising the taste of its inmates and their habits, observing their behaviour at meals, and forming some estimate of the ordinary domestic background of the age.

Scattered here and there throughout the country there were a few fourteenth and fifteenth century houses such as Penshurst and Haddon Hall which showed that the Middle Ages had already realized that comfort and beauty as well as adequate protection might be considered when house planning. Early sixteenth century English building

[1] Readers not already acquainted with the ordinary sources of information such as Harrison's " Description of England " will find the references given in this chapter easier to follow if they will first consult the preliminary bibliographical note on p. 286 (General Section).

4

concentrated still more upon these first two attributes, but it also inclined to keep up its defences. It is not until Elizabeth's reign that the new style becomes really established. Elizabethan architecture means domestic architecture ; it means houses designed and built as dwelling houses, and not designed to withstand a siege.

Elizabethan, as an architectural term, covers two distinct kinds of houses : it includes the timber and plaster manor house and the yeoman's dwelling, and it also includes the stately Italianate palaces erected by such men as Burghley and Hatton, of which a fine though only partially surviving example can be studied in Kirby Hall, Northamptonshire. To both types, however, there were common two ideals, namely, symmetry and domestic comfort. The former was the gift of Italy, the latter of peace at home ; and between them they made possible and characteristic the first—and to many people the most interesting—period of English domestic building. Under their influence the window becomes an element of comfort and also of beauty and design ; the turret and the battlemented coping are retained simply for their picturesque effects. The moat and the drawbridge give way to formal gardens and magnificent terraces ; on nothing did the new age lay its impress of distinction and elegance more effectively than on its houses and their immediate surroundings.

The influence of Italian ideas was at first evident mainly in details of finish, such as tracery and carving ; and throughout the reign it was only in the most palatial buildings that complete symmetry of design really ousted the national preference for a more irregular and haphazard plan. Even when symmetry prevailed the disposition of the rooms followed the English tradition. The popular E- and H-shaped houses, for example, were only the natural result of a further and symmetrized adaptation of our medieval idea of house planning. The essence of the home had been the hall, the common meeting ground for gentle and simple ; then, as society began to develop other needs besides food and sleep, servants' quarters and family quarters had more or less imperceptibly attached them-

selves to opposite sides of the hall, and this relationship
between the different parts of the house was preserved in
both the E and H shaped dwellings. That the former
might also be construed by loyal-minded subjects into a
compliment to the Queen, though it was assuredly not the
origin of the ground-plan, was undoubtedly an extra
attraction.

Apart from its rejection of defensive appurtenances, the
windows, doorways, and exterior ornaments are the surest
signs of Elizabethan origin in a house. Flattened pointed
and semicircular doorway arches are typical of the Tudor
reigns and continue right into the early years of the
seventeenth century ; square-headed mullioned windows
are completely characteristic of Elizabeth's reign and the
following—earlier Tudor windows were flat pointed or
cusped, but the plain, square head belongs to the latter
half of the sixteenth century only. In exterior ornamenta-
tion on the more pretentious Elizabethan and Jacobean
houses the most noticeable and easily remembered features
are the classic pilasters, of no structural value, and the
classic cornice which in these reigns was substituted for
the ubiquitous medieval string course.

The most striking employment of windows as part of
the design of an Elizabethan house is seen in the sym-
metrical use of bays and oriels, neither of them new in
building construction, but found previously isolated where
the Elizabethan architects arranged them in balancing pairs
or groups. Both bays and ordinary windows were
frequently, in large houses, carried up the full height of
the façade ; the ruins of Kirby Hall still show how imposing
and stately an air these long windows—often interspersed,
as in this instance, with pilasters—could impart to the
exterior.

One other feature of the Elizabethan house calls for
mention, and that is the chimney. It impressed contemporaries almost more than any of the other innovations
as being symbolic of the increase in luxury which marked
the trend of the times. Harrison ranks the chimney with
" the great (although not general) amendment of lodging "

and the increasing use of pewter and plate as one of the three remarkable signs of the new way of life. " There are old men yet dwelling in the village where I remain," he writes, " which have noted three things to be marvellously altered in England within their sound remembrance —one is the multitude of chimneys lately erected . . . whereas in their young days there were not above two or three, if so many, in most uplandish towns of the realm (the religious houses and manor places of their lords always excepted and peradventure some great personages), but each one made his fire against a reredos in the hall where he dined and dressed his meat." The beautiful, twisted brickwork chimneys that still decorate a few old houses belong as a rule to one of the earlier Tudor reigns ; they took simpler and less elaborate shapes in Elizabeth's time, but were used in finely massed groups as a striking feature of design.

Despite its distinction it is doubtful whether the grander type of Elizabethan architecture can ever, in English country and for English tastes, have the attraction that belongs to the smaller stone or half-timbered houses of the period. Partly because they assimilated more thoroughly whatever foreign influence there was that touched them, and partly because the way of life in these manor houses and gentlefolks' homes is less alien to our imagination, such a dwelling as Moreton Old Hall, rather than Cowdray's magnificent ruins, has come to typify for us all that we mean by " the Elizabethan house."

The materials with which these smaller houses were built depended, naturally, upon the resources of the locality ; in such counties as Oxfordshire, Northamptonshire, Yorkshire, and Derbyshire, where stone was easily obtained, it was much used ; brickwork, however, was more general in the eastern counties. In the west, and especially along the Welsh border, we find the best specimens of the half-timbered house ; in all the counties from Lancashire and Cheshire down to the Cotswolds there are many beautiful examples of these black and white houses still standing, ranging in style from the lordly Speke Hall

near Liverpool to such attractive cottages as may be found,
for example, in Much Wenlock.

From the point of view of construction an elaborately
ornamented half-timbered house such as Speke or Bramhall
in Cheshire is the same as the simplest specimen of southern
workmanship.   In both cases the framework of the house
is made of upright timbers, strengthened by horizontal
and sloping beams, the interstices being filled in with lath
and plaster.   Moreton Old Hall, illustrated on p. 128,
stands, as it were, midway between Bramhall, with its
richness of curve and pattern, and such a typical south-
country house as Pattenden, near Goudhurst, in Kent.

Leaving the exterior for the interior, however, there are
certain features, typical of the Elizabethan house-plan,
which deserve brief notice, as they are indicative of changes
in the mode of life which became finally established in
this reign.

Great houses still retained the enormous dining halls
that would seat their hundreds, but the typically Elizabethan rooms were the great chamber and the gallery.   In
a large house the latter might be as much as two hundred
feet in length.   To us it seems an awkward apartment,
except for the display of pictures, but it pleased its
Elizabethan inventors more than anything else in their
houses.   Here they listened to music, danced their stately
measures or paced up and down for exercise ; here too
they displayed their choicest cabinets and other treasures
such as fine tapestries.[1]   The great chamber was used for
affairs of ceremony, and corresponded more or less to the
modern drawing-room.   Most house-plans of the period
seem also to have provided a dining parlour for the owner
and his family, the increasing use of which led, by the
middle of the next century, to the disuse of the great hall
as a living room, and its ultimate conversion into a
vestibule.

A vast number of bed-chambers—all leading out of each
other—as well as the gallery and the great chamber,

[1] The " long gallery " at Hengrave Hall contained eleven pictures in
1603.   The " gallery in the tower " boasted seventeen, and a large framed
map which hung over the chimneypiece.—Gage : "History of Hengrave."

occupied the first floor, which was reached in all later
Elizabethan houses by a very fine staircase. These
magnificent and stately flights of stairs, with their elegant
design, their short, shallow-stepped sections, and their
generous landings, were a new and characteristic feature
of the Elizabethan house. Their balustrading was heavy
and substantial, and freely decorated with carving, the
newel posts in particular being as a rule extremely elaborate, and often ending in marvellous heraldic animals.

The general solidity and heaviness of Elizabethan
furniture was well set off by the richness of the interior
decoration of the houses. The plaster ceilings of all
important rooms were of the most elaborate description,
ribbed and patterned in heavy relief, varying from simple
geometrical designs to free flowing curves forming no
repeating pattern at all. The appearance of the windows
was often enriched by panes of stained glass and bright-
hued armorial bearings ; and the walls were either panelled
or else covered with tapestries or the cheaper " painted
cloth " hangings that in many middle-class houses replaced
the older woven ones. Architectural features such as doors
and chimneypieces were further used to enhance the richly
decorative effect of the rooms, and elaborately carved
examples, both in stone and woodwork, still survive in
most considerable houses of the period.

Elizabethan panelled or tapestried rooms gave, of
course, a much lighter and more brilliant effect than they
do to-day. Not only was the colouring of the tapestries
new and unfaded, but the oak wainscot was either new
and therefore light in tone, or else in some cases decorated
with painted designs in brilliant colours such as green or
vermilion. The simple linen-panelling of the fifteenth
century was superseded in Elizabeth's time by small
panels intricately carved with arabesques or animals or
human heads. Here also in the panelling, as in the
windows and over the chimneypieces, heraldry played its
part and added its gorgeous tinctures to intensify the
richly coloured effect given by the room.

Pictures, although much used for the decoration of

rooms in the royal palaces and the halls of great personages, had not, in the sixteenth century, superseded the
" painted cloths " in ordinary households. Portraits and
mythological subjects, however, adorned the galleries and
rooms of such a building as Kenilworth,[1] and Frederick
Duke of Würtemberg,[2] when he visited this country in
1592, commented enthusiastically on the " masterly
paintings " at Hampton Court, and on Burghley's hall
at Theobalds which was " elegantly adorned with paintings." In others of the halls and galleries at Theobalds
he remarked on the " very artistic paintings and correct
landscapes of all the most important and remarkable towns
in Christendom."

One other quaint detail of wall-decoration, which is now
hardly ever found, but was popular in Elizabethan times,
was the posy—a sententious or pithy saying, sometimes
versified, inscribed above the chimneypiece, or around the
panelling. Thomas Tusser of " Good Husbandry " fame
has some curious specimens. His " posy for the parlour "
is probably a typical example :

> Hast thou a friend as heart may wish at will ?
> Then use him so to have his friendship still.

His suggestions for guest-chamber posies, however, set one
speculating as to their authenticity. The Elizabethans
were an outspoken folk, and guests may have had some
very trying habits ; nevertheless the following couplets can
hardly be described either as tactful or cordial :

With curtain some make scabbard clean, with coverlet their
    shoe :
All dirt and mire, some wallow bed, as spaniels use to do.

The sloven and the careless man, the roynish nothing nice,
To lodge in chamber comely decked are seldom suffered twice.

After scanning this " writing on the wall " he would indeed
be an incorrigible sloven of a guest who then persisted—
in spite of Tusser's third distich—in putting his dirty
suit-case on the clean toilet cover !

[1] See Kenilworth Inventories, *Historical MSS. Commission, MSS. of
Lord De Lisle and Dudley*, pp. 278,-295.
[2] See Rye : " England as Seen by Foreigners."

In poorer houses furniture was of the simplest description, and the stone or wooden flooring was left bare. In wealthier houses it was the custom to strew rushes upon the floors ; plaited rush-mats were also used and can be seen in some Elizabethan paintings, but carpets were generally employed as coverings for beds or tables or chests, even in the royal palaces. Paul Hentzner,[1] who visited England in 1598, describes Queen Elizabeth's presence chamber at Greenwich as being " hung with rich tapestry, and the floor, after the English fashion, strewn with hay " ; Shakespeare, too, speaks of " the presence strewed." March appears to have brought to Elizabethan housewives the joys of a spring cleaning ; so one cannot but hope that on such occasions the year's rushes were then removed and used as manure in the garden, if there is any truth in the usual assertion that when the rushes grew dirty and foul a new load was strewn on top of the old. Contemporaries have left us vigorous accounts of the state of these rush-strewn floors, the *locus classicus* being, of course, Erasmus' unflattering description in a letter, in which he implies that this mass of accumulated filth and decaying vegetable matter was allowed to remain for as long as twenty years ![2] Even if the art of perfuming the chambers be taken into consideration, however, one can hardly accept Erasmus quite literally ; perhaps something nearer the truth can be inferred from Tusser's advice to his model husbandman :

While wormwood hath seed, get a bundle or twain,
To save against March, to make flea to refrain.
Where chamber is swept and that wormwood is strown,
No flea for his life dare abide to be known.

The simplicity of it carries conviction, both of the need for wormwood seed, and of the custom of sweeping out

---

[1] See Rye " England as Seen by Foreigners."
[2] " Tum sola fere strata sunt argilla, tum scirpis palustribus, qui subinde sic renovantur, ut fundamentum maneat aliquoties annos viginti, sub se fovens sputa, vomitus, proiectiam cervisiam, et pisciam reliquias, aliasque sordes non nominandas. Hinc mutato coelo vapor quidam exhalatur, mea sententia minime salubris humano corpori."—P. S. Allen : " Selections from Erasmus," 1918, p. 126. (Letter to Cardinal Wolsey's physician, date uncertain.) It must be remembered that the letter refers specifically to early Tudor conditions.

the chambers. There is, further, plenty of evidence to show that in many houses rushes were supplied in considerable quantities every month. In the Earl of Ancaster's manuscripts, for example, we find that the paternal household of Peregrine Bertie " the brave Lord Willoughby " paid every month for rushes, in the year 1561, sums varying from three shillings and sixpence to ten shillings or more. It is hardly reasonable to suppose that each new load was laid on top of the old ; by 1562 the family would have been knee-deep in litter ! In both the Rutland and the Ancaster manuscripts there are, too, various entries in the household accounts of payments made for cleaning rooms, sweeping chambers, and strewing rushes.[1]

Allowing for exaggeration on the part of Erasmus, however, the rushes must have been a happy breeding ground for vermin, especially in the halls of those jolly squires where the dogs were as much at home as their masters.[2] Tapestries, hangings, and curtains must also have become unpleasantly populous. The saving grace of the Elizabethan interior, in these circumstances, would have been a complete lack of upholstery. Covered chairs and stools, however, seem to have been very popular, and throughout the kingdom, in wealthy houses, padded comfort became more and more usual towards the end of the reign. It is almost impossible to turn up any contemporary household accounts or inventories without finding numerous entries of covered chairs and stools and of purchases of material for covering them. In spite of Mr. Percy Macquoid's assertion in " Shakespeare's England " (Chapter XX) that " no stuffing was upholstered to the woodwork before the early part of the seventeenth century," it seems hardly reasonable to suppose that all these covered chairs were entirely unpadded, especially as Sir John Harington, in his " Treatise of Play," written towards the end of the sixteenth century, complains of the stools at Court, which he describes as " so hard that since great breeches were

---

[1] See Historical MSS. Commission ; Rutland MSS., IV, p. 304 ; Ancaster MSS., p. 462.
[2] Sir John Davies in his " Epigrammes " (1590) describes such a country hall as " stinking with dogs, and muted all with hawks."

laid aside men can scant endure to sit on," whereas, he continues, " in every merchant's hall " one may nowadays find " easy quilted and lined forms and stools."[1] In the Duke of Rutland's manuscripts at Belvoir there are several entries which show that covered chairs and stools were in use even at the beginning of the reign ; there are entries in 1558 of the purchase of a stool covered with red cloth which cost fourteen shillings and sevenpence, of two chairs of walnut wood covered with green cloth, and of two black and one red leather covered chairs, the last three costing forty-four shillings.[2] In another year we find entries of stammel bought to cover stools, and of five yards of watchet velvet for a chair, two stools, and a long cushion.[3] Similarly, in the inventory of Sir Henry Unton's goods in his house at Wadley in Berkshire, taken in 1596, practically every chair or stool mentioned is described as a covered one. In the Parlour, for example, there were two chairs in green cloth, one in black wrought velvet laid with silver and gold lace, thirteen stools in green cloth, and six leather stools. In the Great Chamber there was a velvet chair and six stools in tuft taffeta ; another room boasted chairs and stools in green velvet, and one bedroom possessed one yellow velvet chair, two yellow velvet stools, and a yellow velvet cushion for the window seat.[4]

In the great chambers, the halls, and parlours of the Elizabethan house chairs were still seats of honour, few in number, and reserved for the master and mistress of the house and personages of distinction. Particularly beautiful were the oak panel-back arm-chairs of the period, generally high-backed, and well suited to the stiff and dignified costume of the day. Malvolio, in the height of his conceited ecstasy, imagining Sir Toby fetched before him for rebuke, sees himself " sitting in his state " in just such a chair, exercising the authority of the lord of the household. For an uncovered chair of this kind a concession to comfort was usually provided by the cushions,

---

[1] " Nugæ Antiquæ," II, 173: 1779.
[2] Vol. IV, p. 386.
[3] Ibid., p. 423.
[4] ' Unton Inventories," ed. J. G. Nichols ; Berks Ashmolean Soc.

which figure so largely in most inventories of the time,
and which were also used to make the top of a chest or
often the floor itself pleasanter for sitting or reclining.
What was known from its shape as the X chair was, however, the most comfortable seat in an Elizabethan room ;
its woodwork, even if not always padded, was covered in
velvet or silk, and its seat was furnished with a cushion
made to fit. At meals joined- or joint-stools took the
place of our ordinary chair.   These were solidly constructed
and often freely ornamented with carving ; they usually
stood about two feet high, and to the modern idea closely
resemble small tables—as which, indeed, their Elizabethan
owners also used them, particularly in their bedrooms.

Tables, court-cupboards, cabinets, buffets, and chests
made up the rest of the furniture of even the most richly
appointed Elizabethan room.   Chests, inlaid or carved or
merely of plain panels, served many purposes : they were
used as seats throughout the house, and in the bedrooms
they formed the chief receptacles for clothes and household
goods. Standing tables, in all well-to-do families, had
superseded the old trestle tables which had been taken
down after the meal and stacked against the wall in
medieval times. The most popular kind was the draw-
top, which had an extra leaf at each end that could be
drawn out when required. Buffets, cupboards, and
cabinets were, however, the most ornamental pieces of
furniture, and generally the most valuable, with the
exception, perhaps, of beds. They were frequently made
of fine woods, such as rosewood or walnut or oak inlaid
with marqueterie ; coloured woods and carving were freely
used in such pieces, and their whole effect was elaborate
and massive.

Bedrooms in the ordinary house were very scantily furnished : a chest—or perhaps two—did duty for dressing
table, washstand, and chest of drawers. On it the lady
would set up her adjustable mirror ; [1] on it also would
stand her brass or silver basin and ewer. Regular dressing
tables with all their appurtenances were not unknown,

[1] A looking-glass is entered in the Manners' accounts (Rutland MSS.)
for 1586 at 2s.—*Op. cit.*, IV, 390. For an illustration of a dressing-table,
complete with pincushion, jewel box, etc., see *The Elizabethan Home*,
p. 25.

but they were not yet usual or fashionable.   The one really striking piece of bedroom furniture, which figured very largely in bequests at this time, was the four-poster bed. With its carven or inlaid pillars, its elaborate head, its tester, its curtains, its valances and its fringes, an Elizabethan bed, such as would become the room of a person of quality, might cost its owner anything from a few hundreds to a thousand pounds of present-day money.

So much for the surroundings, the appurtenances of living, but what of the way of life itself, the domesticities, and the everyday aspect of things ?   The modern novel, which gives us a complete account of Everyman, from the number of blankets he puts on his bed to the sensations of his wife scrubbing the linoleum, has made us curious in such matters ; and modern scholarship has made us resentful of any fancy pictures of the past, and avid of facts.   Elizabethan literature has given us no equivalent of our novel ; but pen and ink and man's perpetual interest in his own doings and his own property have left us some raw material.

We realize, as a fundamental fact, that life in a well-to-do house had begun to be comfortable.   One awoke in the morning in a bed which would have the hardness of its criss-cross rope framework mitigated by a straw pallet and one or two feather mattresses.   It was then possible to lie and contemplate the fine quality of the linen sheets, the pleasant warmth of a pair of blankets, and the pretty pattern of one's yellow and green coverlet, while waiting for the chambermaid to pull back the elaborately-embroidered curtains of the bed and for the pageboy to light a fire in the room.   Doctors advised one to warm the garments before putting them on, and in front of the bedroom fire the bath could be taken in a wooden tub. Balls of sweet-scented soap were at most people's disposal for their ablutions, and although it could be bought at about fourpence a pound it was generally made at home, where it was perfumed with such essences as oil of almonds or musk.   Sir Hugh Platt has some delightful soap recipes in which rose-leaves and lavender flowers figure prominently. Large households often bought soap by the barrel, the Bertie family, for example, paying fifty shillings for one at Stourbridge Fair in 1562.[1] Tooth soap and a linen cloth were employed for rubbing the teeth—due care of which was insisted on by most physicians. One of them, indeed, suggests in his health manual that one should always retire to one's chamber and clean the teeth after a meal.[2] The barber would scale his customers' teeth for them ; but Sir Hugh Platt bids his friends beware of allowing this amateur dentist to clean their teeth with Aqua Fortis, as if it is not properly diluted and carefully applied the victim " may happen within a few dressings to be forced to borrow a rank of teeth to eat her dinner, unless her gums do help her the better ! " The same authority on the toilet gives in his " Delightes for Ladies " (1602) various recipes for tooth pastes and washes. " To keep the teeth both white and sound," he recommends the Elizabethan gentlewoman to " take a quart of honey, as much vinegar, and half so much white wine, boil them together and wash your teeth therewith now and then." Toothpicks were much used, and when made in the form of elaborate trinkets could be presented to Her Majesty as a New Year's gift. A case of toothpicks of sweet wood cost their purchaser one shilling in 1597 ;[3] and Ben Jonson's advice to a would-be gallant is to pick his teeth when he finds himself with nothing to say.[4]

The toilet, in a word, did not lack its amenities, nor the toilet table its accessories. The lady, when dressing in the morning, demands from her maid her ivory comb[5] and her boxwood comb, which she keeps in a comb-case ; while the maid combs her tresses she wears a *peignoir* to keep the loose hairs off her clothes. When the maid has finished, the combs are handed to the page to be cleaned with comb-brushes, the lady warning him " take heed you do not make them clean with those that I use to my

[1] Ancaster MSS., p. 471.
[2] William Vaughan : " Fifteen Directions to Preserve Health," 1602.
[3] Rutland MSS., IV, 412.
[4] " Everyman out of his Humour."
[5] The cost of this, in 1540, according to the Manners' accounts, would have been fivepence.—*Op. cit.*, IV, 370.

head." She tells her maid to " look in the pin-cushion "
for small pins [1] for her cuffs and a black pin for her gown ;
she demands a clean handkerchief when she is ready
dressed, and as she leaves her bedroom she instructs the
maid to put " all her night-gear " neatly into the " cushion
cloth " or nightdress case when tidying up the chamber.[2]

The Elizabethan breakfast was often taken privately
before issuing forth from one's chamber. It was not
negligible in its proportions, as witness the beef, bread,
and beer consumed each morning by the Queen's maids
of honour.[3] Dinner, however, was the important meal of
the day for all classes, and was generally taken between
ten o'clock and noon. Tusser's good huswife saw no reason
why her ploughmen and neatherds should not have their
meal served upon her well-scrubbed but bare tables, their
country manners and habits not being of the daintiest.
In a well-to-do townsman's household, however, greater
ceremony was observed : a cloth was laid upon the table,
and at every place was set a trencher, a napkin, and a
spoon.[4] Wine, ale, and drinking vessels, Harrison tells us,
stood on the buffet, and the servants filled a clean goblet
or Venetian drinking glass when any guest called for
liquor. In the kitchen quarters the butler took pains to
chip the bread in order to remove any cinders from the
crust, and he also squared each piece neatly before he set
it on the board. Finally, the great salt-cellar would be
placed on the table, and with basin, ewer, and fine damask
towel ready to hand for the diners' ablutions, all was
prepared.

Guests seem frequently to have used their own knives
at table in an ordinary middle class household. In a
dialogue written in the 'seventies we find a late-comer

---

[1] In 1561 we find pins purchased for the use of Mistress Susan, sister of
Peregrine Bertie, at the rate of 1s. 4d. for 1,500 ; in 1574, according to
Rogers' " Hist. Agr. and Prices," they cost about fourpence for 1,000 ; in
1591, according to the Manners' accounts, they cost 1s. 8d. for 2,000.

[2] Erondell : " French Garden " (see Bibliography, III, p. 287.)

[3] Nichols : " Progresses," II, 44. When Elizabeth was entertained at
Cowdray in 1591 the breakfast for the household consisted of 3 oxen and
140 geese.—*Ibid.*, II, 2.

[4] The " Unton Inventories " record two dozen diaper table napkins,
and the same number of plain napkins, also four diaper tablecloths—
evidently the normal equipment for a gentleman's household.

addressing the company with the request, " He which hath two knives, let him lend me one." Forks were introduced from Italy in this reign, but did not come into general use for some time.[1] Well-bred folk cut up their food with their knives, and when they did not use a spoon used their fingers to pick up what they ate ; hence the survival, for some years beyond the Elizabethan period, of the habit of washing both before and after the meal.

The pomp which attached to the serving of a nobleman's daily dinner has been well described in the directions which Anthony Viscount Montague, owner of Cowdray Castle in Sussex, drew up for the guidance of his household in 1595.[2] He and his family did not dine in the great Buck Hall, but in a chamber adjoining it ; and to him, at ten o'clock, repaired his Gentleman Usher, to inquire if his Lordship was ready for his service. Previous to this, however, a large number of his Lordship's enormous retinue had been engaged, under the supervision of the Gentleman Usher, in the elaborate ritual which his Lordship had decreed should accompany the laying of his cloth and the setting of his table. In this complicated business the Yeoman Usher " led off," by conducting into the great chamber the Yeoman of the Ewry—all of them making two bows to his Lordship's table as they approached that honourable piece of furniture. The Yeoman Usher kissed his hand and placed it upon the table to indicate where the cloth should be laid ; this done, the Yeoman of the Pantry then approached, and at each place arranged a trencher, a roll of bread, a silver hafted knife and a spoon, bowing as he placed each article upon the board. The great salt having also been put in its proper position, the Yeomen of the Cellar then set forth upon the buffet the wines and drinking vessels, and all being thus in readiness the Gentleman Usher had at this stage of the proceedings waited upon

[1] 1611 (cf. Coryat's " Crudities ") is usually given as the date of their introduction, but that they were known at any rate as a fashionable novelty from 1582 onwards is evident from the gifts of forks made to Elizabeth on various New Year's Days—e.g. a knife, fork, and spoon of crystal and a fork of coral in 1582, and a spoon and fork of gold in 1588.—See Nichols, II, 25, 26, 37.

[2] See " Sussex Archæological Collections," Vol. VII.

his Lordship to inform him of the fact. Having seen the Carver and the Sewer wash their hands at the Ewry board, the Gentleman Usher then led the Carver to the table, stopping twice on the way to bow. Not being himself of menial rank it was impossible for the Gentleman Usher in person to order the serving of the first mess at this juncture; the most his position allowed of was that he should tell the Yeoman Usher to call for the dinner, so that by the help of various underlings word was carried to the kitchen. Then as the dishes, escorted solemnly by a number of gentlemen in waiting, were carried through the great hall, the whole household stood reverently. Finally, the meat was set before Anthony Viscount Montague, the Gentleman Usher supervising its proper placing, and the Carver then performing his office upon it. Whether or not it was cooked to the Viscount's liking history does not relate; we may imagine, however, that a nobleman who instructed his Clerk of the Kitchen to see that no saucy scullion presumed to affront his lordship's joint by turning his back to it while it roasted would not have been likely to tolerate an inadequate chef.[1]

An Elizabethan dinner was not the gourmandizing affair that one might carelessly imagine it to have been. Contemporary accounts indicate an amazing profusion of dishes—several joints, several kinds of fish, half a dozen different kinds of game, venison, various salads, vegetables, sweetmeats, and fruits. The guest, however, did not work his way right through this formidable menu; rich men, so Harrison explains, furnished their table in this prodigal fashion in order that each man might, in each course, choose the food that pleased him best, and that their large retinues of servants might also have sufficient at the second sitting which followed. Harrison is careful to assure us that gentlemen do not overeat themselves, but are strictly moderate in their diet, although esteeming highly both rare foods and good cooking; in order to obtain this latter, he adds, many of them employed French chefs noted for their skill. To their moderation in drinking a

[1] Hentzner—a German—considered that the English roasted meat "in perfection."

Dutch physician also bears witness : " At their tables, although they be very sumptuous and love to have good fare, yet neither use they to overcharge themselves with excess of drink, neither thereto greatly provoke and urge others, but suffer every man to drink in such measure as best pleaseth himself." [1]

At a pleasant dinner given by the lady of " The French Garden " the guests are offered oysters with brown bread, salt, pepper, and vinegar, which, however, are eventually declined by all on the grounds that shellfish should not be eaten in the dog days. They dine in the great chamber, as fashionable folk should, and upon the cupboard the gold, silver, and silver-gilt plates and cups, which were the pride of all Elizabethan householders, were arrayed beforehand by the butler. A pepper box and a silver chafing-dish figure amongst the table accessories, and a silver fork at every trencher marks the lady's establishment as one of great refinement for 1605. The wine is kept cool and fresh in a copper tub full of water, and each time a guest hands back an empty glass or goblet it is rinsed in a wooden tub before being refilled. The chief guest amongst the ladies is placed by the mistress of the house in a chair ; her nephew, however, is given a stool with a cushion on it.

The fare which the lady provides is plentiful and attractive. Her guests may choose between roast beef, powder (salted) beef, veal, and a leg of mutton with " gallandine sauce " ; there is also a turkey, boiled capon, a hen boiled with leeks, partridge, pheasant, larks, quails, snipe, and woodcock. Salmon, sole, turbot, and whiting, with lobster, crayfish, and shrimps, are set before them ; an eel and a pike are sent from the table untasted. Young rabbits, leverets, and marrow on toasts tempt those who do not care for the " gross meats " ; artichokes, turnips, green peas, cucumbers, and olives are provided as vegetables, together with some attractive salads, including one of violet buds. Finally, their hostess offers them quince pie, tart of almonds, and various fruit tarts, several kinds of cheese, and dessert, including strawberries and cream,

[1] " The Touchstone of Complexions," Levine Lemnie, 1576 ; translated by Thos. Newton.

thus concluding a magnificent banquet of which one of the guests politely and aptly remarks, " In truth I have not seen of a long time (at once) so much poultry nor fowl, nor so good fish." It is hardly surprising, in view of the many dishes and the elegant conversation, that it was after two o'clock before the company rose from the table.

At the midday meal in a good citizen's house we find again many of the dishes provided by the lady for her friends, with the addition, however, of certain coarser cates—sausages, cabbage (badly cooked), and porridge for the children. Here, too, the hospitality which offers the guest his choice of " a pike with a high Dutch sauce," a stewed carp, roasted blackbirds, larks, woodcock, and partridge elicits from one of the feasters the exclamation, " Here is too much meat ; me thinketh that we be at a wedding." [1]

It was customary to spend two or three hours over this chief meal of the day, " the nobility, gentlemen, and merchant men," according to Harrison, commonly sitting at the board " till two or three of the clock at afternoon, so that with many it is a hard matter to rise from the table to go to evening prayers." Supper was supposed to be a lighter meal, and was usually taken about five o'clock. A roast shoulder of mutton, three fried rabbits, bread, beer, and a pint of claret seems, however, to have been the typical and not unsubstantial evening repast of a solitary gentleman living in lodgings in London in 1589. [2]

Country fare was still plentiful and famous, in spite of the decay of " housekeeping " which contemporary literature so frequently laments. [3] Harrison considers that Londoners were not so hospitable as country folk ; " in reward of a fat capon or plenty of beef and mutton largely bestowed upon them in the country, a cup of wine or beer with a napkin to wipe their lips and an ' You are heartily welcome ' is thought to be great entertainment." At Christmas time in particular all countrymen delighted

[1] Hollyband : "French Schoolemaister" (see Bibliography, V).
[2] Darell accounts. See Hall : "Society in the Elizabethan Age."
[3] I.e. the keeping of open house by the nobility and gentry, at whose tables the poor and the stranger had once been able to feast at will.

to provide good cheer for their workers, their neighbours, and themselves :

> Good bread and good drink, a good fire in the hall,
> Brawn, pudding and souse, and good mustard withal.
> Beef, mutton, and pork, shred pies of the best,
> Pig, veal, goose, and capon, and turkey well drest :
> Cheese, apples, and nuts, jolly carol to hear,
> As then, in the country, is counted good cheer.

Except in the holiday season, however, when rich and poor alike indulged in leisure and feasting, the poorer class of farmers and the labouring population fared simply enough. " Good ploughmen," Tusser asserts,

> . . . look weekly, of custom and right,
> For roast meat on Sundays and Thursdays at night.

But for the rest of the week pease and bacon, or fish and " white meat," [1] washed down by a draught of cider or good home-brewed ale, made the husbandman's ordinary dinner. To the haymaking field he and his workers took with them " a bottle or two of good beer, with an apple pasty, potted butter, churn milk, bread and cheese." [2] It contrasts forcibly with the lavish array of meats that Turberville [3] considered necessary for a picnic or a hunt-breakfast for which he bids the butler provide cold loins of veal, cold capon, beef, and goose, pigeon pies, cold mutton, powdered neats' tongues, a gammon of bacon, and finally " sausages and savoury knacks."

London artizans, according to Harrison, profiting by the many adjacent markets, ate more butchers' meat than their fellows in the country. They lent some variety to their meals by such dishes as souse, brawn, bacon, and fowl, and also white meats and fruit. Like their country brethren, again, they too ate salt or fresh fish during Lent and on fish days, but instead of storing it for the season purchased it from the fishmongers as required. In the country, however, one of the farmer's chief duties, as soon

---

[1] I.e. milk, butter, cheese, and eggs.
[2] " Coach and Sedan pleasantly disputing," 1636.
[3] " Booke of Venery," 1575.

as harvest was over, was to ride to his market town and bargain for a store of ling, salt fish, and herring to lay by for the winter.

The well-to-do ate wheaten bread and manchet, a fine white bread also made of wheat ; the poorer classes ate bread made of rye or barley, and in time of dearth of beans, pease, or oats. Jack of Newbury's young wife, in Deloney's pleasant history of that worthy's deeds, was rebuked by her gossip for feeding the work folk on " the best of the beef and the finest of the wheat." She asserted, truly enough, that they were accustomed to the coarse brown bread of " barley or rye mingled with pease," and also to " necks and points of beef, which because it is commonly lean they seethe therewith now and then a piece of bacon or pork, whereby they make their pottage fat."

In the popular coupling of "food and clothing" we tacitly assume that the former comes first in importance. In Elizabeth's time, however, such was the inordinate love of gay apparel amongst all classes that many a gallant preferred to prank it in his silks and velvets rather than to provide himself with a good solid meal. Many are the gibes that contemporary pamphleteers level at the youth who has " so little in his purse, so much upon his back." Bishop Hall [1] in particular cries out upon the stupidity of such :

> The maw, the guts, all inward parts complain
> The back's great pride, and their own secret pain.

In no age, perhaps, has there been seen in this country greater extravagance of apparel than in the latter part of Elizabeth's reign. The Court presented a brilliant spectacle, as all visitors bore witness. Silks, satins, velvets, brocades, jewels, feathers—nothing was lacking that might by rarity, texture, colour or quality give pleasure to the eye. But at no period in the history of English costume have the natural line and true proportions of the human body been more curiously disguised and distorted by padding, stiffening and cut. The simpler forms of dress were often comely enough,

---

[1] " Virgidemiarum," Lib. III, Sat. vii ; 1597.

but at their most extreme, Elizabethan fashions have style and magnificence rather than beauty.

It is the age of doublet and hose, ruff and farthingale. The fashionable doublet was always padded to get the smooth fit shown in Elizabethan portraits, but it did not acquire the characteristic " peascod-bellied " shape until about 1575, when it became paunched out in front with the overhanging, stiffened protuberance which we associate with Mr. Punch. In its earlier form (see illustration, p. 210) it came down to a V-shaped point in front but fitted the body. It was fastened down the front by closely-set buttons, and attached by points (tagged laces) to the breeches. Its collar—which at times came right up to the nape—was finished either with a small ruff or a lace-edged turn-over collar. The sleeves were similarly finished with wrist-ruffs or turned-back cuffs. Close-fitting sleeves were worn throughout the reign, but during the eighties the fuller " leg-o'-mutton " type was more fashionable. The armhole join was concealed by a padded roll of material or a double or single row of tabs called pickadils (see illustration), and later by epaulette-like projections called wings. The sleeves of women's dresses were similarly trimmed. At the end of the reign the fashionable doublet lost the peascod-belly but generally kept the pointed waist-line and often acquired longer bases (or skirts).

Breeches were of various kinds and were worn with hose (" netherstocks "=stockings) : when sewn together the garment was known as " whole-hose." In the earlier part of the reign the most usual type was the short, puffed, slashed and paned round- or French-hose, coming to mid-thigh, now generally called trunk-hose. Panes are the longitudinal strips of material, attached at top and bottom and revealing the lining at the widest part. One very characteristic shape is illustrated at p. 210, worn with canions and separate netherstocks. The canions are the tubular extensions of the trunks coming down to the knee : the netherstocks can be gartered either over or under the canions. The other equally characteristic shape for trunk-hose is the rounded pumpkin form, smaller and shorter, generally worn without canions and sewn to the nether-stocks. In the last part of the reign trunk-hose were often worn so short that they hardly came below hip-level.

Venetians were breeches which varied from the almost skin-tight to the very full, gathered, padded, melon-shaped kind. Whatever their width, they always fastened below the knee. They were particularly fashionable in the eighties. Galligaskins, apparently, were very full, loose breeches, fastening above the knee. Slops appears to be a general term for any wide, loose breeches, whether short like trunk-hose or long like Venetians.

Cloaks, throughout the reign, were among the most costly and beautiful garments for men. A gentleman was not considered fully dressed for society unless he wore his cloak. The typical short, full cloak with a high upstanding collar was a fashion adopted from Spain. Linings were often as costly and beautiful as the actual cloaks, which were made of the richest materials, frequently faced with gold or silver lace and even embroidered with pearls. The earlier cloak often had dummy sleeves and was worn on both shoulders : the later, very short kind could be worn on one shoulder only. They were kept in place by cords which passed under the armpits and were tied behind the back.

Women's dress, in the early years, differed little from that worn in Mary's reign. The gored skirt fitted smoothly over the bell- or cone-shaped Spanish farthingale and was frequently made with an inverted V-opening in front, from waist to hem, revealing either a petticoat or a " forepart " of another rich material. The Spanish farthingale was an under-petticoat, held out by a series of cane hoops increasing in size from top to bottom. Worn with a long-waisted, pointed bodice, it gave the wearer an hour-glass appearance. Some bodices were cut with high necks. Those that were cut low and square, as in the reign of Henry VIII, generally had the decolletage filled up by a high-necked chemisette, finished by a small ruff.

The Spanish farthingale was worn till the end of the century, but was supplanted in fashionable society in the eighties by the French and " wheel " farthingales. For the

French style a thick roll or hip-bolster was tied round the waist so that the skirt was held out at almost a right-angle to the figure and then fell vertically to instep level. It varied in shape from a complete circle or an oval to a half-circle at the back only—the " semicircled farthingale " that Falstaff thought would look well on Mistress Ford. The wheel (or Catherine-wheel or Italian) farthingale appears to have been a wired or whaleboned shelf-like structure, which could hold the skirt out at right angles to a width of a couple of feet or more. A flounce of the same material as the skirt was arranged in radiating pleats on top of this framework, which gave a ruff-like appearance to its edge. These farthingales all tilted up slightly at the back and down in the front, and the stumpy appearance given by their width to the lower half of the figure was still further accentuated by the exaggeratedly long stomachers of the bodices which became fashionable in the eighties and nineties for full Court wear.

The ruff, worn by men and women alike, grew to enormous dimensions in the latter part of the reign. It was made of the finest materials, lawn and cambric being especially favoured, and it was frequently " got up " with coloured starches, yellow being popular at one period. The three-piled ruff, literally three ruffs one on top of another, was one of the more extravagant kinds, and in width some extended as much as nine inches from the neck of the wearer. Some of them were jewelled, others were ornamented with costly lace. Some were worn fitting closely to the neck ; others were open in the front, and yet others were worn with a stiff, upstanding collar which is to be seen in most of the Queen's later portraits, such as the well-known one by Zucchero at Hatfield House. Sumptuary laws were useless to check this particular extravagance, and ruffs continued to be worn right through the next reign, yielding at last in the time of Charles I to the simpler " falling bands " or flat lace collar which had been worn, indeed, throughout Elizabeth's time, but had not then been able to vie with the ruff in popularity.

The satirists of the day lashed mercilessly at the extrava-

gance of clothing. Ruffs to Stubbes were the invention
of the devil and the starch with which they were got up
" the devil's liquor." The farthingale drew the ridicule
of every one ; and Stubbes poured scorn on men who wore
long doublets so stiffened, stuffed, and quilted that they
could hardly bend. He laughs a little less fiercely at
the diversity of hats affected by men and women alike :
some are " sharp on the crown, peaking up like a spear
or shaft of a steeple, standing a quarter of a yard above
the crown of their heads " ; " others be flat and broad on
the crown like the battlements of a house." Velvet
hats, fine beaver hats, and hats of taffeta are worn by all
classes : " Every artificer's wife (almost) will not stick
to go in her hat of velvet every day, every merchant's
wife and mean gentlewoman in her French hood, and every
poor cottager's daughter in her taffety hat." [1] In spite
of sumptuary laws and high prices all classes were infected
by the extravagance that was in the air ; every poor man
must have his finely wrought shirt, the cheapest costing
as much as a crown or a noble, and many costing even
ten pounds or more.

It is perhaps needless to point out that although this
mood of extravagance in clothing overran the whole land
there were plenty of men and women both in town and
country who had neither the means nor the desire to ape the
fantastic habits of the wealthy. Rowlands the satirist [2]
describes a typical country fellow:

> . . . plain in russet clad
> His doublet, mutton taffety, sheeps' skins . . .
> Upon his head a filthy greasy hat,
> That had a hole ate thorow by some rat.

He carries a plain leather pouch, wears kersey stockings and
knitted hose, heavy shoes with two hundred hobnails
in them, and his whole outfit would hardly fetch twelvepence. Similarly, the typical maidservant in a country
gentleman's house is described by the poet Churchyard [3] as
boasting only a very modest wardrobe :

---

[1] " Anatomy of Abuses."   [2] " Dr. Merryman " ; 1609.
[3] " Chippes " : " The Spider and the Gowt."

Two fair new kirtles to her back.
The one was blue, the other black.
For holy-days she had a gown
And every yard did cost a crown ;
And more by eighteenpence I guess.
She had three smocks, she had no less,
Four rails, and eke five kerchers fair,
Of hose and shoes she had a pair,
She needed not no more to have,
She would go barefoot for to save
Her shoes and hose for they were dear.

She wore the bodice of her petticoat " laced before " in the old-fashioned guise of King Henry's or Queen Mary's time, and her greatest vanity was a purse with " fair tassels " which she wore on a green ribbon when she took her annual Easter holiday.

Farthingales and ruffs, great breeches, and stuffed doublets were not for ordinary folk, or sober lower and middle class men and women. Elderly men as a rule wore a long gown with hanging sleeves over their doublet and hose, and quiet colours and older fashions were always to be seen in any street crowd. But in some form or another extravagance made itself felt everywhere. Lodge, for example, in his " Wits Miserie " (1596) makes us realize this : " The Ploughman that in times past was contented in russet must nowadays have his doublet of the fashion with wide cuts, his garters of fine silk of Granado[1] to meet his Sis on Sunday ; the farmer that was contented in times past with his russet frock, and mockado (i.e. cloth) sleeves now sells a cow against Easter to buy him silken gear."

Of underclothing in the modern sense of the word the Elizabethan knew little. The lady wore her linen smock, the gentleman his linen shirt[2] ; then they donned their ordinary garments, solving the problem of cold weather simply by putting on more of them—a jerkin or jacket or gown on top of the doublet, a long gown, either loose or

[1] Granado silk was costly, too. In 1561 the Bertie household, purchasing ten ounces for shirts, paid for it at the rate of two shillings and eightpence an ounce.—Op. cit., p. 460.
[2] Dr. G. B. Harrison has pointed out to me a unique mention of " two pair of linen breeches next the skin, three pair of linen hose under the stockings," in the first dialogue of Minsheu's " Spanish Grammar " (1599), where the servant checks the laundry. Obviously, it is not necessarily evidence of English underclothing.

fitted, on top of the dress. Andrew Boorde, a physician, advised his patients to wear a jacket of black and white lambskins when extra warmth was needed. A multiplicity of petticoats, an extra shirt, fur-lined cloaks, and the corsets and quilted garments worn by men and women alike seem to have been all the resources even of the rich.

Having thus surveyed his house and his furniture, his food, his clothing, and his domestic habits, we may for a concluding glimpse see our Elizabethan retire to his magnificent four-poster. We may rest assured that his clean sheets will have been aired before the bed was made ; all well instructed servants saw to that point.[1] He will, further, have had the bed warmed by a warming pan— perhaps by a silver warming pan, if he is a wealthy man, and his wife as fastidious as Lady Compton, daughter of one of London's Lord Mayors and heroine of a runaway match with the first Earl of Northampton. His nostrils will not be insulted by the stink of tallow candles ; his attendants may use them, but will be careful to whisk them away and bring in good wax lights before the master approaches. Whether or not he will wear a night-rail will depend on his personal tastes ; people were only just beginning to adopt the new habit of wearing a garment in bed.[2] He will certainly, however, wear a night-cap, perhaps one wrought with gold costing some twenty-two shillings ; [3] or perhaps one with a hole in the top of it, if he is a reader of Vaughan's treatise on the preservation of the health. And the dressing-gown [4] that he will doff before he steps into bed will be certainly of some rich material, perhaps " black damask furred with cony." [5] Perhaps he is averse to sleeping in the darkness, when fears of ghosts and evil spirits may the more easily assail one, and so has a watch-light burning by him as he sleeps ; the Bertie family paid sixpence in 1560 for a supply of rushes for

[1] Hugh Rhodes : " Booke of Nurture," 1577.
[2] The Queen, in 1588, accepted a present of " a night-rail of cambric wrought all over with black silk."—Nichols, II, 103.
[3] See Duke of Rutland's MSS., p. 412.
[4] Generally referred to as a "night gown." [5] Ancaster MSS., p. 457.

watch-lights.[1] If he prefers to have "light by him continually," his attendant will kindle one of these tiny wicks,
place it in a holder,[2] and stand it probably on a ledge made
by the elaborate carving of the bed's head. Then the
heavy fringed curtains will be drawn closely around so that
he is well protected from the draughts, and commending
his master to God his attendant will then draw out from
under the four-poster his own little truckle bed, place it
at the foot of the big one, and tumble into it as quickly as
possible. If, like many servitors, he has only one blanket
and one old coverlet to his master's several, he will probably
redress matters by sleeping in some of his day clothing.
And even if the "children of the kitchen" sleep on straw
pallets,[3] the cook in his chamber retires to a "plain bed-
stead" with a feather mattress. He rejoices in a bolster,
a blanket, and two rug coverlets ; and "one old cupboard
and one joined stool" give his room quite a furnished
appearance.[4] Master and man alike have forsaken the
ways of their forefathers and grandfathers, when, as
Harrison tells us, men lay on "straw pallets, on rough mats
covered only with a sheet, under coverlets made of dag-
swain and a good round log under their heads instead of a
bolster or pillow. As for servants, if they had any sheet
above them it was well, for seldom had they any under
their bodies to keep them from the pricking straws that
ran oft through the canvas of the pallet, and rased their
hardened hides."

So from the pages of Harrison and Stubbes, private
inventories, the journals of foreigners, and the casual
comments of the average writer there gradually emerges a
picture of the Elizabethan at home. As one reads, it takes
on life and colour, and the details fall into a truer per-
spective. Looking at this everyday aspect of things the
life of the ordinary man seems near enough to our own to
evoke at once our sympathy and understanding. Stubbes

[1] *Ibid.*, p. 470.
[2] *Ibid.*, p. 462 ; a candlestick for a watch-light 3s. 10d. ; 1562.
[3] *Ibid.*, p. 462 : 1561, straw for the children of the kitchens' beds cost
2s., and 54 yards of Irish rug for servants' coverlets was bought at 7d. a
yard.
[4] "Unton Inventories," p. 8.

may lash the wickedness and the worldliness of the age,
and Erasmus may complain of its filthy habits, but the
desires and ideas of ordinary men took shape in comely
buildings and beautiful furniture ; and another Dutchman,
writing perhaps half a century later than the uncompli-
mentary scholar, admits that on his visit to England " the
neat cleanliness, the exquisite fineness, the pleasant and
delightful furniture in every point for household, wonder-
fully rejoiced me, their chambers and parlours strawed
over with sweet herbs, refreshed me, their nosegays finely
intermingled with sundry sorts of flowers in their bed
chambers and privy rooms, with comfortable smell cheered
me up and entirely delighted all my senses." [1]   We balance
the two opinions, and we form a credible image ; their
fearsome enthusiasm for bear baiting, and two-headed
pigs and other monstrosities, becomes less alarming when
we remember this delight the Elizabethans had in pleasant
bunches of flowers for their houses.   The picture is in some
respects a familiar one, but it is not modern, nor was the
Elizabethan quite the same man as his Tudor fathers ; he
demanded greater luxury in his home, and created a new
standard of comfort, but the present age would be hard
put to it to accommodate itself to his way of life.   He
thought and felt quite differently on some important
subjects, as we shall see in succeeding chapters ; and he
lived quite differently in some respects—as witness those
rushes with which he insisted on littering a perfectly good
floor, notwithstanding the obvious drawbacks.   In spite
of the differences, however, Elizabethan England becomes
very recognizably English when we explore its house ; and
the final touch of familiarity is added by Bishop Jewel's
description of the English domestic weather.   Stow makes
us shiver with accounts of a frozen Thames, but with Jewel
we are in the familiar country whose climate men delight
to curse, where, as the Bishop has it, " Nec sol, nec luna,
nec hyems, nec ver, nec æstas, nec autumnus, satisfecit
officium suum." [2]

---

[1] Levine Lemnie : *op. cit.*   [2] In a letter to Bullinger in 1562.

CHAPTER III

LONDON TOWN

AN Elizabethan who did not live in London lived in the country. Technically he might inhabit a township or a city of no mean importance, but in essence London was, as the fourteenth century Scots poet had called it, " of townes *A per se.*" It stood alone, unique ; it was " the town "—town life was London life. Never before or since has it bulked quite so large in the imagination of the people. Always it has lured and will be able to lure its provincial Dick Whittingtons, but at no other time has it so focused, so concentrated, so dominated the national being.

Although Elizabeth continued the custom of making royal progresses throughout the realm the Court in her reign may be said finally to have lost its original migratory character. It became once and for all essentially associated with and situated in London. It was in this reign therefore that the Government and the Privy Council came to regard London as their permanent abode. Thus naturally there gravitated to the source of all advancement and the seat of power the ability, the culture, the wisdom, and the riches of the whole kingdom ; London took to itself the resurgent energies of the nation. Norden the mapmaker and topographer speaks of it as " that adamant which draweth unto it all the other parts of the land, and above the rest is most usually frequented with her Majesty's most royal presence." It drew men to it, and it made them or it marred them ; it delighted, it amazed, it disgusted them. Some it wearied and broke ; to others it gave fame and fortune. Some, disheartened or disgraced, it sent back to the peace they had forsaken when they yielded to its seduction.

In Tudor times London was still the City of London,

bounded on the south by its river, and on its other sides by the old city wall, the useless relic of its battlemented past. We still trace the line of it to-day on the north in Aldersgate, Cripplegate, Moorgate, Bishopsgate, and Aldgate, which were then ponderous gate-house towers or posterns, closed at nightfall with heavy doors or portcullises. Eastward the wall ended in the Tower, State prison, mint, and treasury, and still nominally a royal palace. On the west the City was entered by Newgate or Ludgate, both used as prisons. Even before Elizabeth's reign, however, the City had begun to spread beyond its fortified limits. Temple Bar, then as now, marked its real western boundary, where the jurisdiction of the Lord Mayor ended ; and on the north side in the reign of Mary little groups of houses had begun to spring up along the highways just outside the gates. We have only to compare Wyngaerde's map of 1543 with Ralph Agas' of about 1560 to realize that in the intervening decades the growth of outer-London had begun in earnest. By the time of Norden's map of 1593—famous because it represents the London that Shakespeare knew—we find that large tracts outside the northern gates have been closely built over, and London has already started to swallow up its country, although these districts were still for some time to remain rural ones, giving easy access to the villages of St. Pancras or Islington in a short walk.

London's main thoroughfare in Elizabeth's time was still the Thames. Every one used the river : it was certainly pleasanter and in many ways safer than road travel. The Queen had her State barge, so had the Lord Mayor and the great livery companies of the City. All the nobles whose houses lined the river front between the City and Westminster had their boats waiting ready at their landing stairs. Watermen plied for hire up and down the river with every kind of craft, and the shipping of the world discharged cargoes at the city wharves. London's river was a lovely thing—a " silver christall stream " one poet calls it—clear, bright water on which in very truth floated Spenser's " goodly swans " of snowy plumage.

" The broad river of Thames most charming and quite
full of swans white as snow " was an Italian traveller's
description. While still in the country, it flowed past
Chiswick House, where the Westminster scholars retired in
time of plague to avoid the contagion. Then it flowed
through the fields of Chelsea, " so called of the nature of
the place, whose strand is like the chesil which the sea
casteth up of sand and pebble stones " [1]—Chelsea, where
Queen Elizabeth had " a fair country house," as had also
the Lord Dacres. Past Westminster and the stately gardens of Whitehall and the Queen's orchard the river flowed,
and then from the royal palace took its way past a line of
palaces—York House, where Francis Bacon was born ;
Durham House, tenanted in 1566 by Leicester, and from
1584 until 1603 by Sir Walter Raleigh ; Russell House,
where the Hotel Cecil now stands ; and then the Savoy,
from which even then its ancient glory had long departed,
and of which to-day only the beautiful chapel remains.
Somerset House it passed next—where distinguished
foreigners were sometimes lodged—occupied towards the
end of the reign by Lord Hunsdon, the Queen's cousin on
her mother's side ; then Arundel House, lower built and
less conspicuous than its neighbours ; and then the princely
structure known first as Exeter House while it belonged to
that see, then as Leicester House while occupied by the
favourite, lastly as Essex House when it passed into the
hands of that rash and unfortunate nobleman.

By the Temple, with its famous gardens, the river passed
next, then on to Whitefriars stairs, the water exit from
Alsatia of ill-repute, one of the refuges of the worst scoun-
drels in the kingdom. From Whitefriars, past the old
palace of Bridewell, once the residence of the eighth Henry,
but in his daughter's time a house of correction, it flowed on
by the Blackfriars ; only the wall of the old monastery was
left standing, and already the site was becoming associated
with one of Shakespeare's theatres. After Blackfriars it
washed the gloomy base of Baynard's Castle, palace, and
stronghold, and residence in Shakespeare's time of the Earl

[1] Norden. See Bibliography to Chap. VI.

of Pembroke.   Then came Paul's Wharf, and after it many
another wharf or quay, busy with merchants and sailors,
and piled high with bales.   So the river took its way,
past the palaces of Queen and nobles, past relics of an older
London, past the thronging City, prophetic of the future,
on past the Tower, and finally the Queen's palace of
Placentia at Greenwich, said to have been Elizabeth's
favourite residence, as it had been her father's.

All London used its river in those days.   The Queen
herself would take the air upon the Thames ; pageants of
all kinds were enacted upon its waters ; foreigners who had
landed at Dover would post to Gravesend, and thence take
boat to London to avoid the fatigue and the dangers of
the road.   Boats left for London with every tide, and the
charge for passage in the " common barge " was only twopence, sixpence for the tilt boat.[1]   Ferries plied to and fro
at various points, and although the famous London Bridge
spanned the river most Londoners whose pleasure led them
to the Bankside would hail a small boat and be rowed across
to some one of the landing stairs, generally Paris Garden.
Merchants whose business took them to another quarter of
the City preferred rather to call a boatman, crying, " Westward ho ! " or " Eastward ho ! " than to pick their way
along the dirty narrow streets.

London Bridge was in several ways a unique structure.
It was the City's only bridge across the river : it was built
on twenty arches—said by some authorities to have been
of different widths—and it had a covered way right across
it from bank to bank, enclosed on either side by houses
and shops, and roofed above.   The actual roadway was a
narrow one, hardly wide enough to allow two carts to pass ;
and about the middle there was a drawbridge which could
be raised for high-masted vessels to sail underneath.   The
piers of the arches were all protected with a curious timber
framework which is seen very clearly in the illustration on
p. 66.   These erections—called " starlings "—made the
waterway between each pier very narrow indeed, with the

---

[1] I.e. boats with a " tilt " or canopy.   They could carry twenty or
thirty passengers.

result that at high tide the swift rush of the current was terrific in its force—shooting the bridge was always dangerous, and was impossible at the flood tide. As it rushed through the narrow arches the water by its own force created a fall of some five or six feet, so that going under London Bridge meant quite literally shooting a small rapid.

Foreign visitors remarked on the beauty of the bridge, and its " quite splendid handsome and well built houses," as Frederick Duke of Würtemberg described them. These, according to Stow, were inhabited mainly by wealthy merchants and haberdashers. Fynes Moryson, an English traveller, with even greater enthusiasm puts it amongst the prime miracles of the world, allowing the Rialto a place only in the second class, and relegating Florence's Ponte Vecchio to the fourth. One feature which is to be remarked in all contemporary views is the horrible spectacle presented by the gate-house tower which guarded the middle drawbridge. Here on poles were erected the rotting heads of those executed as traitors—a crude and savage warning to malcontents. The sight drew comments from most of the foreigners, who appear to have been sufficiently interested to count the number of heads displayed. The thirty-four noted by Duke Frederick in 1592 had been reduced to thirty by the time Paul Hentzner of Brandenburg made his reckoning in 1598.

Tudor London, more particularly towards the end of Elizabeth's reign, was an overcrowded and insanitary city, but it was, as a whole, undeniably picturesque and parts of it were beautiful. The Thames with its bridge, its palaces, its gardens, its swans, and its multitude of vessels was the pride of every Londoner ; old St. Paul's was the finest ecclesiastical building in the country, and was, indeed, England's pride. When the disastrous fire destroyed it we lost what had been the largest of English cathedrals and the most magnificent. The way in which it dominated the City can well be realized from the contemporary views, and before it lost its graceful spire, struck by lightning in 1561, this had soared high above all the hundred and twenty church spires which rose from every quarter of the City.

Elizabeth's stately Whitehall, like old St. Paul's, has vanished, leaving only the memory of its splendour. In her day the palace covered many acres, and through the centre of its grounds ran the road from London to Westminster, entered at either end under a magnificent archway. Westwards its buildings fronted St. James' Park ; along the river it stretched practically from Charing Cross to the present Whitehall Gardens. Whitehall stairs, which still exist, and the corner of Richmond Terrace mark the bounds of that portion of the palace occupied by the Queen. Her orchard fronted the river and her garden stretched to where Parliament Street now runs.

Although the Tudor period saw much building in and around London, as well as the erection of noblemen's palaces and of Sir Thomas Gresham's famous Royal Exchange, it saw also the beginning of the overcrowding of the metropolis, with which problem the authorities have found themselves confronted ever since. Not only had the population steadily increased, but it had been augmented by the influx of all those restless spirits who flocked to Court to make their fortunes and who generally forsook the country and took up their permanent abode in London. Many a ballad echoed the lament that landlords were leaving their estates to look after themselves :

> Great men by flocks there be flown . . .
> to London-ward. . . .
> Houses where music was wont for to ring
> Nothing but bats and owlets do sing,
> Welladay. . . .
> Houses where pleasures once did abound
> Nought but a dog and a shepherd is found. . . .
> Places where Christmas revels did keep
> Is now become habitations for sheep.[1]

" The use and ancient custom of this realm," says one of the speakers in the dialogue of " Civil and Uncivil Life," [2] " was that all noblemen and gentlemen (not called to

[1] Roxburghe Ballads.
[2] W. C. Hazlitt : " Inedited Tracts," Roxburghe Library.

attendance in our prince's service) did continually inhabit
the country, continuing there from age to age, and from
ancestor to ancestor, a continual house and hospitality."
Now, he complains, the country is deserted ; and he might
have added that London, wholly unprepared for this new
state of affairs, was suffering also.

Overcrowding had already begun to create slums.
Nothing creates a slum quarter more quickly than old
houses that have come down in the world. The palace
that was originally designed for some nobleman and his
enormous establishment becomes first the tenement house
and then the rabbit-warren, the plague spot, crowded from
garret to cellar with dirty, poverty-stricken wretches. The
tide of fashion, ebbing westwards, had left stranded many
such city houses. Elizabeth tried to enforce the rule of
" one house one family," but not even a Tudor could arrest
this inevitable process, whilst others of her measures literally forced such cohabitation upon the poorest section of
the community. Elizabeth, and James after her, feared
the natural growth of London, feared the growth of the
City's power ; and their legislation forbade the erection of
new buildings upon hitherto unoccupied sites in the City,
and also within a three mile radius beyond the gates.[1] A
letter written in 1602 really gives the whole situation in a
nutshell : " The Council have lately spied a great inconvenience, of the increase of housing within and without
London, by building over stables, in gardens, and other odd
corners ; whereupon they have taken order to have them
pulled down ; and this week they have begun almost in
every parish to light on the unluckiest, here and there one,
which, God knows, is far from removing the mischief." [2]

Gardens and open spaces admittedly there were throughout the length and breadth of Elizabethan London. They
helped to sweeten the air in slum localities, but, as the letter
just quoted admits, they were being encroached upon, so
that the bad condition of the streets of the town intensified

[1] See, for example, Acts of the Privy Council, Vol. XIX, pp. 278–80,
quoted Tawney and Power, " Tudor Economic Documents," I.
[2] See " Letters written by John Chamberlain," Camden Soc. Publ.,
p. 142.

the evils resulting from the bad housing conditions. Except for its two or three main thoroughfares London was a network of narrow, badly paved lanes, half darkened by the overhanging fronts of the houses, and rendered wholly unsavoury by the unpleasant habit which prevailed of depositing all the garbage in the kennel or in front of one's door. Some of these lanes were not even paved ; the Strand, for example, not until Elizabeth's time. In such parts the pedestrian picked his way along a path of trodden, rutted soil, " soaked," says one modern sanitary authority, " with the filth of centuries." When one of the plague's many visitations occurred the city authorities would bestir themselves and order every citizen to make a bonfire in front of his house and burn his own rubbish three times a week at seven o'clock in the evening. In 1563 the Mayor and Council even asserted themselves so far as to order that " the filthy dunghill lying in the highway near unto Finsbury Court be removed and carried away " ; they further instructed the inhabitants that their monstrous garbage heap was not to be renewed. Even so, in spite of these spasmodic efforts, the filth and mud of these lanes in wet weather and their stench in the summer was indescribable. The very names of some of them are horribly suggestive : Chick Lane near Smithfield, Stow notes, was popularly known as Stinking Lane.

At nightfall each householder was supposed to hang up a lantern for the benefit of the passers-by ; but even when this ordinance was strictly observed these very primitive affairs, with their thick, discoloured horn panes and their guttering candles, did little to reveal either the condition of the path underfoot or the lurking assailant, crouching in the deep shadow, and as willing to cut a throat as a purse. A prudent body preferred not to go unaccompanied after dark, and the habit of hiring link-boys or of equipping servants with torches to light the way was general. Gallants who had spent a convivial evening at the tavern would hire one of the drawers to carry a lantern and light them home.

From east to west, however, ran a fine highway, the

Cheapside-Holborn route that London still uses. It was the main arterial road, as the Strand had only recently ceased to be a muddy lane in front of noblemen's stables. The most important section of this great road was Cheapside, famous for its open market, and honoured by the passage of every civic pageant or royal progress. On the south side it boasted what the annalist Stow considered to be one of the finest buildings in London—the splendid block of ten houses and fourteen shops known as Goldsmith's Row. Standing between Bread Street and the Cross these houses were all four storeys high, uniformly built, and decorated with the goldsmiths' arms—fitting residences for members of one of the oldest of the city companies, the bankers of their age, and amongst the most prosperous of the citizens. Howes, the continuator of Stow, speaks of Cheapside as " the beauty of London," a description well merited by the broad, open, well-paved street. The foreigner Paul Hentzner considered it surpassed all the other streets both in handsomeness and cleanliness, adding, after a eulogy of the gold and silver vessels displayed for sale in the shops, the quaint item of information that it was here the best oysters were sold.

Streets and districts had each their peculiar repute then as now—a point on which Stow in his " Survey of London " supplies much useful information. Printers were only just becoming associated with Fleet Street, which was still more famous for its taverns and its " motions " or sideshows of all kinds. Paul's Churchyard was almost entirely appropriated by the booksellers, Bucklersbury by the grocers and apothecaries. East Cheap was still famous for its cook-shops, but the butchers were encroaching upon it in addition to occupying most of the shops in St. Nicholas Shambles [1] and the Stocks Market, where the Mansion House now stands. Cook shops shared Thames Street with the stock-fishmongers.[2] The " wet-fishmongers " were to be found in Knightrider Street and Bridge Street, or Fish Street Hill as it was sometimes called ; they also

[1] Leading from Newgate to Cheapside.
[2] " Stock-fishes, so called for dried fishes of all sorts, as lings, haberdines, and others."—Stow's " Survey."

overflowed into Friday Street, off Fleet Street. Bread
Street and Milk Street indicated their inhabitants' calling
by their names, as did Goldsmiths' Row ; Milk Street,
however, perhaps contrary to what one would expect,
boasted " many fair houses " in Stow's time. Lothbury
was almost entirely given up to the founders who cast such
things as candlesticks and chafing-dishes. Some of the
best haberdashers were to be found on London Bridge ;
Houndsditch and Long Lane were mostly occupied by old
clothes vendors and brokers. The poulterers, Stow tells us,
were in his time leaving the Poultry for Grass (Gracechurch)
Street and St. Nicholas Shambles. Turnbull Street [1] was
known as a haunt of prostitutes ; and Turnagain Lane was
more or less appropriated to the Billingsgate fishwives, who
in those days, however, shared their market with most
other victuallers except the grocers.

The suburbs had a curious double reputation in Elizabeth's time and her successor's. The assertion usually
made, that they were the most disreputable quarters of
the town, needs to be accepted with some reserve. The
townsman in the dialogue of " Civil and Uncivil Life " tells
the countryman that " the manner of the most gentlemen
and noblemen is to house themselves (if possibly they may)
in the suburbs of the city, because most commonly the air
there being somewhat at large, the place is healthy, and
through the distance from the body of the town, the noise
not much, and so consequently quiet." In the suburbs, he
points out, the water is pure and excellent, and the risk
from that ever-recurring menace, the plague, much
lessened. " Also for commodity," he adds, " we find many
lodgings both spacious and roomy, with gardens and
orchards very delectable."

The bad repute of the suburbs, however, to which one
finds so many allusions in contemporary literature,[2] arose
mainly on account of the number of brothel houses to be
found in some of the poorer outlying quarters. Similar
ill-fame attached to the Bankside and the whole unruly

[1] I.e. Turnmill Street, Clerkenwell.
[2] Particularly in the pamphlets of men like Dekker.

district of Southwark. Here were the " stews," and here
also was Paris Garden, whither men flocked for the bear or
bull baiting and for other animal shows. Several theatres
helped to attract troublesome crowds, ready for brawling
and the breaking of heads. Here too were no less than five
prisons—the King's Bench, the Marshalsea, the White
Lion, the Borough Counter, and the Clink.

Southwark gave sanctuary to many a rogue and law-
breaker ; so too did Alsatia, bounded on the south by the
river, on the north by Fleet Street, and on the east and
west by Whitefriars Street and Carmelite Street. Here
many a cutpurse and murderer found refuge—not, indeed,
the sanctuary of the Roman Church, but a lurking place
where in a known criminal quarter he could probably evade
discovery until the hue and cry had died down. Southwark and Alsatia were not the only rogue quarters, however ; according to Fleetwood, the Recorder of the City,
the two chief haunts of the criminal population, round
about the year 1581, were the precincts of the Savoy and
the brick kilns near Islington ; in 1594 the Lord Mayor
similarly indicated Newington Butts and others of the
southern suburbs.[1]

During Elizabeth's reign the suburbs encroached steadily
upon the open country ; in the seventeenth century one
had to walk as far as Islington before the cuckoo could be
heard. Again and again Stow laments the state of affairs.
Towards Ratcliffe he had seen growing up " a continual
street or filthy straight passage with alleys of small tene-
ments or cottages . . . inhabited by sailors' victuallers."
Just beyond Whitechapel Church he had seen the common
field, " which ought to be open and free for all men,"
" pestered with cottages and alleys." As a good Londoner
he felt it a disgrace that the stranger should thus come
upon his city by such an " unsavoury and unseemly
entrance."

[1] All sanctuaries, except churches and churchyards, were abolished in
1540 (by 32 Hen. VIII, cap. 12). During Elizabeth's reign sanctuary·
could still be claimed by debtors. This privilege was abolished in 1623,
(21 James I, cap. 28, sect. 6 and 7), although it struggled for survival
until 1727.

Nevertheless, in spite of Stow's complaints, Elizabethan London was still surrounded by fields, and within its bounds it boasted many gardens and open spaces, so that as one poet wrote :

> Some say the fairies fair
> Did dance on Bednall Green.

The Rat-catcher's song reminds us in an amusing fashion of the countrified aspect of many parts of the town :

> Rats or mice, ha' ye any rats, mice, polecats, or weasels,
> Or ha' ye any old sows sick of the measles ?
> I can kill them, and I can kill moles, and I can kill vermin that creepeth up and creepeth down, and peepeth into holes ! [1]

Gerard the herbalist went botanizing in " the fields of Holborn near unto Gray's Inn " ; fields lay between Tower Hill and Ratcliffe ; and there were fields around the tiny village of Charing Cross, an outpost of the country lying forgotten and stranded between the cities of London and Westminster.   Gallants and prentices, flocking to the playhouses, rode or walked through the fields by Finsbury to reach The Theatre or The Curtain ; arable ground and meadows lay all around Paddington ; Queen Elizabeth hunted in Hyde Park and at Marylebone ; and young men went hawking where now are the British Museum and Liverpool Street Station.   Woods, too, were everywhere ; north of the outlying village of Kentish Town was some entirely uncleared forest land ; there were woods by Hampstead, Highgate, Islington, and Hornsey, and in Finchley Wood whortleberries could be picked in their proper season.   Hampstead Heath was a real heath, where one might find cotton grass, orchises, and lilies of the valley, and where juniper and bilberry bushes grew thickly.

Islington, Hampstead, and Highgate were real country villages.   Hackney was one of the country places which supplied London with turnips ; the women of the village brought them to the Cross in Cheapside, and sold them in the market.   Hoxton, or " Hogsden," was country too,

[1] British Museum, Addit. MS. 29376, f. 73.

separated from London by the as yet undrained Moorfields, marshy and in many places impassable. To Islington Ponds, so we are informed by Master Matthew, Ben Jonson's country " gull " who dwelt at Hogsden, the good citizens resorted for an afternoon's sport, shooting wild ducks. South of the river the aspect was equally countrified : west of London Bridge there was little more than a single row of houses along the Bankside and for perhaps half a mile along the main road from the Bridge ; all around lay St. George's Fields, and beyond these the open country. East of the Tower on the north side there was again a line of houses along the road for about half a mile, then the open. At the farms by Stratford Bow beyond Whitechapel one might buy cakes and cream, and " the Oxford Road " began at the village of St. Giles (in the Fields), of whose position Londoners have recently been reminded by the newly-named St. Giles' Circus.

Most houses had their gardens even in the old and crowded quarters of the City. As London had grown and the noblemen gradually moved westwards, raising new palaces along the banks of the river between Westminster and the City, many of their old residences were acquired by the wealthier merchants, who prized lovely gardens as much as their predecessors had done. In 1602, for example, we find the Marquis of Winchester offering his house near London Wall to the worthy John Swinnerton, knighted in 1603, Lord Mayor in 1612, at the price of some five thousand pounds—this much to the dismay of Fulke Greville, Sir Philip Sidney's friend, and of Lady Warwick, neither of whom appeared to relish the idea of " such a fellow " for their next-door neighbour ! [1]

Both in the new gardens and in the old grew abundance of flowers and fruit. Hatton Gardens were famous, as were those of Gray's Inn, planted by no less an enthusiast than Francis Bacon. In Old Broad Street, and around Drapers' Hall, as round most of the other city companies' halls, there were spacious grounds, fairly laid out. Gerard grew

---

[1] Letter from Greville to the Countess of Salisbury ; see Nichols " Progresses (Eliz.), " IV, 29 ; Talbot Papers, Vol. M, f. 75.

his herbs in his own plot in Holborn, and took care of
Burghley's garden in the Strand.[1] In Tothill Street,
Westminster, there were flourishing pear orchards. Apples,
cherries, pears grew in most gardens, and there were goose-
berry bushes everywhere. Roses, wild roses, sweetbriar,
Spanish broom, the saffron crocus, gilliflowers, daffodils,
narcissi, primroses, lilies, and peonies regularly made
the London gardens gay as their seasons came round.

Such was Elizabeth's London—a proud city, unique
in its constitution and its power.[2] Alike in its squalor and
its splendour, it makes a fitting background to the literature of the age. Our understanding of the parts men played
is quickened by a realization of how the scene was set.
Chaucer's London had been a medieval town like any other,
inhabited by its own citizens, and not overshadowing the
rest of the country; Shakespeare's London was still
" an ornament to the realm by the beauty thereof," but
it was also something more : it was already the new
London, " that adamant which draweth unto it all the
other parts of the land "; John Lyly's encomium [3] may
not have been precisely accurate but it gives the Elizabethan point of view : " A place both for the beauty of
building, infinite riches, variety of all things, that excelleth
all the cities in the world, insomuch that it may be called
the storehouse and mart of all Europe."[4]

---

[1] There is no complete modern edition of Gerard's " Herball ". The
edition published by Marcus Woodward in 1927 is a good selection, containing the best and most characteristic passages. " Leaves from Gerard's
Herball " (1931), by the same editor, is a useful abridged version of the
1927 edition.
  [2] See Appendix I.   [3] " Euphues," 1579.
  [4] For an admirable collection of drawings, derived from and executed in
the manner of the sixteenth century pictorial maps of London, see *Old
London Illustrated. London in the XVIth century.* Drawings by H. W.
Brewer. Text by H. A. Cox. 8th ed. 1946. Published by " The Builder ".

CHAPTER IV

ROUND THE TOWN

THE literature of the day abounds in sketches of town life and character. From the gallant to the water carrier the Londoners jostle their way through the pamphlets, the comedies, the ballads and the broadsides ; the realistic impulse in letters was not slow to make use of the motley crowd of them. Naturally the result was by no means always literature ; this impulse turned first and foremost, as it generally does, to the exploitation of the sordid and the sensational. But the picture, if crudely limned, is nevertheless a vivid one. If we know Paul's Walk, the theatres, and the taverns, we need have no difficulty in peopling them. Individual after individual steps forth, naïvely assertive and self-confident—brave or sorry, each cuts a figure and challenges our attention. Just so must they have challenged the gaze of many an honest countryman, setting foot in the city for the first time. If in imagination we may follow such a one as he wanders from street to street, seeing " the sights " of London, we shall find ourselves rubbing shoulders with them all, may watch them intent upon their lawful—and unlawful—occasions.

Lodge has drawn our countryman's portrait for us in his " holiday suit "—a russet jacket, faced with red worsted, with a pair of blue camlet sleeves and a dozen pewter buttons, hose and stockings of grey kersey, large " slop " breeches, and a green bonnet. We may picture him riding into London early in the morning along the Holborn-Cheapside route, leaving his horse at some hostelry, and then sallying forth again to accomplish his business and see the sights of the town. Already the streets are crowded and busy, although it is barely eight o'clock. There is a general hubbub on all sides : " hammers are beating in one place, tubs hooping in another, pots clinking in a third, water tankards running at till in a fourth." [1]   Every now and again the notes of the street cries fall pleasantly upon the ear, piercing the more discordant noises ; men and women are crying hot apple pies and hot mutton pies, live periwinkles, hot oatcakes, fresh herrings, fine potatoes.[2] The sweep announces himself with a lengthy call :

" Swepe chimney swepe, mistris, with a hey derry swepe from the bottom to the top, swepe chimney swepe.   Then shall no soote fall in your poridge pot, with a hoop-dery, dery, dery swepe ! "   No sooner has he passed than a pretty girl comes calling " Fine Seville oranges, fine lemons," to be drowned by the prosaic demand " Ha' ye any corns on your feet or toes ? " and " Will ye buy any starch or clear complexion, mistress ? " followed by " Ripe hartychokes ripe, medlars fine ! "

The prentices are busily taking down shutters, opening the shops, setting up little stalls outside the house doors, and getting ready their wares for the day's business.   As he passes an open doorway, the countryman sees a small boy with a satchel in his hand come racing down the stairs.   His father, standing in the shop, calls to him, " Are you up ?   Is it time to rise at eight of the clock ?   You shall be whipt."   Then he dismisses the sleepy scholar with his blessing, providing him with an invitation to dinner for his schoolmaster to save him from the beating which his late arrival would otherwise earn him.[3]

Walking on eastwards along Cheapside the countryman watched the schoolboy alternately running and loitering ahead of him.   Presently the youngster came up with a small companion of a similar truant disposition, and they stopped for a friendly contest in top scourging.   Then as an old woman came round the corner crying, " Cherry ripe, apples fine, medlars fine ! " they forsook their play to tease her to give them some of her fruit.   As the countryman

[1] Dekker : " Seven Deadly Sins of London " ; 1606.
[2] The cries quoted in this chapter have been taken from manuscript music in the British Museum, i.e. Addit. MSS. 29372-77, 29427.   See Appendix II.
[3] Hollyband : " French Schoolemaister."

drew near he heard her protesting that she herself had to buy everything, whereupon one of the lads asked cheekily, " Canst thou not have of gift the filth which is painted on thy hands and neck ? " and snatched a handful of cherries from her basket.   The dialogue terminated with a shrewdly aimed box on the ear from the justly irritated fruit-seller. " If thou get thee not hence, thou shameless boy, thy cheeks shall feel these filthes.   Restore the cherries that thou hast stolen from me, little thief ! " [1]   The country-man heard no more, but in a few moments the boys dashed past him again.   He lost sight of them as they turned down a side street and when he reached it they had vanished— into Paul's Churchyard, he surmised, and some school there, as above him towered the huge bulk of the cathedral. He meant to visit Paul's, but for the moment he had business to transact in Cheapside, so he retraced his steps —the cathedral must come later.

When about an hour afterwards he again stepped forth into the street it seemed even busier and more crowded than before—carts and coaches rattling up and down, and everywhere throngs of people, laughing, gossiping, quarrel-ling, men, women, and children in such shoals that, as Dekker says, " posts are set up of purpose to strengthen the houses, lest with jostling one another they should shoulder them down."   As he stood for a moment in the doorway three apprentices in the shop behind him started a catch :

O the month of May, the merry month of May,
So frolic, so gay, and so green, so green, so green.[2]

From the next house came the notes of a viol de gamba— some good citizen's daughter at her music lesson, perhaps. Then yet another of the tuneful cries caught his ear : " I ha' ripe cowcumbers, ripe, ripe, ripe ! " and in every doorway that he passed stood a ready-tongued apprentice, adver-tising his master's wares.   One deep-voiced fellow called to him : " Will ye buy a very fine cabinet, a fine scarf, or a

[1] Hollyband : " Campo di Fior."
[2] Dekker : " Shoemaker's Holiday," III, v.

rich girdle and hangers ? " A woman's persuasive notes were inveigling a fine lady into her shop : " See here, madam, fine cobweb lawn, good cambric, or fair bone lace." A lad piped in his ear : " Will ye buy any very fine silk stocks, sir ? " and his helper took him up with : " See here a fair hat of the French block, sir." As he passed on they called after him in unison : " What do ye lack, do ye buy, sir, see what ye lack ? Pins, points, garters, Spanish gloves or silk ribbons ? " [1]

The diversity of things to hear was only rivalled by the astonishing variety of the things to see. As he stood admiring the handsome buildings of Goldsmiths' Row every imaginable kind of personage came passing by, and he stared at them all in frank delight. Porters staggering and sweating under enormous burdens hurried past ; there seemed no limit to the size of the trunk one man would hoist on to his back. Gravefaced merchants, bound for the Royal Exchange, paced slowly by, their prosperity betokened by their fine gold chains and their long, richly furred robes. Then came a noisy group of gallants swaggering along with much elbowing of their way and a perfunctory " By your leave." Resplendent in silks and satins and jewels they make a glittering show, but the countryman comments to himself on the folly that bears its lands on its back, and thinks nothing of paying the price of three fields for a pair of breeches, or of a farm for its shoestrings.

As he walked towards the conduit at the far end of Cheapside he noticed that a large crowd had gathered around it. On inquiring the cause he was told that the Lord Mayor and the Aldermen and " many worshipful men and divers of the masters and wardens of the twelve companies " according to an old custom were inspecting all the conduit heads upon which the City's water supply depended. All were on horseback, and dogs and huntsmen accompanied them ; before dining they would hunt and kill a hare. After dinner, so our countryman was to hear that evening

---

[1] Richard Deering : " A Fancy : What d'ye lacke ? "—B.M. Addit. MSS. 29372.

in his tavern, they roused a fox : " and there was a goodly cry for a mile and after, the hounds killed the fox at the end of St. Giles, and there was a great cry at the death and blowing of horns." [1]

As our countryman turned into Paul's Churchyard, and began to look about him the first thing that attracted his attention was the number of signs above the booksellers' shops. From every house swung a gaily painted sign —some of them appropriate enough to their surroundings : the Bible, the Angel, the Holy Ghost, the Bishop's Head, and the Holy Lamb. The exotic Parrot was matched by the Black Boy, and a Mermaid kept the Ship in countenance. Keys and Crowns, Roses and Blazing Stars confronted the sign of the Gun ; and in whatever year one came to the Churchyard there was always a delightful menagerie of Green Dragons, Black Bears, White Horses, Pied Bulls, Greyhounds, Foxes, and Brazen Serpents, with Tigers' Heads, and a unique and short-lived Goshawk in the Sun. Outside the shops stood the trestle stalls on which the booksellers displayed their wares ; on them books newly come from the press lay side by side with firm favourites and neglected volumes which had never caught the general fancy. As the passers-by went to and fro the prentices stationed by the stalls to keep an eye on the books did their best to shout each other down and attract attention. " What lack you, gentleman ? " could be heard on all sides. " See a new book, new come forth, sir ; buy a new book, sir." [2] In some of the doorways stood the masters of the shops themselves. Nashe draws the portrait of one of these worthies whom he knew, " with his thumb under his girdle, who, if a man came to his stall to ask him for a book, never stirs his head, or looks upon him, but stands stone still and speaks not a word, only with his little finger points backwards to his boy who must be his interpreter." [3]

One such bright lad, having successfully drawn the countryman's attention to his stall, assures him that he

[1] Machyn's " Diary," (1550-63), Camden Soc. Publ.
[2] See Samuel Rowlands : " Tis Merrie when Gossips Meet," 1602 edn. only ; reprinted in Hunterian Club's " Collected Works "
[3] " Pierce Penniless," 1592

can show him " as many of all sorts as any in London."
Upon the countryman's demanding " all Greene's books in
one volume," however, the voluble little salesman is driven
to admit that he unfortunately lacks the " Conny-Catching "
and some half-dozen more. Not to be beaten, he eagerly
offers to obtain them for his customer and assures him
that he can supply him with the " Two parts of Pasquil,"
or a second-hand copy of " Pierce Penniless," both of which
are lying on the stall, and which he displays hopefully,
trusting that the gentleman's demand for Greene has
enabled him to size up his taste in popular literature, and
that Nashe may meet the case equally well.[1]

At most of the stalls men are fingering newly printed
volumes and discussing their authors' merits. Shabby
individuals, with one eye on the proprietor, stand reading
the latest success ; such fellows return time after time until
they have skimmed through the book and can prate of it
glibly when the talk turns to such topics. And often
enough, while the poor scholar catches his glimpse of
the book he cannot afford to purchase, inside the shop
there ruffles it the pretender to learning—such a gallant as
Ben Jonson[2] describes who " will sit you a whole afternoon
sometimes in a book-seller's shop, reading the Greek, Italian
and Spanish when he understands not a word of either."

But our countryman will not linger unduly by the
book-sellers' stalls : he is doing the sights, and he will
undoubtedly take us up the steeple of St. Paul's. For a
penny he can climb to the top, and when he has admired
the view, and has pondered the truth of the story of Banks's
horse, who was reputed to have made this very ascent, he
will certainly " draw his knife and grave his name in great
characters upon the leads." Already, Dekker tells us,
in his time, the steeple of Paul's boasted more names than
Stow's " Chronicle," so our countryman will descend well
content at having added his to their number.[3]

---

[1] The customer with whom the dialogue was conducted in Rowlands'
tract is eventually represented as going away with a copy of it, for which
he pays sixpence (*ut supra*).
[2] " Everyman out of his Humour."
[3] Frederick Duke of Würtemberg carved his on the leads at Windsor
Castle.

As he nears the bottom of the twisting little stair a babel of conversation greets him, and in a moment he finds himself in the crowd, borne along towards the middle aisle, the Mediterranean—Paul's Walk, as they call it, known even to him by bad repute, as the haunt of needy knaves and tricksters, pickpockets, soldiers of fortune, and all other disreputables. Dekker has made a lively sketch of the scene in his " Dead Term " : " What swearing is there, what facing and out-facing ? What shuffling, what shouldering, what jostling, what jeering, what biting of thumbs to beget quarrels . . . what casting open of cloaks to publish new clothes, what muffling in cloaks to hide broken elbows . . . foot by foot and elbow by elbow shall you see walking the knight, the gull, the gallant, the upstart, the gentleman, the clown, the captain, the apple-squire, the lawyer, the usurer, the citizen, the bankrupt, the scholar, the beggar, the doctor, the idiot, the ruffian, the cheater, the Puritan, the cut throat."

And so our countryman finds himself jostled and pushed by the press of people into the notorious Paul's Walk, half bewildered by the noise, half fascinated by the gaiety and colour of the spectacle. That it was indeed " the land's epitome . . . the whole world's map, which you may here discern in its perfectest motion, jostling and turning " he could hardly be expected to realize ; the lawyers chattering with their clients, the merchants discussing their affairs, the gallants exchanging jests and anecdotes, are all, to him, potential conny-catchers. If one of them should accost him in pure politeness he fancies himself the victim of a plot ; his hand is all the time thrust into the pocket of his slop, clutching firmly at his purse for fear of the Nip or the Foist.[1] He has not forgotten the story told by Robert Greene of an honest country fellow who, in spite of a similar precaution, was cozened of his purse in Paul's. " A proper young gentleman," who was no other than the cutpurse's " Stale " or decoy, sank down at the farmer's feet in a pretended swoon, calling for help. The farmer, greatly concerned, picked him up, rubbed him and chafed

---

[1] I.e. the cutpurse and the pickpocket.

him ; and then, as people crowded round, the Foist saw his opportunity, neatly picked the poor man's pocket and got away with the purse.[1]

The mere remembrance of the anecdote was enough for our sightseer ; he began to elbow his way out of the crowd, excusing his faint-heartedness to himself by the assurance that it was near upon the hour for dinner, and that he had first to call upon a merchant who dwelt in one of the houses on London Bridge, to deliver to him a packet of letters entrusted to his care by a friend in the country. As he neared the door, however, his attention was attracted by a loud-voiced, gaudily dressed fellow who had buttonholed two callow youths, come to exhibit their new cloaks in Paul's fashion parade. He was declaiming upon the subject of food, talking

> . . . much against excess
> Swearing all other nations eat far less
> Than Englishmen,

and proceeding to praise the French and Spanish fashion of dining, where four or five persons content themselves with twenty figs and half a pint of wine.[2] Our countryman, amazed at such curious opinions, glanced at the orator's lean visage and summed the matter up in his own mind— rightly, had he but known—as a case of " sour grapes." He knew from his conny-catching literature what " to dine with Duke Humphrey " meant ; and here in the flesh, he was sure, was one of those frequenters of Paul's, who when unable to cadge a meal from anyone had perforce to fast and to spend a doleful dinner hour skulking unobtrusively in the neighbourhood of Duke Humphrey's tomb, until such a time as the more fortunate returned from their ordinaries, and might perhaps be successfully spunged upon for a cup of wine or a supper.

Proud of having identified a real Paul's " character," and half relieved, half disappointed at having seen nothing of the conny-catchers, the countryman took his way towards the Bridge. As he descended the steep slope of

[1] Greene : " Second Part of Conny-Catching " ; 1592.
[2] Samuel Rowlands : " Letting of Humours Blood," Satire I ; 1600.

LONDON BRIDGE

From Visscher's "View," 1616

Fish Street Hill he saw people running and a crowd quickly gathering in front of a shop just by the Bridge gate. He hurried on to share in the excitement, and learnt from an informative fellow in the buzzing throng that the shop was a bookseller's, and that folk had collected because the word had spread abroad that the searchers of the Stationers' Company were inspecting the stock of the owner, one Thomas Gosson. His informant enlarged on the troubles of the London printers and booksellers; the trade was plagued beyond bearing, he declared, by the monopolies granted to the richer members of the Stationers' Company; they had the sole rights of printing and selling all the most profitable books, those for which there was a continual demand. If anyone else tried to print and sell such a thing as an A B C book, for example, he got into trouble for it with the Company, as apparently Thomas Gosson was doing at the moment.

As he spoke a little procession began to emerge from the shop, and everybody craned to see what was happening, the countryman and his informant elbowing their way to the front. First came the Wardens of the Stationers' Company, talking together; Gosson the bookseller escorted them out of the shop, not looking so downcast as might have been expected; then came two of his apprentices staggering under enormous armfuls of small books. The countryman's acquaintance stretched out a long arm, and picked the topmost book off the pile. " A B C and the Little Catechism," he announced as he threw it back to the scowling boy, and the crowd murmured sympathetically as it began to disperse. The countryman gathered that most people thought the monopolist a fair prey, and that the general hope was that Gosson had made his profit before he was unfortunate enough to be caught.[1]

Hurrying on to his destination our countryman found that the merchant whom he sought was not at home, but

---

[1] " The A B C and Little Catechism " was the property of the well-known printer John Day, and his brother Richard; and this little predatory excursion made by Gosson and others into Day's preserves is a matter of history. It cost this particular pirate a fine of one pound. See Arber: " Stationers' Register," II, 791, 826.

was expected back for the midday dinner in a short time.
As he waited he fell into talk with the lively little apprentice who was tidying up the shop.   He had always thought
of the London prentice as rather a dangerous fellow, throw-
ing stones at foreigners, abusing strangers, and ready at
the terrible cry of " Clubs ! " to seize his cudgel and join
his fellows in his favourite game of breaking other folks'
heads.   This lad, however, was a quiet, pleasant mannered
child.   He inquired the boy's name, and was told " Eustace."   He then asked him how he enjoyed learning his
trade, and what it was like to be a prentice.   Eustace
allowed that the learning of the trade did not irk him, but
complained that his master kept him hard at work from
morning till night, so that he could never get any time to
himself.   He no sooner sits himself down to breakfast with
his mates than " Eustace ! Eustace ! " echoes through the
house, and he has to leave his food and run and see what is
wanted.   Worst of all is the way in which his master keeps
him from all the delights of London :

> He will not let me see a mustering,
> Nor on a Mayday morning fetch in May.
> I am no sooner got into the fencen school
> To play a venue with some friend I bring,
> But " Eustace ! Eustace ! " all the street must ring.
> He will allow me not one hour for sport,
> I must not strike a football in the street
> But he will frown ; nor view the dancing school
> But he will miss me straight.[1]

Eustace had barely concluded the catalogue of his woes
with a final lament upon his master's inability to see eye
to eye with him in the matter of a joyous bout at fisticuffs
in the street when the merchant entered.   The countryman
explained his errand, and produced his packet of letters.
The merchant was about to break the seal when from within
came the voice of the mistress of the house : " All is
ready ; the meat marreth ; where have you tarried so
long ? "   Turning to the countryman he thereupon pressed

---

[1] Thomas Heywood : " Four Prentices of London," 1632 : first published 1615.

him to dine with him and his family, to which invitation
the visitor only too gladly assented, having proposed to
himself nothing but the plain fare of a shilling ordinary.[1]
They passed at once into the chamber where the table was
laid, and after he had greeted his host's wife the children
appeared and their mother in a hasty aside bade the eldest
little boy " Take your sister by the hand, take off your cap,
and make curtsey." [2] When they had washed and were
seated at the board the little fellow said grace, and then
amid much bustle on the part of the servants the dishes
were set before them.   The fare was good and plentiful,
and the countryman was especially struck by the number
of meat dishes provided ; at home he was accustomed to
more simplicity and less variety.

At dinner the talk turned, amongst other things, to the
Royal Exchange, which the countryman expressed himself
desirous of seeing.   His host promptly offered to conduct
him there after the meal, and dilated upon its handsome
appearance and its general utility both as a bazaar and as
a meeting place for the merchants of the city for the transaction of business.   He recalled the inconvenience of the
old days before the Exchange was built, when one met one's
fellow-merchants in the open, if fine, and took refuge in an
adjacent tavern if wet.   When they bade farewell to the
good lady and left the house he was still holding forth upon
the munificence of the founder and builder, Sir Thomas
Gresham.   As they took their way up Fish Street Hill, he
branched off, however, on to other topics and took care to
point out to the visitor all the places of interest that they
passed.   He led him on up Gracechurch Street, and at the
Cornhill and Leadenhall corner called his attention particularly to the fine vista of houses and gardens as they looked
up Bishopsgate.   He took him a little way past the corner
in order to point out, on their left, Gresham's own dwelling,
where, on the occasion of the Queen's memorable visit to
his Exchange, he had had the honour to offer her a banquet.
Crosby Hall, too, he pointed out, almost opposite to

[1] I.e. a tavern where the price of the ordinary or table d'hôte dinner
was fixed at a shilling.
[2] Hollyband : " French Schoolemaister."

Gresham's house, a fine fifteenth century building, belonging towards the end of the century to Sir John Spencer,
but the lodging in earlier days of many a foreign ambassador
to the English Court.

And all the time coaches and carts rattled by, with that
peculiarly sharp, penetrating clatter made only by horses
and wheels upon rough paving or cobbled streets.   Always
in his memory our countryman would hear the melodies of
the London cries against a background of noise—the noise
of the London streets :

> There squeaks a cart wheel, here a tumbrel rumbles,
> Here scolds an old bawd, there a porter grumbles,
> Here two tough carmen combat for the way.[1]

Everybody cursed the coaches as they rumbled through
narrow lanes and drove the foot passengers into the doorways of the houses, splashing every one with mud if the
weather was bad.   If you were Sir Francis Drake himself
you must needs stand flat against the wall when the coach
comes past, or its wheels will go over your toes.   " Let a
man but come from St. James to Charing Cross and meet a
coach in his way, one would swear by his dirty cloak he
had come post from St. Michael's Mount in Cornwall."
The way the coaches were allowed to block the streets was
becoming daily more of a scandal.   Two or three of them
might cumber up the thoroughfare for half an hour, while
their fair owners bargained in the shops for ear-rings for
themselves or collars for their pet dogs.   The gate that led
from Paul's Churchyard into Cheapside was badly pestered
with coaches, and by the seventeenth century, whenever a
play was toward at the Blackfriars, Ludgate and Ludgate
Hill were entirely choked by these clumsy conveyances.[2]
Years earlier Stow had remarked the problem of the London
traffic ; shod carts were forbidden, and the fore-horse was
supposed to be led when inside the city precincts, " but
these good orders are not observed," he complains, and the
coachman simply lashes at his horses and takes no heed

---

[1] Guilpin : " Skialetheia," 1598.
[2] " Coach and Sedan pleasantly disputing," 1636.

of other users of the road, while " the drayman sitteth and sleepeth on his dray and letteth his horse lead him home." [1]

Such was the gist of the good merchant's strictures on the coaches and carts that every now and again drove them into doorways even in such a fine thoroughfare as Bishopsgate Street. The countryman began to understand why it was that the Londoner always preferred to travel by river rather than road. And as they drew nearer to the Exchange the coaches clattered past them more frequently than ever, taking the ladies of London to the finest shopping centre in the town, where in Gresham's princely building the merchandise of the world lay awaiting the purchasers.

Retracing their steps along Bishopsgate they turned into Cornhill and passed into the quadrangle of the Exchange, the merchant regretting that the countryman would not be able to hear the music of the city waits, who by express order of the Court of Aldermen played there after seven o'clock in the evening, but only on Sundays and Holy days. Looking about him the countryman saw that the large quadrangle was surrounded by a cloister walk with shops opening off it. His guide explained to him, however, that most of these shops were too dark and damp for the shopkeepers and their clients, and were only used as storage vaults ; to find the best shops he would have to follow the fine ladies and the gallants, who, on entering, made straight for the first floor or " upper pawn " as it was generally called. [2] Glad to escape from the noise of the crowded quadrangle, where they could scarcely hear each other speak, and where swarms of small boys dashed in and out between the throngs and bumped into every one and generally made a thorough nuisance of themselves, the countryman followed this advice ; and bidding farewell to his host, with many compliments and protestations on both sides, mounted to the upper walk to make some small purchases for his family at home and to see the shops of which he had heard so much.

In the upper pawn prentices and serving-women were

[1] Stow : " Survey of London," 1603.
[2] Stow's " Survey," ed. Strype.

standing in the doorways of the shops, calling their wares
to attract the attention of customers.　Every kind of costly
trifle was on sale :

> Such purses, gloves and points
> 　　Of cost and fashion rare,
> Such cutworks, partlets, suits of lawn,
> 　　Bongraces and such ware ;
> Such gorgets, sleeves and ruffs,
> 　　Linings for gowns and cauls,
> Coifs, crippins, cornets, billaments,
> 　　Musk boxes and sweet balls ;
> Pincases, pick-tooths, beard-brushes,
> 　　Combs, needles, glasses, bells,
> And many such like toys as these,
> 　　That Gain to Fancy sells.[1]

At the shop of a seamstress a neat girl was talking at the
passers-by :
　" Would ye have any fair linen cloth ?　Mistress, see
what I have, and I will show you the fairest linen cloth in
London ; if you do not like it you may leave it ; you shall
bestow nothing but the looking on, the pain shall be ours
to show them you."　A young gallant, escorting two ladies,
was obviously attracted by her vivacity, and suggested
that they should enter the shop.　The ladies, admitting
that the wench was " reasonable fine and pretty," agreed,
and they passed within to bargain.　The countryman,
watching through the open window, saw them turning over
hollands and cambrics, pricing the latter at twenty shillings
the ell, vowing they would never pay more than fifteen,
and finally compromising at sixteen, the seamstress protesting the while that she was giving the material away.[2]
　As he turned from the window he heard a voice which he
recognized.　Looking round he saw standing near him,
again holding forth to the inevitable pair of gallants, his
" Paul's man " of the morning.　The fellow was now
obviously trying his luck at the Exchange, and he was still
playing the great traveller ; he was boasting, as our

[1] Breton : " The Fort of Fancy," from " A Flourish upon Fancy."
[2] Erondell : " French Garden."

countryman loitered past him, that he possessed a piece of the chair in which Julius Cæsar had been stabbed, and that he had trodden upon the stones which Satan brought to Christ when tempting Him to turn them into bread.[1] Then the eddying crowd bore him and his would-be victims away, and the countryman heard no more.

Having made his purchases he decided to finish up his sightseeing with a glimpse of the Queen's palace. He walked down to the river again to take boat for Westminster, finding the streets less crowded than they had been in the morning—the gallants had gone to the play, the ladies had gone to the Exchange, the boys were in school, shopkeepers were enjoying an afternoon nap. When he had sufficiently admired the splendours of Whitehall, he entered the Abbey to gaze upon the tombs and monuments of the dead kings and queens of England, " covered all over with gilding and executed in a most beautiful manner." [2] In company with two or three other country cousins like himself he paid his penny [3] to the verger, but refused to be inveigled by that worthy into buying a guide-book [4] to the monuments, much to the latter's disappointment, as he regarded the sightseer as fair game, and took care to make a pretty profit upon every copy he sold. Then by the time he had been the round of the monuments the countryman's zeal began to flag. He decided he would walk back to the City, sup at a tavern in Fleet Street on his way, and then repair to his lodging in Cheapside for a night's rest. Some half-dozen inn signs caught his eye as he walked east from Charing Cross—the Bear and Ragged Staff, the Angel, the King Harry Head, the Golden Bull—but he did not stop until he reached Temple Bar. There he came across a small crowd which was collecting around a ballad singer, who had taken up his standing at this favourite spot. Just

[1] Rowlands, *op. cit.*

[2] This, at any rate, was the impression they gave to that noble sightseer Duke Frederick and his retinue.

[3] See Peacham's preliminary verses to Coryat's " Crudities."

[4] The guide-book in question was Camden's " Reges Reginæ, Nobiles et alii in ecclesia collegiata B. Petri Westmonasterii sepulti 1600." According-ing to a traveller who visited the monuments in 1617 the verger asked too much for the book, being " after the manner of his nation eaten up with avarice."

such a crowd it was as Sir John Davies describes in one of
his " Epigrams " (38), listening to " an ale house story " :

> First stands a porter, then an oyster-wife
> Doth stint her cry, and stays her steps to see him ,
> Then comes a cutpurse, ready with a knife,
> And then a country client passeth near him.
> There stands the constable, there stands the whore,
> And harkening to the song, mark not each other.

Our countryman listened for a moment, and then walked on ;
he had heard many such at every fair he had ever visited.
In Fleet Street he hardly noticed what he passed : at the
Fleet Bridge he had gone by without seeing the " new
motion of the city of Nineveh with Jonas and the whale,"
although a gaudy picture was displayed to lure one in, and
a raucous-voiced individual was advertising the sight with
all his lung-power. He had seen so much and heard so
much in the one day that his faculties felt stunned. He
could not take in any more impressions ; he must sup, and
so to bed.

In the distance he could hear two street vendors crying
alternately, one going up the street and the other down.
One was calling : " Salt—salt—white Worcestershire salt,"
and the other, a man's voice, answered her with, " Will ye
buy any straw ? Ha' ye any wood to cleave ? " The
noise of the town which had surrounded him all day
seemed to be lessening. The sun was getting low ; every
one seemed to have gone indoors. There was a creaking
above his head ; he looked up and saw another swinging
tavern sign ; he pushed open the door and went in for his
supper.

Inside all was bustle and confusion. From upstairs
came the noise of a roystering party in one of the private
rooms, and in the large parlour that he had entered men
were supping or drinking in small groups, while busy
drawers ran to and fro with glasses and tankards, wine
and ale, responding invariably to impatient customers' calls
with their " Anon ! Anon, sir ! " In one corner a company of some half-dozen men were listening to a tall fellow

who was reading a play aloud. He sat down at the table nearest to them, watching them as they commented gravely or boisterously on the matter and the manner and made suggestions to the reader. Each had a cup of wine before him, but their meeting was obviously a business one, and the drink did not circulate freely. Listening to their discussion he realized that they were players, and that they were considering a new play. Parts were being apportioned by the tall man as he read, and details of stage business were being discussed. The countryman ate his supper, and listened hard as their voices rose and fell ; he was surprised at their quietness and at the small amount of wine consumed. He had believed that these players were troublesome rogues, but this little group was the most serious in the room, and the man who was reading might well, by his clothing and his general sobriety of demeanour, have been taken in any assembly for a prosperous merchant ; evidently, however, he was the chief actor in the company, and when the little group finally dispersed, the countryman noticed that it was he who paid the reckoning, two shillings in all.[1]

When the players had gone he turned his attention to another table, where two smartly dressed fellows, who were plying their companion with more than his fair share of the drink, had just summoned one of the drawers to fetch them dice and " a pair of cards." [2] He watched them as they fell to play. The young man seemed to be winning most of the stakes, in spite of the fact that he was manifestly drunk while the other two were quite sober. He was just preparing to settle his own score and leave the tavern, when he noticed that the players' luck was beginning to change ; they were at the dice, and the young man who had been winning was now losing every cast. His opponents' throws were amazing ; they had already more than retrieved their losses, and the countryman felt con-

[1] See Henslowe's " Diary," ed. Greg, F.105ᵛ : " Layd owt for the companye when they Read the playe of Jeffa for wine at the tavern ii₃." Two shillings would probably have paid for a gallon of white wine about this time (i.e. 1602).
[2] I.e. a pack.

vinced they must be using false dice. He gazed keenly to
see if he could detect any sleight of hand, but the gamesters,
if cheats, were too skilful both for him and for their victim ;
he could see nothing suspicious.   Then his attention was
distracted by the entry of two boisterous serving men.
They called for drink, kissed the hostess, cursed the drawer
for his slowness, and began a vivid narration of a scene
they had just witnessed. A young girl had committed
suicide in the town-ditch by Moorfields, and they had seen
men drawing out the drowned body as they came by.[1]

When they had told their tale the countryman glanced
again at his neighbours, but they were gone, and the next
moment the two serving men seated themselves at the
adjoining table, saluting him in a friendly fashion. Taking
advantage of their already loosened tongues and obvious
readiness to talk he opened the subject of false dice and
cheating at cards. The serving men became voluble at
once. There were false dice everywhere, they informed
him ; there were regular workshops for their production
in the King's Bench and the Marshalsea prisons ; they
could even be bought by any would-be cheater.   " Bird in
Holborn is the finest workman," one of them interpolated.[2]
A favourite device, they told him, was to set a small bristle
on one face of a dice, which effectually prevented that face
from lying on the table when it fell ; another trick was to
hollow out one side for the same purpose. From false dice
they went on to roguery in general, and the countryman
listened with delight—here at last was the London of the
conny-catching pamphlets and the ballads, the city where
wickedness and cozening stalked the streets.   They told
him how highway robbers took refuge in the Counters,[3]
and how thieves and strumpets could lodge for the night
in the prisons on paying fourpence to the gaolers, in order
to escape the searches that were made for them by the
watch.[4]   Then they told him of the places where the rogues

[1] See Machyn's " Diary," Camden Soc.
[2] " Manifest Detection of Dice Play," 1552, Percy Soc. Publication,
LXXXVII.
[3] I.e. prisons in Wood Street and the Poultry, and Southwark.
[4] See Stow's " Survey " ; also W. Fennor, " Compters Commonwealth,"
p. 58, 1617.

of the city were harboured—the Falcon in Grace Street, the Gun at Billingsgate, the Rose at Fleet Bridge, Muggleston's House in Whitechapel, the Pressing Iron in Southwark, and the Bear and Ragged Staff at Charing Cross.[1] The countryman was particularly thrilled at their mention of this last ; he had passed it himself, that very afternoon, little guessing the kind of inmates it lodged.

Eager to hear more of this underworld of London, the countryman plied them with a cup of wine apiece, and each vied with the other to produce a more amazing yarn than the last speaker.   What astonished their enthralled auditor most, however, was the account they gave him of a training school for thieves, set up at Smart's Quay, so they averred, by one Wotton : " There was a school house set up to teach young boys to cut purses.   There was hung up two devices, one a pocket, the other a purse.   The pocket had in it certain counters, and was hung about with hawks' bells, and over the top did hang a little scaring bell, and he that could take out a counter without any noise was allowed to be a public hoyster, and he that could take a piece of silver out of the purse, without the noise of any of the bells, he was adjudged a judicial nipper."[2]

The countryman would willingly have listened longer, but the tavern was emptying and his acquaintances offered to put him on his homeward way and see him safely past the watch if he would accompany them.   They set out through the dark streets, guiding their steps by a lantern that one of the men had brought with him.   Light gleamed occasionally through chinks in doors and window shutters, but most of the houses were already in darkness.   Every now and then they passed small parties hurrying home, armed like themselves with lanterns or else with flaring torches.   Suddenly one of the men stepped aside and drew the countryman and his companion after him into the darkness of a tiny alley between tall houses.   They heard a heavy trampling, and round the corner came the watch armed with their brown bills and a lantern each.

[1] See Wright : " Queen Elizabeth and her Times," II, p. 249 ff.
[2] Wright, *ut supra*.

Two people, coming in the opposite direction, ran straight into their arms, almost in front of the alley where the three were hidden. " Who goes there ? " demanded the constable, and the watch gathered round, holding up their lanterns to get a better view of the night-walkers. " Where have you been so late ? " was the next demand, whereupon the hidden watchers heard a woman's voice reply, " At supper, forsooth, with my uncle here, and he is bringing me home." " Are you married ? " then came from the constable. " Yes, forsooth," was the reply, and after a few more questions the two were allowed to pass on.[1] Then when the watch too had left the coast clear the three slipped out of their alley mouth and sped on homewards. In Cheapside they parted, and after much knocking at the door of his inn our countryman eventually roused a sleepy ostler, who admitted him with many grumbles and provided him with a candle. A few minutes more and he was in bed, and as he pulled the clothes over him he heard steps coming down the street. Chime after chime rang out from the city churches, and as he settled his head on his pillow the voice of the watchman floated up to him : " Twelve o'clock, look well to your lock, your fire and your light, and so good night."

---

1 Dekker : " O per se O.'

CHAPTER V

THE QUEEN'S HIGHWAY

TO travel, for an Elizabethan, did not always mean to arrive, but it usually meant to adventure, for the risks of the road were many. Travelling was an arduous undertaking and much might befall a man before he came to his journey's end. The highway itself was an ideal right of passage rather than a substantial track giving solid footing to man and beast. It is scarcely an exaggeration to say that, judged by modern standards, roads were almost non-existent. The four great Roman highways and their dependent roads remained, but apart from these there were only customary tracks across the country, often impassable in winter, rutted and uneven in summer. The wise traveller guided his horse off the beaten pathway, and cantered alongside, on the edge of somebody's field. No one could deliberately travel for pleasure ; people took to the road when it was necessary to get from one place to another, and men travelled about their business. Even in the towns, moreover, the streets were generally in a worse condition than the average farm track is to-day. Roads were not made ; they happened, because a sufficient number of people and horses trod out a track.

The Roman roads had carried the traffic of the Middle Ages, its trade and its pilgrimages, with the help of newer cross roads and bypaths which were more or less kept up by the manor. With the suppression of the old religion and the gradual decay of the manorial system in the late fifteenth and early sixteenth centuries the roads became less generally used and were allowed to fall into a hopeless state of disrepair. Bridges were left to become ruinous, holes and ruts were mended with a few faggots and some brushwood which looked substantial enough but often created a veritable death-trap for man and horse. The

Kentish roads leading from the ports to the capital were probably as good as any in the kingdom ; nevertheless they are described in Henry VIII's reign as passable only at " great pains, peril, and jeopardy." When the way-faring life of the Middle Ages came to an end the roads of the country began to fall into a state of decay which was not arrested till the reign of Mary Tudor.

In 1555 a statute for amending the highways described them as " very noisome and tedious, to travel in and dangerous to all passengers and carriages." [1] The statute was a memorable one, because by it the responsibility for the repair of the roads was apportioned. Hitherto it had been possible for a locality to avoid collision with the law by the most inadequate or perfunctory repairs. The provision of the necessary funds had been left to anybody or nobody. Bequests in wills occasionally furnished the necessary gravel or stones for repairs, but they had become less frequent in the sixteenth century, and taxation was applied to many purposes, but not to this. In 1555, however, the responsibility for providing the necessary funds, materials, tools, and labour was definitely laid upon each parish in the kingdom and upon each of its inhabitants. They had to choose one of their number each year to be their Surveyor of Highways ; the richer members of the community had then, when called upon, to furnish him with teams and men for the work ; the poorer sort had to give their labour for eight hours a day on four consecutive days.

The reform was thus more or less adequately begun, and the office of Surveyor thus created must have been quite one of the most unpleasant that could fall to the lot of any good Tudor citizen. It was an age in which there was no lack of public spirit amongst high or low, but it must have taken a very considerable amount of it to prevent the relations between the unfortunate surveyor and his neighbours from being anything but strained. To be compelled, under penalty of a forty shilling fine for neglect of duty, to make the whole village turn out and mend the roads, when per-

" Statutes of the Realm," 2 and 3 Philip and Mary, cap. VIII.

haps every second individual ought to have been working
on his own holding, was no happy task for any man.
Refusal of the office, however, was no solution of the
difficulty for most people, as that cost no less than five
pounds ; and refusal of work was no solution for those
called upon, as that meant an appearance before the Justice
and a fine . . . so the roads of England began to be more
or less continually, if amateurishly, repaired, and the actual
passageway became a little safer than it had been. In
theory the method would appear a sufficient one, but upon
the practical results Harrison, as usual, has some illuminating remarks. " The intent of the statute," he admits,
" is very profitable," but in practice the rich evade their
share, and the poor so loiter in their labour that scarcely
two good days' work gets accomplished. Individual sur-
veyors, too, had a habit of mending the lanes and ways
that led to their own pastures, instead of concentrating
upon the highway.

Fifty years later complaint was still loud. Thomas
Procter [1] in 1607 reports that there was a great lack of
good roads, " to the daily continual great grief and heart-
breaking of man and beast, with charges, hindrances,
wearing and tiring of them, and sometimes to the great and
imminent danger of their lives, and often spoil and loss of
goods." Procter was a sensible and practical man, and
from his recommendations we realize that since the Romans
made their great ways nobody had bothered either to lay
any foundations for the English roads or to drain them.
" One principal and chief cause of all bad and foul ways is
that the rain water or other water doth lie and rest upon
the highways (not orderly and soundly made) which with
the working of cart wheels and others, doth pierce down
more deeper into the said ways, and so more and more doth
soften and rot the same." Not only did travellers in their
desire to find a fair track ride through the fields to the
" great hurt and spoil of fences and grounds with riding
and going on the corn," but in some places they would

---

[1] " A Worthy Worke Profitable to this whole kingdom. Concerning the
mending of all high-waies," 1607.

refuse to use an old highway at all, as in the case of the road that once led from Gray's Inn to High Barnet. This, Norden tells us, "was refused of wayfaring men and carriers by reason of the deepness and dirty passage in the winter season," so that a new way had to be laid through the park of the Bishop of London from Highgate Hill direct to Whetstone, for the use of which all travellers as they passed through the gate on Highgate Hill paid toll to the Bishop. Foreigners were equally emphatic in their condemnation. Frederick Duke of Würtemberg, for example, who travelled from Oxford to Cambridge in 1592, does not mince matters : " On the road we passed through a villainous boggy and wild country, and several times missed our way, because the country thereabouts is very little inhabited and is nearly a waste, and there is one spot in particular where the mud is so deep that . . . it would scarcely be possible to pass with a coach in winter or rainy weather."

Besides the ruts and the mire and the ruinous bridges there were other dangers which threatened the life and the property of the Elizabethan traveller. In the belts of forest which so often surrounded the cultivated areas lurked highway robbers ready to hold up the solitary rider or even a small company of travellers. Generally the victims would escape with their lives, sometimes not ; the penalty for highway robbery was the same as for highway murder, and with the gallows ready for either offence there was no particular reason why the gentleman of the road, the " High Lawyer," should restrict himself solely to the former, if he happened to lose his temper with an unwilling or stout-hearted prize.

Gadshill, near Rochester, the scene of Falstaff's exploit with the men in buckram, was long notorious as the resort of highway robbers. Shooter's Hill near Blackheath was another danger zone for the traveller, as were the deserted stretches of Salisbury Plain and Newmarket Heath. Prudent men made haste to reach their destination before nightfall involved them in a passage perilous ; Shakespeare himself must often, as a " lated traveller," have

" spurred apace to reach the timely inn " while " the west yet glimmered with some streaks of day." A French conversation manual of the time, in one of its " familiar talks," gives as a matter of course the following picture of the perils of the road ; one of the travellers wishes for a guide to conduct them as the way is so dangerous, and they overtake a horseman and inquire their right road. He replies that they have not far to go, but that the way is " very tedious to keep, furthermore it is so dirty and miry that your horses will be therein to the girths." They tip a poor ploughman for leading them to the village, and before they dismiss him the following conversation ensues :

Traveller. I pray you set me a little in my right way out of the village.

Ploughman. Keep still the right hand until you come to the corner of a wood, then turn at the left hand.

Traveller. Have we no thieves at that forest ?

Ploughman. No, sir, for the provost-marshal hung the other day a half dozen at the gallows which you see before you at the top of that hill.

Traveller. Truly I fear lest we be here robbed . . . we shall spur a little harder for it waxeth night.

On arrival at the inn, however, a good reception awaited such travellers. The next dialogue shows them welcomed by the mistress of the house, who promises that they shall want for nothing. Their horses are handed over to the ostler for a rub down and a " bottle of hay," and the gentlemen enter the inn-chamber where they call for sack and for a man to pull off their riding boots.[1] Upstairs in the bedroom Jane the chambermaid is kindling a fire and getting her warming pan ready, clean sheets are being put upon the feather bed, and every one is bustling round to provide for the new arrivals that good cheer for which the English inns were famous.

The inns in the towns which lay on the great main roads, so Harrison tells us, were " great and sumptuous." " Every man," he asserts, " may use his inn as his own house in England." He has special praise for the napery, the

---

[1] Hollyband : " French Littleton," 1576.

bedding, and the tapestry, and assures us that "each comer is sure to lie in clean sheets, wherein no man hath been lodged since they came from the laundress." Some of these inns seem to have been able to lodge over a hundred people—three hundred, according to Harrison—" and their horses at ease, and thereto with a very short warning make such provision for their diet as to him that is unacquainted therewithall may seem to be incredible." In some of the large towns there were " twelve or sixteen such inns at the least," each with a brightly painted signboard which Harrison condemns as a costly vanity. " It is a world," he exclaims, " to see how each owner of them contendeth with other for goodness of entertainment of their guests, as about fineness and change of linen, furniture of bedding, beauty of rooms, service at the table, costliness of plate, strength of drink, variety of wines, or well using of horses."

While a traveller sojourned in his house the master of the inn held himself responsible for his guest's belongings : " If he lose aught whilst he abideth in the inn the host is bound by a general custom to restore the damage, so that there is no greater security any where for travellers." On the other hand, however, Harrison admits that the inn servants, and the ostlers and tapsters were often in league with gangs of highwaymen. They had many sly ways of discovering whether a man was a likely prize or not.

When a traveller arrived and dismounted from his horse the ostler would busily take down the capcase (or travelling bag) from the saddle-bow, judging by its weight whether the contents were worth robbing. If the ostler failed in his plan, then the man who saw to the guest's chamber would make his attempt, moving the bag ostensibly to a more convenient position in the room ; and " the tapster . . . doth mark his behaviour, and what plenty of money he draweth when he payeth the shot, . . . so that it shall be an hard matter to escape all their subtle practises." Then the word would be conveyed to their purse-cutting con-federates " to the utter undoing of many an honest yeoman as he journeyeth by the way."

Travelling, as we have thus seen, had its manifold

dangers ; it had also its fatigues. Those who could take
to the road on foot were perhaps the luckiest ; horses meant
speed, but the saddles of those days were small and hard
and so uncomfortable for a heavy rider that one distinguished foreigner—that Duke of Würtemberg, who complained of our villainous boggy ways—actually took one
home with him as a curiosity. Women frequently travelled
on horseback, either riding on a pillion or else on a man's
saddle. Coaches were sometimes used for long journeys,
but these too must have been extremely tiring as they had
no springs to them, the body of the coach resting directly
on the axles. The jolting and the jarring must have been
intolerable, but for anyone with a family of women-folk to
transport these lumbering conveyances were both convenient and cheap, and during this reign they came more
and more into favour. In spite of the discomfort the
Queen herself frequently used a coach for travelling, and
so set the fashion for others of her sex. It even became
possible, according to Fynes Moryson in 1607, to hire a
coach for journeys near London at the rate of ten shillings
a day.

Carts, both two-wheeled and four-wheeled, were used by
the country-people for transporting their goods and farm
produce. They were also necessary for the moving of a
large household, or for the Queen's annual progresses. On
such occasions as these latter the roads must have been
churned into an even worse state of mud and ruts than
usual, by the long train of wagons required to carry the
goods and provisions which accompanied each stage of the
journey. Harrison comments on the fact that sumpter
horses had been given up in his time, because " Our Princes
and the Nobility have their carriage commonly made by
carts, whereby it cometh to pass that when the Queen's
Majesty doth remove from any place to another there are
usually 400 carewares which amount to the sum of 2400
horses appointed out of the countries adjoining, whereby
her carriage is conveyed safely unto the appointed
place."

The regular frequenters of the road were the posts and

the carriers. The latter during this reign began to use carts as well as horses, and would occasionally carry passengers besides goods. The service was a well-organized and regular one ; the great towns all had their carriers, who kept them in communication with London. The Oxford carrier,[1] for example, in 1575, left for London on Wednesday each week, and had to be back again by Saturday at the latest. He charged 2s. 4d. for each hundredweight of goods carried. While this transport service was at the disposal of all, however, the post as a means of conveying correspondence was restricted to the use of the Government. It was, literally, the Queen's post. The private person who wished to send a letter from London to Bristol had to rely either on a private messenger or on the carriers, or even on such an extremely dubious personage as a chapman or pedlar. There was only one way in which the public was able to benefit by the postal system—the individual as well as the official was allowed to hire the post-horses for his journeys, if he did not possess a horse of his own, or if his business required greater speed than could be obtained from one horse. By travelling " post " he could hire horses at threepence a mile, and could do seventy miles or more in a day if necessary, each horse being taken back after a ten-mile stage by a mounted postboy. Many travellers, however, who could not afford the post charges bought themselves horses for the purpose of a journey, and sold them when they returned home again.

The footpad was not the only rogue who haunted the highways, though from most others of the vagrant tribe the able-bodied passenger had little molestation to fear. The Elizabethan tramp was a much more picturesque personage than his modern descendant ; he was a member of a very highly organized profession, with a jargon of its own and its own distinct social ranks. Of the habits and way of life of this curious confraternity of vagabonds we have many detailed accounts. Dekker the dramatist has set forth in his pamphlets an anatomy of roguery

[1] See Mallet : " History of Oxford University," II, 109.

which gives us an extraordinarily vivid picture of this aspect of Elizabethan life. He is rivalled perhaps by his predecessor Greene, while any mention of rogue-literature would be sadly incomplete without reference to the two yet earlier pamphlets—Awdelay's " Fraternitye of Vacabondes " and Harman's " Caveat for Commen Cursetors."

The vagrants and beggars who roamed the countryside were to some extent quite distinct from the " connycatching " rogues who haunted the streets and taverns of London. They had their own organization, and their canting tongue differed from that of the town rogues, although not greatly. Of all the unsavoury specimens of humanity to be met with in a day's travel these must certainly have been the worst—filthy, verminous beings, dressed in tattered, weather-stained garments and disfigured often enough by every imaginable kind of sore, wound, or mutilation. Their conny-catching brethren of the town contrived to present as prosperous an appearance as they could : the rogues of the highways were destitution incarnate.

By Elizabeth's time vagabondage had increased to such an alarming extent that the regulation of it was one of the chief problems with which the Government was confronted. The wandering beggars numbered in their ranks all kinds of men and women, from the real gipsies—the Romanys—to the impotent poor and the sturdy rascals whose one aim in life was to avoid honest work. Amongst them was many a " wild rogue," vagabond by birth, born to the road, and sometimes boastful of three such generations behind him. Discharged serving men, old soldiers, ruined smallholders, out-of-work agricultural labourers, masterless men of all kinds helped to make up an almost unbelievably numerous crew of rascals, who swarmed over the whole country-side practising the gentle art of living on nothing a year at the expense of the respectable members of the community.

The most fantastic and horrible of these creatures to be met on the high road were the Palliards, the Abraham-Men, and the Counterfeit Cranks. The Palliard, who was also known in the canting tongue as a Clapperdudgeon, was the kind of beggar who deliberately covered his limbs with loathsome running sores to rouse compassion and elicit alms. To make these raw and bleeding places they would tie arsenic or ratsbane on an ankle or an arm. When it had produced its corrosive effect they would then leave the sore exposed, and surround it with bloody and filthy rags, and so take their way from fair to fair and market to market, sometimes obtaining as much as five shillings a week in charity. Sham " old soldiers " used much the same method to produce " wounds," applying unslaked lime, soap, and iron rust, which made the arm appear black, while the sore was " raw and reddish but white about the edges like an old wound." [1]

The Counterfeit Crank was another rogue who also dressed himself in the filthiest rags imaginable, daubed his face with blood, and pretended to have the falling sickness or some other dreadful affliction. One of the favourite tricks in his repertoire was to fall grovelling in the dirt at the feet of a passer-by, counterfeiting froth at the mouth by judicious sucking of a piece of soap! Harman tells us in his " Caveat " of one such rogue who earned 14s. 3½d. in a day.

The Abraham-Man was perhaps the most terrifying figure of the three, as he pretended to be mad. Tom o' Bedlam and Poor Tom were other names for him. These impostors roamed the country half-naked. " He walketh bare armed and bare legged," Awdelay tells us, " and carrieth a pack of wool or a stick with bacon on it or such like toy," " Poor Tom's a-cold," wails Edgar in " King Lear " when counterfeiting one of these madmen. " Who gives anything to poor Tom ? . . . Do poor Tom some charity, whom the foul fiend vexes. . . . Who is whipped from tithing to tithing, and stock-punish'd and imprison'd. . . . Tom's a-cold." On his journeys between London and Stratford Shakespeare must often enough have come across these " Bedlam beggars " :

[1] Dekker : " O per se O," 1612. When desirous to heal it again they would apply to such a " wound " brown paper covered with butter and wax.

> who, with roaring voices
> Strike in their numbed and mortified bare arms
> Pins, wooden pricks, nails, sprigs of rosemary ;
> And with this horrible object, from low farms,
> Poor pelting villages, sheep-cotes and mills
> Sometime with lunatic bans, sometime with prayers,
> Enforce their charity.

Dekker several times describes the devices of these " Abraham-Men." In " O per se O " he tells how they terrify the women and children of the country villages more than " the name of Raw Head and Bloody Bones, Robin Goodfellow or any other Hobgoblin " ; " crackers tied to a dog's tail make not the poor cur run faster than these Abram Ninnies does the silly Villages of the Country, so that when they come to any door a begging, nothing is denied them." According to his " Belman of London " some of them used even more violent methods ; they are " dogged and so sullen both in look and speech, that spying but a small company in a house they boldly and bluntly enter, compelling the servants through fear to give them what they demand." Alexander Barclay in his " Ship of Fools " gives a vivid description of the beggars of his own time which may be applied equally well to these Abraham-Men and Counterfeit Cranks of Shakespeare's day :

> Some ray their legs and arms over with blood,
> With leaves and plasters though they be whole and sound ,
> Some halt as cripples, their leg falsely up-bound ;
> Some other beggars falsely for the nones
> Disfigure their children, God wot unhappily,
> Mangling their faces and breaking their bones,
> To stir the people to pity that pass by.

Thus they wheedled and terrorized the country folk and sometimes the wayfarer into a reluctant almsgiving.

A disreputable life they led, these rascals of the highway, but merry enough, so long as they achieved their main object, which was the avoidance of work in any shape or form. The Anglers amongst them would fish for linen off the hedges and trifles from inside a room with an open window, their tackle consisting of a long stick with a hook at the end of it. The Prigger of Prancers had an eye for a good nag, and woe to the farmer who left his horse loose in a meadow when one of these rogues was about. The Rufflers ruffled it after the manner of their kind, begging from the able-bodied, openly robbing the un-protected. The Rogue would put his hand to anything, picking the pockets of poor fools like Perdita's brother, turning ballad-monger or pedlar or pilferer as occasion served. And at the head of their profession, chiefs of the gang, were the Upright Men, who being the strongest and most influential members of the vagabond community not only had their choice amongst the women but frequently lived by extorting contributions from members of their own lower orders !

More or less identified with this motley throng of beggars and their wenches were the minstrels, pedlars, tinkers, and bear-wards, fortune-tellers and jugglers. They too led the vagabond life, roaming up and down the highways and frequenting the country fairs. The minstrels fiddled on the village green, in the streets, outside the alehouses, singing their " bawdy songs, filthy ballads, and scurvy rhymes " whenever they could gather an audience. Often enough the pedlars and tinkers used their apparent trades merely as a protection—many of them were as ready as any Rogue or Ruffler to " work " their way by thieving and trickery. The bear-wards, with their half-savage beasts, added a real terror to life for the country children ; the jugglers and the fortune-tellers awed and thrilled the country audiences with their legerdemain and their prognostications. Rascals all of them, disturbers of the peace, enemies of law and order, they were none of them pleasant companions for an honest and prosperous citizen as he trotted his comfortable cob along the Queen's highway. The fraternity of the open road constituted perhaps the most pressing social problem of the day, and the traveller had little chance to overlook it. Even the Queen herself was confronted by it. Anecdote tells that one evening

In 1581,[1] as she rode out towards " Iseldon, commonly
called Islington, a country town," she was surrounded by
swarms of these begging rogues " which gave the Queen
much disturbance." Romantic enough at a distance
of three hundred years, picturesque enough in literature,
the Queen's highway must have had little to recommend
it to a contemporary ; it is not surprising that one hears
more of the joys of taking one's ease in one's inn than of
the pleasures of going a journey. Having seen it at its
worst, however, it is time to turn to a happier aspect,
and to look at Elizabethan England through the eyes of
one who rode along these highways with a relish of the
country-side that appears to have compensated, at any rate
in retrospect, for his probable discomfort as a traveller.

---

[1] See Strype's edition of Stow's " Survey," II, iv. 61.

CHAPTER VI

THE QUEEN'S MAPMAKER

SOMEWHERE about the year 1593 travellers or carriers whose business led them to frequent the London roads of the Home Counties must often have passed the time of day with a fellow-wayfarer of a quick, observant eye and an inquiring turn of mind. A middle-aged, pleasant-spoken man, he readily drew folk into conversation, listening with particular attention when the talk turned upon the locality in which he found himself. Likely enough the horse he rode was none of the best ; his dress was simple, his riding boots old, and his cloak threadbare and weather-stained, for although he rode about Her Majesty's business, Her Majesty proved herself such a tardy paymaster that more than once he was, as he tells us himself, "forced to struggle with want." Riding through the English country-side was doubtless a congenial occupation for a mapmaker and surveyor, " authorised and appointed by Her Majesty to travel through England and Wales to make more perfect descriptions, charts and maps." Nevertheless inns and horse-hire ran away with good money, and expenses were almost impossible to recover, so that we shall perhaps be hardly exceeding the warrant of fact if we surmise that this particular surveyor—who was indeed none other than the now-famous John Norden—undertook his great task of a " survey of Britain " [1] not merely from business motives but prompted equally by his own real love of the country-side itself. Only a fraction of his project was ever completed, and only about half of his manuscript found its way into print in his lifetime ; but in spite of his lack of art and his awkward style, Norden stands alone as the one topographer who made a real, if crude, attempt to

---

[1] See special bibliography to this chapter, p. 101.

describe what English country looked like in Elizabeth's time.

In the literature of the age it is difficult to find much " landscape painting " to help us to picture for ourselves the appearance of the country-side. At the most it is a few scattered details, such as Shakespeare's brief but graphic reference to the " high wild hills and rough uneven ways " which drew out the miles for a traveller in Gloucestershire. Often, too, such details as there are, though picturesque, are hardly pictorial, as when we are told of the county of Northamptonshire that it is " much inhabited by the nobility," or of Lancashire that it is a district " plentiful of oats and great-bodied beeves." Occasionally our vision is aided : Buckingham, then as now, we are told, was " full of beech trees." Sussex was " divided into downs full of sheep, and woodland full of iron mines, and some good pasturage." Northumberland is neatly summed up as " chiefly noted for swift horses and sea coals, a rough country and hardly tilled, inhabited by a fierce people." [1] Even in the " Britannia," that vast wilderness of Camden's antiquarianism, there are glimpses of the things he had seen. Saffron Walden, he tells us, stood " in the midst of fields smiling with the most beautiful crocus " ; the great woods of north Wiltshire were beginning to grow thin in his time ; the air of Somerset was pleasant, but the county was bad for winter travelling— " so wet and weely, so miry and moorish it is." But pictures such as these are far to seek ; with the sole exception of Norden the topographers were all too interested in imparting their knowledge of an England that had been to take the time to describe for our delight the England that lay around them. Nor are we any better off if we take refuge with the poets. Michael Drayton's " Polyolbion " leaves us with the impression that England was composed of innumerable rivers, and little else.

Happily for us Norden was chiefly interested in the present ; he saw beautiful country around him and he

[1] All these quotations are taken from the British Museum manuscript, Harleian 3813 (a description of Britain, with maps, c. 1599).

recorded the crops it bore and the commodities for which it was famous ; he saw stately houses, and he liked to discover who lived in them ; he watched the country-folk going forth to their work, and he wanted to know how they earned their living. In print he appears to have been intimidated into conforming to the antiquarian method, but his manuscripts betray him. When in his printed survey of Middlesex he writes a note upon the history of the church at Pancras he is as dull as any other. Turn to the manuscript, however (Harl. 570), and read what the book omits : " Although this place be as it were forsaken of all, and true men seldom frequent the same but upon divine occasions, yet is it visited and usually haunted of Rogues, vagabonds, harlots and thieves, who assemble not there to pray, but to wait for prey, and many fall into their hands clothed that are glad when they are escaped naked. *Walk not there too late.*" Here is that interest in humanity and in his own day that gives Norden his unique position. Willingly we sacrifice the discussion of the (probably fanciful) philological derivation of a place-name, such as his fellows delighted in, when Norden gives us in an anecdote that far more interesting fact— the character and reputation of the place in his time. We do not forget Knightsbridge,[1] " near Hyde Park Corner," after Norden has told us that there he would wish " no true man to walk too late without good guard, unless he can make his party good, as did Sir Henry Knyvet knight who valiantly defended himself, there being assaulted, and slew the master thief with his own hands."

As one would have imagined of such a man, John Norden appreciated a good inn, for he has left it on record that in his opinion no other English county, in his time, could rival Hertfordshire in this respect : " I take it, (though it be one of the least) no shire in England for the quantity comes near it, for thoroughfare places of competent receipt." At the end of his ride, seated in the inn parlour, he must often, while he waited for his supper, have jotted down the facts he had gathered that day.

[1] Kingsbridge in the MS.

We may picture him on one such occasion eager, after his solitary perambulations, to enter into conversation with the only other occupant of the room. This latter, however, is busily engaged in writing ; propped up in front of him is a French book, " Gerileon d'Angleterre " [1]—Norden has been able to read the title as he crossed the room, and to see that the writer was rapidly translating the book into English. His suspicion of the man's identity was confirmed ; he knew him by sight and by repute as Anthony Munday, author and playwright, and also pursuivant and recusant hunter. Men told unpleasant anecdotes of his activities in this latter capacity. He was probably bound upon an errand of that nature at the moment, and, unable to proceed farther that night, was industriously making use of his enforced leisure to produce some more of that romance-stuff which sold so well to the citizens' wives and daughters. Little chance of conversation there ; so out comes the surveyor's notebook, and down go his gleanings. Market days are easily forgotten, so they must be entered : St. Albans and Barnet,[2] Monday ; Rickmansworth, Saturday ; Stortford, Thursday. . . . And there are fairs too—Watford's, which began on Trinity Monday, and lasted for three days, and Rickmansworth's on Lady Day in harvest time ; and St. Albans and Stortford boasted three apiece. . . . Perhaps after supper there would be an opportunity to talk to the landlord or his good dame ; he has not yet discovered who owned that fine house he has passed at sundown. . . .

John Norden was not a Londoner. He lived in the little country village of Fulham, far removed even from the out-

---

[1] See bibliographical note, p. 101.
[2] Barnet has been delightfully described by the dramatist Thomas Heywood in his " English Traveller " :

> " This Barnet is a place of great resort,
> And commonly upon the market days
> Here all the country gentlemen appoint
> A friendly meeting ; some about affairs
> Of consequence and profit—bargain, sale,
> And to confer with chapmen ; some for pleasure,
> To match their horses, wager on their dogs,
> Or try their hawks ; some to no other end
> But only meet good company, discourse,
> Dine, drink and spend their money."

skirts of the capital, with its noise and its smells. If we follow him as he sets out from his home one fine summer morning we can view the country-side through his eyes. Perhaps his objective is some hamlet such as Ruislip on the northern boundary of the county ; his journey, there-fore, will take him through the richest vale in Middlesex, and leaving the main Uxbridge Road at Hanwell he will follow a small track that leads northwards across country. It is fair enough going on a day like this, and the rider contrasts in his mind the road's present condition with the state in which he found it when he came that way in winter. Then it was " dirty and deep " after the heavy autumn rains; he had arrived at his journey's end spattered with mud from head to foot. That, he would admit, was one of the drawbacks of the very clayey soil of Middlesex ; but the traveller's discommodity was the husbandman's joy, as Norden was fully able to realize on this particular journey. On all sides of him stretches one of the finest tracts of wheat in the whole country ; from Heston, near Hounslow, it runs north to Harrow-on-the-Hill, and then on to Pinner. To-day it is still young and green, but he remembers the first time he saw it, from the summit of the hill at Harrow, just before the harvest. Ripe almost to whiteness it had stretched as far as his eye could reach. It was then he had learnt that Heston wheat was famous throughout England for its purity : so pure and fine it was that none but Heston wheat was used for the manchet bread for Her Majesty's own diet.

The people in this part of the country live chiefly by husbandry. The yeomen farmers who have become wealthy only oversee the work, and " give directions unto their servants, seldom or not at all setting their hand unto the plough." They generally acquire their riches by cattle dealing at Smithfield Market ; they are great breeders and own extensive tracts of pasture. Even the poorer sort who do their own work are commonly " so furnished with kine " that the huswife twice or thrice a week " con-veyeth to London milk, butter, cheese, apples, pears, frumenty, hens, chickens, eggs, bacon, and a thousand

NORDEN'S MAP OF MIDDLESEX
(*From "Speculum Britanniæ," 1593*)

other country doings which good huswives can frame and find to get a penny. And this yieldeth them a large comfort and relief." In all parts of the county, too, there are many who live by the carriage of goods : they keep carts, and transport "meal, malt, and many other things to London, and so furnish themselves in their return with sundry men's carriages of the country. whereby they live very gainfully." Down by the Thames, however, the "meaner sort" live mainly by river-work with barge, wherry, or sculler. They also fish, and act as ferrymen, and all "live well and plentifully and in decent and honest sort relieve their families." With such details, which never found their way farther than his manuscript, might Norden beguile the journey for his companion. Many a gentleman's house, too, he could have pointed out on that or any other expedition, for in his time the great London merchants had just begun to discover Middlesex. Not only was it honoured by several of Her Majesty's residences, such as Enfield house, but in many of its choicest spots these good citizens were rearing fine "houses of recreation," and surrounding them with beautiful orchards and spacious gardens "with delectable walks, arbours and alleys." Pleasant indeed must the surveyor's memories have been when in 1593 he drew his map of this fair shire and marked so carefully on it the roads by which he himself had often travelled.

Norden, however, rode farther afield than Middlesex, and for its neighbour on the east he has even higher praise. Essex, he exclaims, "is most fat, fruitful and full of profitable things, exceeding (as far as I can find) any other shire for the general commodities and the planting." He calls it "the English Goshen, the fattest of the land : comparable to Palestina that flowed with milk and honey." The generosity of his tribute is rendered all the more striking by the confession he makes of the scurvy treatment meted out by this English Goshen to her enthusiastic topographer : "But I cannot commend the healthfulness of it, and especially near the sea coasts, Rochford, Denge, Tendering hundreds, and other low places about the creeks, which gave me a most cruel quartain fever."

In Essex, he notes, there are no great flocks of sheep anywhere, though the wool produced is of the finest quality, especially that which comes from Kingswood Heath, Tiptree, and Alresford. The south-eastern parts deal chiefly in milk and butter and " great and huge " cheeses ; in the north they grow hops and corn, and there are fine pastures. Round Chelmsford there is corn ; Waltham and Ongar are woody districts, and red deer and fallow deer are to be found in their forests.

Surrey, when Norden surveyed it, could boast no rivalry with its neighbour Middlesex. It was too barren a county to be thickly populated : " Few places are to be commended for fertility " is his comment. Every here and there by the Thames, he admits, there are corn lands and good meadows for pasture ; " The greatest places of corn are . . . between Farnsham and Guildford, and on the north side of the downs between Guildford and Leatherhead, and so to Croydon, reverting towards Kingston." In the west and the south, however, the soil only yields to the most strenuous cultivation. The forest regions are " healthy and hilly " but not fertile. It was a very well-wooded county, and Norden remarks the great woods of box which surrounded Dorking, and the walnut trees which grew in " extraordinary abundance " about Croydon. It was from the ubiquitous coppices, however, that the inhabitants profited most, as by means of them they were able to provide London with its fuel supply.

Hampshire Norden knew, and its hills, valleys, and parks stand to him for " health wealth and pleasure," in which respects he held that it rivalled any other shire in the country. Cornwall he visited, and of some of its antiquities, such as Tintagel and St. Michael's Mount, he made quaint little water-colour sketches for the edification of King James, to whom he presented his manuscript. Some of the facts that he records are of the greatest interest. The mining villages of the tin districts were much poorer than those in the parts where the country-folk lived by tillage. He found the Cornishmen a very personable folk, strong, sturdy, and extremely long-lived. He speaks of their fame as " wrastlers," and of the quarrelsome nature of the peasantry : " Many of them are of harsh hard and of no such civil disposition, very litigious." By their perpetual lawsuits, indeed, they appear to have made Cornwall an earthly paradise for the pettifogging attorneys and second-rate lawyers of Norden's time. As many another traveller since, he found the Cornish folk very sufficient unto themselves, and inclined to look upon English " foreigners " with a hostile eye. They still spoke their own Cornish " language " as well as English, and Norden found it hard to procure good inn, lodging, or diet amongst them, as there was " no great haunt of travellers in those parts." Where he came upon a gentleman's house, however, he was well received, and found the place as well furnished of all comforts as in any other part of the country.

According to Norden, King John was responsible for the disafforestation of Cornwall, which had left it as bare of trees then as it remains to this day. He admits that frost and snow are never of long duration there, but it is bad country for travellers in winter time, for " the fierce and furious winds sharply assail the naked hills and dales, having no defensive woods for shelter." A grim, uncomfortable shire he found it, after the pleasant homeliness of Middlesex or Hampshire. He must have been glad to start on his homeward journey again, and to forget the litigious Cornishmen and their bleak moors and their iron coast-line. As he rode he might well remember the adventure that befell him on this very journey, many years before, when by chance he fell in with " Don Antonie, the supposed King of Portugal "—the pretender to the throne who landed in this country in 1581,[1] seeking Elizabeth's help against the King of Spain. Then in company of the Don and his followers he had ridden Londonwards at a leisurely pace, for the foreigners were

[1] Cf. Cecil Papers in Lodge's " Illustrations," II, 254. Earl of Sussex to Burghley, 27 June, 1581—" the arrival of Don Antonio."

full of interest in all they saw, and in Norden they had found an ideal guide who could point to everything worthy of their notice. As forgetfulness came upon him with the years and he told the same story twice over there were perhaps friends who began to weary of the King of Portugal. It must have been an anecdote dear to his heart, for it occurs in no less than three of the dedications he penned for different manuscripts.

Having thus seen something of the Home Counties and of the western extremity of the land, we may follow Norden on a last journey, when he rides northwards to the Midlands to make his survey of the county of Northampton. He comments, as do all his fellow-topographers, on the number of noblemen who have chosen this county for their seats ; he is struck also by the great number of parish churches which he passes in a day's journey along the highway. He finds it a very prosperous and well-cultivated shire : no other " within this land hath so little waste ground," and here " the baser sort of men prove wealthy and wade through the world with good countenance in their calling, least beholden generally to the monied men of any other shire whatsoever that I know."

Northamptonshire appears to have been very thickly populated for the period, so that Norden writes that he finds the country " most comfortable for travellers, not only in the delightful perspects which are delightful to wayfaring men : but also in regard of plenty of towns, parishes and villages, which are so universally dispersed that in every two or three miles at the most is found a place of ease to the wearisome traveller." What impressed him more than anything else, however, were the enormous flocks and herds : " I cannot but wonder to call to mind the great herds of cattle, longing to every small parish, village and hamlet, which when in my small travel I did behold such general multitudes I persuaded myself of an impossibility, that so small parishes and places of so slender accompt could yield so great a number of kine and other cattle, such main flocks of sheep, and which made me most to marvel were the great herds of swine."

On his return from Northamptonshire we must bid Norden farewell. We might follow him through Hampshire and to the Isle of Wight, but he has already given us his best, and we should need to resuscitate more than his manuscript if we think to profit further by his pleasant company. So far as we are concerned he may now retire to his house at Hendon, to which he moved in the reign of James I. If we are to take to the road again it must now be in the company of a hypothetical traveller only. Lacking Norden's humanity he will not be able to distract our attention from such things as the problems of enclosure and rural depopulation ; he will have no anecdotes to divert us from a strict pursuit of facts. Such things, however, demand a chapter to themselves ; neither they nor Norden would gain if they were to be forced to compete for interest with the personality of the Queen's surveyor and mapmaker. [1]

---

[1] Quotations throughout this chapter are from Norden's own writings. The (conjectural) remarks upon his personality and doings can be deduced by any reader from the same source. The following books and MSS. have been used :—(i) " Speculum Britanniae. The first parte. An historicall and chorographicall discription of Middlesex. 1593 ". (ii) " Speculi Britanniae Pars. The discription of Hertfordshire. 1598." (iii) " Speculi Britanniae pars altera ; or a delineation of Northamptonshire. 1610." (printed 1720). (iv) " Speculi Britaniae pars ; an historical and chorographical description of the County of Essex." ed. H. Ellis. 1840. (v) Harleian MS. 570 (Middlesex). (vi) Addit. MS. 31853 (Middlesex, Essex, Surrey, Sussex, Hants., Wilts., Isle of Wight, Guernsey, Jersey.) (vii) Addit. MS. 33769 (Essex ; differing from Hatfield MS. ed. Ellis, no (iv). (viii) Harleian MS. 6252 (Cornwall).

The meeting between Norden and Munday is an imaginary one. Munday himself is evidence for his frequenting of inns while hunting recusants round about this date, and also for his habit of getting on with his literary work at the end of a day's ride : see introductory remarks to " Gerileon of England " (1592), where he speaks of himself as " compelled to catch hold on such little leisures, as in the morning ere I went to horseback or in the evening coming into mine inn, I could compass from company."

Note.—Since this chapter was written, in 1925, two valuable topographical studies of Tudor England have appeared—E. G. R. Taylor's " Leland's England " and " Camden's England," in " An Historical Geography of England before 1800 " : (ed. H. C. Darby : 1936). For the work of Norden, Saxton and other English map-makers see E. Lynam's *British Maps and Map-Makers* (1944), and his *English Maps and Map-Makers of the 16th Century* (*Geographical Journal*, cxvi, 1950). For a vivid and comprehensive account of the country and its appearance, see Chaps. II and III of Rowse's *The England of Elizabeth.*

CHAPTER VII

COUNTRY LIFE AND THE COUNTRY-SIDE

THE Tudor period was an age of sweeping social changes affecting every class, both in town and country. Office, lands, and wealth were all changing hands. At Court, as we have seen, a new kind of statesman, chosen for his address and merit and ability, was ousting the older aristocracy ; in the country a new race of land-lords had arisen for the troubling of their tenants—land-lords who enclosed the common lands, absentees and rack-renters, business men out to make money by investing in land and farming on a large scale, middlemen and specula-tors who bought only to sell at an enhanced value, and land-lords whose sole object was to bleed their lands and tenants of every possible penny to supply their own extravagance in London.

These changes, which affected the life of the rural popu-lation so vitally, had been largely due, in the first instance, to the suppression of the monasteries and the transference of their enormous estates to the ownership of Henry VIII, from whom they had passed, by gift or purchase, to these new owners, whose main idea was to make money out of their ill-gotten land. In the Middle Ages land had been valued because it supported men or enabled a village to supply its own needs ; in the Tudor period, on the contrary, land came to be regarded as a commercial asset, to be exploited for profit. The ready and easy way to wealth in the early years of the Tudors was by the conversion of arable into grass lands. English wool was in great demand in the foreign market, and at home the cloth trade had developed enormously. Hence, throughout the country, landlords converted their acres to sheep pasture wherever possible—more profitable in itself than agricul-ture and more economical in its use of labour. It was a policy which undoubtedly brought wealth to the country, particularly to the merchants and the landlords; but it was the cause, especially during the reigns of Elizabeth's immediate predecessors, of a terrible amount of unemployment, destitution, and misery in the rural areas.

The commercial attitude to land having been fully accepted it was inevitable that those who had some land should try to acquire more. When this meant the reclaiming of waste land it was all to the good; when it meant land-grabbing by the rich at the expense of their poorer neighbours the results were disastrous for the peasant population. There were various ways of jockeying a tenant out of his holding. A copyholder who, on the death of his father, came to take up his inheritance would find that a new landlord had doubled or trebled both the " fine " for the transference of the tenancy and the actual rent, and that it was " pay or go." The complaint of the seventeenth century ballad called " Mockbeggar Hall " applied only too often to all the Tudor reigns :

> Young landlords when to age they come,
> Their rents they will be racking,
> The tenant must give a golden sum,
> Or else he is turned packing,
> Great fines and double rent beside.

For those turned out of doors there was little chance ; at the best they might become hired servants, but in general they went to swell the ranks of the vagabond population which was yearly becoming more and more serious as a social problem.

Harrison writes feelingly of the distress thus caused by the land-grabbing of the rich. Many a poor man, he says, thinks himself lucky if he is able to keep a roof of any kind over his head and can secure one acre of ground upon which to keep his cow and to plant his " cabbages, radishes, parsnips, carrots, melons, pumpkins . . . by which he and his poor household liveth as their principal food, sith they can do no better." Another writer, Thomas Bastard, in his "Chrestoleros," a book of epigrams published in 1598, complains of the thief who

> Steals away both subjects from the Queen,
> And men from his own country of all sorts.
> Houses by three and seven and ten he razeth,
> To make the common glebe his private land :
> Our country cities cruel he defaceth.

He gives a picture of what must have been only too frequent an occurrence :

> The grass grows green where little Troy did stand,
> The forlorn father hanging down his head,
> His outcast company drawn up and down
> The pining labourer doth beg his bread,
> The ploughswain seeks his dinner from the town.

Perhaps the best-known account of the misfortunes which had thus overtaken so many smallholders is the passage in Latimer's first sermon preached before Edward VI, in which he contrasts the present state of affairs with that of his youth. His father had been a yeoman, owning no land, but renting for £3 or £4 a year a farm of a hundred sheep, thirty cows, and sufficient tillage to support half a dozen men. He was able to educate his son, and to give his daughters good portions on marriage. He was hospitable to his poorer neighbours, and gave alms to the poor. But his successor "payeth £16 by year or more, and is not able to do anything for his Prince, for himself, nor for his children, nor give a cup of drink to the poor."

Legislation to restrain sheep-farming helped the situation only to a small extent. Nevertheless, during Elizabeth's reign arable farming took on a new life, because the price of English wool fell and the price of wheat rose. By the later years of her reign the latter was as much as six times higher than it had been in her father's. Wool, on the other hand, which from 6s. 8d. per tod in 1540 had risen to 20s. 8d. in 1546, had by 1561 fallen to 16s. Naturally the sheep declined in popularity, and the agricultural labourer found his services more in demand than they had been. This did something to remedy the distress in the rural areas by natural means ; for the remaining individuals who could not be re-absorbed into the agricultural community, and who represented that large or small number of persons who must always suffer in any time of transition such as this, there was called into existence the important machinery of the Elizabethan poor laws. To these we must return subsequently. It is of more immediate importance, however, first to understand the changes in the methods of English agriculture which bulked so large in the domestic history of the reign owing to this revival of tillage, and which were responsible to some extent for the distress as well as the prosperity of the country-side.

It is difficult at first to realize that our hypothetical Elizabethan traveller, whom we may for our own convenience dispatch at this juncture upon a somewhat lengthy journey, saw in many parts of the country as he rode through the cultivated areas a vista that was quite different from anything that we should see to-day if we followed the same route. In some parts he would see flocks of several thousand sheep grazing over nearly a quarter of a county ; in other parts he would be confronted by huge stretches of woodland or waste that have all, by now, been either cut down or reclaimed or else reduced to comparatively insignificant dimensions. If he rode between Brandon and Peterborough he would pass by " the great level "—an enormous stretch of fen more than three thousand acres in extent. He would find Lancashire three parts morass, or " moss," and Cannock Chase in Staffordshire still a mighty oak forest, covering, with Needwood, a third of the county. It is strangest of all, however, to realize that in many counties English ploughland and meadow presented a completely different appearance then from what they do to-day.

Nowadays, if we describe English country to one who has never seen it, we think first of its irregular patchwork of fields and meadows of every conceivable shade of green and yellow, divided from each other by lines of dark green hedges in the south and grey stone walls in the bleaker north. But the country our Elizabethan traveller rode through was still largely unenclosed; it lacked our familiar hedges, and it lacked as a rule that irregularity of size and shape which so pleasingly distinguishes almost any extensive view to-day. The larger part of the country was still farmed upon the medieval system, by which the land was held in common by the inhabitants of the district. Emerging from a strip of woodland and looking down upon a cultivated area our traveller would see before him a cluster of cottages, forming a small village, with perhaps a church and a large manor house near by. By the river he would see the meadows where grass for the hay harvest was growing, and where the village flocks and herds would find pasture during the autumn and winter. Between the meadows and the woodland he would see three enormous fields, all of which were divided into innumerable half-acre strips, separated each from the other by narrow grass-grown paths which the country people called "balks." The field which lay nearest to him was lying fallow; the one next to it had a fine crop of wheat, just beginning to turn from green to gold; the last one was under barley. And through them all ran those narrow ribs of green turf. Perhaps someone standing near enough might have heard our Londoner humming snatches of a pleasant ditty as he looked down upon the fields:

> It was a lover and his lass
> That o'er the green cornfield did pass.
>
> . . . . .
>
> Between the acres of the rye
> These pretty country folk would lie. . . .

To his right, on the edge of the woodland and the fallow, was some rough downland pasture; a herd of swine was rooting about beneath the trees and among the scattered gorse clumps. If we could take our stand beside him and gaze upon the same scene we might look at the meadow [1] and at the woodland and downs and imagine we were in

---

[1] The meadow was also divided into strips, but it would not be so apparent at a little distance.

twentieth century England. The distinctive and curious feature of the landscape—to our eyes—would be that tract of arable land of over a thousand acres, divided into one thousand two hundred and thirty-eight narrow strips ! [1]

Farming in common appears to have been the original method of English agriculture, and more than half of the country was still cultivated under this system until the eighteenth century. Land held thus in common lay open and unfenced, and those who cultivated it all contributed to and owned in common the necessary ploughs and implements. Everybody's cattle grazed on the common pasture. The strips into which the arable land was divided were redistributed amongst the holders every year. As the strip system was meant originally to ensure that the fertile and unfertile areas should be equally distributed, each holder who found himself in possession of perhaps ten acres in a field would have these ten acres cut up into twenty half-acre strips, no two of which would be adjacent to each other.

It is easy to see that in some respects this system was both wasteful and unprofitable. An appreciable amount of land was wasted by the balks, and a considerably greater amount of labour and time was wasted by the scattered position of the strips. There are cases on record in which men sowed their neighbours' strips by mistake, and there are even instances of a man completely losing one of his half acres. The method depended for its success upon the unity and the co-operative spirit of all the holders. If one man was slack about the draining of his strips his neighbours' ground might suffer ; another, too lazy to manure properly his scattered sections, would impoverish the land for its next holder. Unless all were agreed on the policy of letting one field lie fallow each year, of sowing the second with rye or wheat, and the third with beans, barley, or pease, the land was spoilt by the taking of too many grain crops in succession. Yet a further drawback was the herding together of the flocks of all the holders in the

[1] These were the actual figures for South Luffenham in Rutland when it was enclosed in 1879.

common pasture. The resultant indiscriminate breeding reduced the size and the value of the animals, and the danger of cattle diseases was greatly increased.

Open country cultivated on this common-field system was known as " champion." If we may imagine our traveller making a circular tour, riding north through Suffolk into Norfolk, then turning west across Cambridgeshire, Rutland, and Leicestershire, striking south again through Warwickshire to the middle of Gloucestershire, then riding eastwards and homewards to London through Berkshire, the cultivated portions through which he would pass in these counties would be almost without exception of this nature. At the beginning of his journey, however, while he rode through Essex, and here and there at other points in his journey, he would have been able to observe the working of the newer system, and the landscape would have presented to him an appearance much more nearly resembling that of to-day.

The disadvantages of the common-field system had become apparent to some parts of the country long before Elizabeth's reign. Here and there, in various counties, men who were a little wiser than their neighbours had begun to see that it was much more economical for each man to cultivate a compact holding. When all the holders of the common field arrived at the same conclusion they proceeded to divide up their land so that each man's holding should be a consolidated instead of a scattered one, fenced off from the neighbouring plots, and continuing in what was virtually his private ownership from year to year. Where this newer method of farming in " several," as it was called, had been adopted, the landscape would be cut up into fields, divided from each other by hedges or fences as they are to-day ; and our imaginary traveller, provided he approved of such newfangled ideas, would be able to comment to himself upon the finer crops and the greater prosperity in all such areas. In fact, if he knew his " Five Hundreth Points of Good Husbandry " he might very well have quoted to himself Tusser's doggerel praises of Essex .

> More plenty of mutton and beef,
> Corn, butter and cheese of the best,
> More wealth anywhere (to be brief)
> More people, more handsome and prest
> Where find ye—go search any coast,
> Than there where enclosure is most.

Farming in " several " was advocated by all those who realized that more intensive methods of cultivation were necessary if English agriculture was to become remunerative as a commercial venture. Thomas Tusser is emphatic in his commendation :

> More profit is quieter found
> Where pastures in several be
> Of one silly acre of ground
> Than champion maketh of three.

Norden, whose opinion is possibly more accurate, puts the comparative value of several and champion lower—one acre enclosed being worth one and a half in the common field. Nevertheless, all the experts seem to be agreed on the main issue—that several was the more profitable farming, for both great or small landowners.

Obvious as the case for the universal adoption of farming in several may now appear, we have only to look at the history and the literature of the Tudor period to realize that this change from medieval to modern methods was accompanied by protest and even rebellion on the part of the agricultural population. It was obviously profitable to the landowner and to the country as a whole ; and when it merely meant that each tenant of the common field was able to farm a compact instead of a scattered holding, then it was obviously beneficial to the smallholder as well. Unfortunately, however, for this particular section of the population enclosing meant a great deal besides the parcelling out of the village farm into various small farms. As often as not it meant the land-grabbing by the rich to which reference has already been made, it meant encroachment upon and the pilfering of the common land, and it meant fencing in land for the express purpose of converting arable into pasture, and the consequent unemployment of the cottagers, who, having been turned out of their holdings, were reduced to the status of the agricultural day labourer or the hired servant, and could yet find no man to employ them.

Conditions varied, of course, in the different counties. Kent and Essex in the east, Cornwall and Devon in the west, had early forsaken the older method, and contemporary writers on agriculture generally attribute their exceptional prosperity to this fact. Norden speaks of Dorset, Wiltshire, Hampshire, Berkshire, and Northamptonshire as still being typically champion districts in 1607, and by the end of the seventeenth century the Midlands were still the least enclosed of any portion of the country under cultivation. Enclosing had begun early in Berkshire, and was most common in the middle, north-west, and east, but the county as a whole was largely open at the end of the eighteenth century. Wiltshire, according to its historian Aubrey, was a lovely champion country until the middle of the sixteenth century ; it had very few enclosures, except in the neighbourhood of some of the great houses. Year by year, however, during his lifetime, more enclosures had been made. In his grandfather's time all the ground between Kington St. Michael and Dracot Cerne had been common field ; " then were a world of labouring people maintained by the plough, as yet in Northamptonshire."

Leland the antiquary and topographer, writing towards the middle of the sixteenth century, makes every here and there in his " Itinerary " notes which help us to realize what parts of the country were open and what enclosed. In his peregrinations in Oxfordshire, for example, he covered most of the tract lying between Caversham on the south-east, Hasely on the north-east, and Oxford on the north-west. Riding from Caversham to Ewelme he passed five or six miles of great woods ; then for the last four miles to Ewelme, over the hilly ground, the country was all champion. Riding on in a northerly direction to Hasely he passed by five miles of " champion ground somewhat plentiful of corn but mostly laid to pasturage." From Hasely he struck south-west to Chiselhampton, passing by three miles or more of "plain ground fruitful of corn and grass, but barren of wood as all that angle of Oxfordshire is." From Dorchester he rode south again to Wallingford, "by marvellous fair champion and fruitful ground of corn." From Oxford, by way of Hinksey Hill, he rode south-west to Farringdon in Berkshire, a good ten miles, "all by champion," some corn, but mostly pasture.

Leland covered a great deal of ground in the Midlands, in Leicestershire, Lincolnshire, Rutland, and Northamptonshire, and generally he describes the country as champion. Rutland was rich champion all around Uppingham; and striking north to Ancaster along Ermine Street he found the whole tract on each side of him between Deane in the west to Oundle in the east of Northants all fine corn or grass champion. From Higham Ferrars to Bedford, and from Bicester on to Brackley and Banbury all was champion; from Banbury to Warwick he passed two miles of enclosed and wooded ground to twelve of champion, corn, and grass.

Warwickshire, on the other hand, was almost divided into two portions: to the south of the Avon, which runs more or less obliquely from north-east to south-west, lay what was known as the Fielden, champion country whose "fertile fields of corn and verdant pastures," Camden assures us, yielded a most delightful prospect when viewed from the top of Edgehill. To the north of the Avon, however, the well-wooded district known as Arden was much enclosed and chiefly given up to pasture.

Times were changing; the old order of life in the country was breaking up; communal farming was giving place to the modern system, and in at least one county industrialism also was helping to change the appearance of the land. The mighty forest which had once spread over the whole of Sussex was being devoured by the iron foundries and glassworks for which the district was famous, and Norden in 1607[1] reports that those who know the Weald well say that

---

[1] "Surveyor's Dialogue."

the trees have decayed greatly during the last thirty years. He has fears for the complete destruction of the supply of wood for timber and fuel, but admits that in Sussex the country-side has also benefited by this cutting down of the woods : " Where in former times a farm stood in those parts wholly upon these unprofitable bushy and woody grounds, having only some small and ragged pastures . . . now I see as I travel and where I have had business that these unprofitable grounds are converted to beneficial tillage ; in so much as the people lack not, but can to their great benefit yearly afford to others both butter, cheese and corn, even where was little or none at all."

Before leaving the land itself mention must be made of the crops which it bore. Besides the ordinary grain crops of the two-, three-, or four-course systems in vogue for both champion and several, a great deal of hemp was grown for use in the farm-house, especially, Norden tells us, in Sussex, Dorset, Somerset, Norfolk, and Suffolk. Kent and Devon were, of course, famous for their orchards then as now, and other counties that Norden singled out, which, like both these, also grew pears, apples, and crabs in the hedges between the enclosed fields, were Shropshire, Worcester, Gloucester, and Somerset. Such was the profit from these extra hedgerow crops that, as he says, " a good mind will not grudge at a wayfaring passenger taking for his refection and to qualify the heat of his travel, an apple or a pear." In the north and east of Middlesex and in the south of Hertfordshire he had also noted similar fruit-bearing hedges, and while speaking of orchards comments on the amazing profusion of cherries and pippins that grew about Faversham and Sittingbourne.

Root crops, of course, were impossible under the common-field system, not because anything else was grown in the fields in the winter, but simply because by custom the arable land was thrown open for all the cattle from Lammas Day in August till seed time. Even those farming in several, however, had hardly realized the utility of roots, which were still grown more in the huswife's vegetable garden than in the husbandman's fallow.

The art of manuring the ground was yet in its infancy. Marl, a clayey soil containing carbonate of lime, was still used, though not as freely as it had been in the Middle Ages. Norden says that the counties where marling was most employed in 1607 were Lancashire, Cheshire, Shropshire, and Somerset to the north and west, Middlesex, Surrey, and Sussex in the south. Sea sand was used for land near the coasts, as in Cornwall, especially along the north coast and about Padstow. In some of the Welsh counties lime was still used, and in Sussex, from Eastbourne and the shores about Camber near Rye, pebbles were collected and burnt for the same purpose. In Hertfordshire fern was cut and laid in the highway to become dunged and decayed, and then in March spread upon the fields. Farmers in Middlesex, Buckingham, and Hertfordshire prized very highly a peaty soil called " moore-earth," which they gathered from the river between Colebrook and Uxbridge, and which if put on barren ground was said to ensure twelve years' good tilth. In Hampshire " mawme," or malm, a light loamy soil obtained from the " slub " or slushy mud of the River Avon between Fordingbridge and Ringwood, was used by many ; and the dung of the London stables was taken by water to such places as Chelsea, Battersea, and Putney to fertilize their sandy soil. No proper and systematic use appears to have been made of the household garbage heap, which was allowed to decay in front of the door until it became too offensive to be tolerated any more and was then usually burnt. In 1607, however, Norden wrote that " of late the farmers near London have found a benefit by bringing the scavengers' street soil, which being mixed as it is with the stove coal dust is very helpful to their clay ground." [1]

Having dealt at some length with the appearance of the country-side and the cultivation of the soil it will be as well to consider next the different classes that went to make up the rural population. From the eleventh to the fourteenth century the manor was the unit of land distribution in England. Under the manorial system the property of any

[1] " Surveyor's Dialogue."

tract of land, large or small, was vested in a "lord," and ultimately, of course, in the King. In a typical manor the lord would divide the land into two parts—his own *demesne* and the common fields. With holdings in these latter the lord recompensed his dependants for their services ; and by means of these holdings the villein population was able to support itself. Whether the system originated in a free community or a slave-owning one is too remote a question for present consideration ; the point is that, till Elizabeth's time and after, the manorial system, though much altered, still survived to the extent that all tenants of land were manorial tenants, standing each in his particular relationship to the lord of the manor.

There were still in Elizabeth's reign four main classes of such tenants. In the most enviable position were the freeholders, virtually owners of their lands in return for certain payments to the lord of the manor. Socially, this class contained two strata—the gentleman-freeholder and the tenant of free but not gentle birth ; tenurially it perpetuated the original relationship between the overlord and the freeman-tenant who held his estate for life.

Next in importance came the leaseholders—farmers, for the most part, who held their land either from the lord of the manor or some freeholder in return for a fixed rental. Their tenancies were for various periods—a term of years, a life, or a series of lives. The largest part of the rural population, however, consisted of what were known as customary tenants. The relation between the lord and these tenants (as contrasted with the freeholders) had originally been that of the overlord and the villein. Often a family of such tenants would have held its land just as long as the family of the lord of the manor. It passed by inheritance from father to son simply on the ground of ancient custom. Rent was paid to the lord of the manor instead of the labour-service originally given ; and a son taking up his dead father's holding would pay a small fine to his overlord. From the custom of entering this latter transaction in the manorial court roll arose the title of copyholder—that is, holder by copy of the court roll—by which such tenants were more generally known from Tudor times onwards. Lowest of all in the scale came a small-holding labouring class, consisting of men who worked on other people's land for wages, but who also cultivated for themselves either two or three acres in the common fields or, after 1566, the regulation four acres which the law required to be attached to every cottage that was built.

All these people were attached to the land either by temporary or permanent ownership. With the growth of enclosures, however, and the consequent decay of the class of smallholders, many of whom lost their shares in the common field, there had grown up a distinct class of hired labourers who worked on the land but had no part or lot in it. Such labourers hired themselves out at the annual hiring fairs for varying periods of service. Many, such as harvesters, hedgers, ditchers, and thatchers, were day labourers, paid at a daily rate ; others, such as shepherds and milkmaids, took service for a year at a time. Breaking of agreement on the part of either master or servant was punishable, unless just cause could be proved. Wages varied in different districts, but those given in the 1589 accounts of the Darell family for their Littlecote and Axford estates in Wiltshire may be taken as fairly typical. There we find field-workers being paid at the rate of two-pence or threepence a day, and ploughmen at one shilling a week with board. The shepherd received sixpence a week and board, and his boy twopence halfpenny. Hedgers were paid for their skilled work at the rate of sixpence a day ; threshers earned from threepence to sevenpence according to the grain ; thatching for five days was entered at two shillings.[1] In the Chester wages assessment for 1594 thatchers are to be paid at the rate of a penny a day, and reapers at twopence, without meat and drink. In the East Riding assessment for the previous year a mower in harvest time is rated at tenpence a day without food, and common labourers for hedging, ditching, or threshing at one penny a day in winter and twopence in summer, with their meat

[1] See Hall : " Society in the Elizabethan Age," pp. 22, 23, 203.

and drink. A woman servant taking charge of " brewing, baking, kitching, milk house, or malting that is hired with a gentleman or rich yeoman " was not allowed to receive more than seventeen shillings a year in addition to her board and lodging. In the Oakham assessment for Rutland in 1610 a common shepherd is rated at twenty-five shillings a year, and a mower at tenpence a day, without meat and drink.[1]

Of the wealth and position of these sections of the community little needs to be said. The freeholders were in a secure position legally ; they could not be made to pay more for their lands, and they could only be turned out of their holdings by purchase. They stood to gain by the change in agricultural methods, and if anything their position in this century was distinctly an improved one. The copyholders and leaseholders were the ones who suffered, together with the labouring class. Copyholders and leaseholders could be made to pay exorbitant fines and rent ; the poorest cottars were simply evicted and their cottages destroyed.

In those parts of the country where the enclosing movement had begun early and by consent of the community, all classes of tenants stood a better chance of survival, as in Devonshire, for example, where the smallholders flourished. Nor did all the smaller farmers necessarily go under in the districts where land-grabbing was most rife. It was a commercial age, and those who had better business instincts than their neighbours often managed not only to survive the storm but to thrive. Harrison tells us that there were many smallholders who, even when their rents had been raised from £4 to £50 or £100, yet managed to save enough to purchase a new lease when the old one ran out, and were able to live in a much more extravagant fashion than their fathers before them. The poem " Vox populi Vox dei " [2] (1547/8) denounces these "upstart gentlemen" as devourers of the goods of the poor and speaks scathingly of the luxury of their homes :

---

[1] Rogers : " History of Agriculture and Prices," VI, p. 686 ff.
[2] See " Ballads from Manuscripts," Furnivall ; Ballad Soc., I, 124-46.

> For they that of late did sup
> Out of an ashen cup
> Are wonderfully sprung up ;
> That nought was worth of late,
> Hath now a cupboard of plate,
> His table furnished too
> With plate beset enow,
> Parcel gilt and sound
> Well worth two hundred pound.

The lives of all these classes of country folk were organized and controlled by that famous Tudor system of local government which was already well developed when Elizabeth came to the throne. The suppression of the monasteries, with its far-reaching social effects, had amongst other things thrown upon the State a burden formerly borne by the Church—that, namely, of provision for the poor. It had also, as we have just seen, been, at any rate indirectly, responsible for a large increase in the number of those needing such relief. When this responsibility was finally recognized by the Government, it solved the problem by making each parish undertake the administration of poor relief within its own bounds, thus transforming what had originally been the unit of the ecclesiastical organization of the Middle Ages into the unit of the Tudor scheme of social legislation. As a measure this was typically Tudor; it weakened rather than strengthened whatever remained of the feudal authority of the lord of the manor ; it delegated local affairs to local control; but it kept everything under the eventual supervision of the central authority. The justice of the peace was set in authority for his particular country area ; but if he went beyond his statutory powers he was made answerable in the law-courts for his transgression.

Equally typical of Tudor methods was the way in which the new system took over the personnel and the machinery of the ecclesiastical unit and adapted them to the new conditions and needs. The churchwardens and the constables of the medieval parish were confirmed in their offices, and with them were associated two new officials—

a surveyor, whose business it was to see to the upkeep and repair of roads and highways, and an overseer, who was to administer the poor relief for the district. They all carried out their duties under the general supervision of the justices, and served for a year at a time, being elected annually by the parishioners. They were unpaid, and unless specially privileged were obliged by law to serve in these capacities for the year of their election. Beneath them were various minor functionaries who received yearly salaries. Such were the scavenger, the hog-ringer, the swineherd, and of slightly higher standing such officials as the clerk of the markets and the searcher of broadcloth, all of whose duties have their nature sufficiently indicated by their titles.

First in importance amongst the local officials who managed the affairs of rural England were the justices of the peace, residents of high standing, possessed as a rule of wealth and influence, and endowed with considerable administrative and judicial powers. Established as far back as the reign of Edward III, the office had developed into a most efficient instrument for the centralizing policy of the Tudor dynasty. The Tudors did not need to create an official class ; they found it ready to hand in this body of gentlemen already trained in the work of governing and already accepted by the nation as a part of the social fabric. The justices for each county were appointed by the Crown and were strictly controlled by the central authority ; they had sufficient power and independence to make them thoroughly efficient in their administrative and governing work, but they were so definitely and watchfully controlled from the centre that there was no fear of independent action upon their part endangering the absolute authority of the monarch.

Gradually the whole administration of the government of the counties came to be concentrated in the hands of the justices. They have been called, without exaggeration, " the State's men-of-all-work," and it was mainly owing to their efforts that the unsettled condition of the country-side, due to the increase of enclosures and vagabondage, gradually gave way to an improved state of affairs, in which, as the Statute Roll of Henry VII anticipates, it was possible for the King's subjects to live " in surety under his peace in their bodies and goods."

In Tudor times the justices were required to undertake a great deal of administrative work which now falls to the lot of the county councils. They were responsible for the construction and upkeep of the highways, and for the building and maintenance of bridges. In many counties they were responsible for the erection of the gaol and for deciding in which town it was to be built. The control and licensing of public-houses was in their hands ; orders for the whipping of vagrants had to come from them ; they were even required to see that every person occupying tillage land should sow with flax a quarter of an acre in every sixty, in order that weaving should be encouraged, and employment given to the poor. In the hands of the justices lay the regulation of labour, wages, and trade, as well as the oversight of the administration of the Poor Law. They nominated annually the overseers of the poor who were charged with the duties of supplying materials for the employment of the destitute ; of putting the children of parents, who were too poor to support them, into employment ; of taxing the inhabitants of their parish for the support of the poor ; and of seeing to the erection of poorhouses where necessary. All complaints against the overseers had to be referred to the justices, to whom also these officials had to render a strict account of their performance of their duties.

The churchwardens were, as their name implies, the legal guardians of the property belonging to the church and the parish. They were responsible for the parish accounts—kept for them by the parish clerk at a charge of a shilling a year—and they had to provide a strong chest with three keys for the safe keeping of the moneys and valuables in their charge. They were usually two in number, although both this and the manner of their election varied from parish to parish according to ancient custom. As an office it was not regarded with disfavour, being not particularly onerous, and having attached to it none of the unpleasant duties which fell to the lot both of the overseer of the poor and the surveyor of the highways. The churchwardens had to allot the seats in the church according to rank, sex, and age ; they had to provide " a comely and honest pulpit " for the preacher, and proper service books and a Bible in English " of the largest volume." [1] They had also to report to the ordinary upon the incumbent's performance of his duties, the state of the church and its furniture, and finally upon the moral and religious backslidings of the members of the community.

Very important in his own eyes, though perhaps rather less so in other people's, was the village constable, Dogberry or Goodman Dull. His office appears to date back to the reign of Edward III, when one of the tithing men, reeves, or headboroughs of each township was made responsible under the constable of the hundred for the preservation of law and order within his township. Curiously enough, it was an unpaid office, and its duties naturally made it one which most people were eager to evade. Any man who was a householder, however, was liable to be chosen for the unpleasant job, which usually went by rotation. If he were a " privileged " person, such as a peer, a member of parliament, a clergyman, an attorney, or a justice of the peace, he could plead exemption. If he were wealthy enough he could pay a deputy to undertake the work for him. But if he could fall back on neither of these resources the law set him in the stocks and fined him six and eightpence if he refused to execute his duties when elected !

The post was indeed no sinecure. Peace had to be preserved amongst a remarkably hot-blooded, quarrelsome set of folk, as ready with a knife or a dagger as their descendants with the tongue. Breakers of the peace had to be followed if they tried to escape, and it was the constable's duty to raise the " hue and cry " after a fugitive and rouse all the inhabitants to join in the chase. Punishments

---

[1] For a typical specimen list of " the furniture, implements, and books requisite to be had in every church " see " Injunctions and other Ecclesiastical Proceedings of Richard Barnes, Bishop of Durham from 1575 to 1587," Surtees Soc., Vol. XXII, p. 25.

ordered by the magistrates were executed by the constable. It was his business to duck the village scold in the nearest stream or pond, to thrust thieves and brawlers into the stocks, and to whip rogues and vagabonds, men and women alike, either at the whipping post or through the streets. He had to watch over the manners and morals of the villagers, and see that flesh was not eaten on fast days, and that every one went to church on Sundays as the law demanded. Cursers and swearers stood in danger of his authority, so did the drunkard and the player of unlawful games. The constable saw to it that the rate of wages paid and received was that ordained by the justices. He was also required to see to such diverse matters as that fathers apprenticed their children to some calling and that no looting took place if a fire broke out in anybody's house.

There is one more parish official who calls for some mention, and who was certainly a person of importance in his day. This is the parish clerk, practically the only representative of the minor orders of the Roman Church left to us by the Reformation. From that time onwards he became a functionary of all work, and took upon himself many of the duties hitherto performed by such persons as the sub-deacons and acolytes. Originally the clerk was intended to aid the incumbent with the singing at service time, and to teach the children of the parish ; after the Reformation he continued these offices, and became sexton and verger as well in most small churches. He had to be able to read the Epistle and the First Lesson in church, and it was his duty to begin the Communion service by singing a psalm,[1] and to lead the responses in the lesser Litany. He frequently accompanied the parish priest when the latter visited the sick.[2]

---

[1] For full accounts of the parish clerk and his duties see " The Clerk's Book of 1549," ed. J. Wickham Legg ; also " The Parish Clerk," by P. H. Ditchfield.

[2] One of the best Elizabethan anecdotes is that told by Edward Topsell, chaplain of St. Botolph's, Aldersgate, about one of these clerks and his incumbent : " I may remember you of a country tale of an old mass-priest in the days of Henry VIII, who reading in English after the translation of the Bible, the miracle of the five loaves and two fishes, and when he came to the verse that reckoneth the number of the guests or eaters of the banquet, he paused a little and at last said, they were about five

Such, in brief, were the local officials and their servants who, between them, controlled the doings and the life of the genuine rural community in Elizabeth's time. Parishes might vary enormously in extent, from the tiny hamlet of two or three dozen inhabitants to a vast but sparsely inhabited district or a small but densely populated one. Whatever the size, however, the personnel and the administration remained the same. With some of these officials and their tasks we shall be concerned again when inquiring into social conditions. For the moment, however, we may leave them for the pleasanter occupation of making the acquaintance of various good country folk of whom the literature of the time affords us some entertaining glimpses.

hundred ; the clerk that was a little wiser, whispered into the priest's ear that it was five thousand, but the priest turned back and replied with indignation, ' Hold your peace, sirra, we shall never make them believe they were five hundred ! ' "—" The Historie of Foure-Footed Beastes," 1607.

Note.—R. H. Tawney's *The Rise of the Gentry 1558-1640* (*Economic History Review*, XI, 1941) is the classic exposition of its subject. For a contemporary account of the various sections of the upper classes, their incomes, etc., see Thomas Wilson, *The State of England, Anno Dom. 1600* ; ed. F. J. Fisher : Camden Miscellany, xvi : 1936. For day-to-day business and the work of the J.P. in his county and the work of a City Council the following items will be found characteristic, useful and illuminating : *Wiltshire County Records. Minutes of Proceedings in Sessions, 1563 and 1574 to 1592.* ed. H. C. Johnson : Wilts. Archaeol. and Nat. Hist. Soc. Records Branch, Vol. IV ; (1949 for 1948). *York Civic Records* (Vols. 6 and 7) ed. A. Raine. Yorks. Archaeol. Soc., Record Series, cxii, cxv : (1948, 1950) ; N.B. has helpful subject-index.

CHAPTER VIII

COUNTRY FOLK AND COUNTRY WAYS

E VEN in Elizabethan times, when to our way of thinking London itself presented almost a pastoral aspect, there is sounded in literature that note of longing for the simplicity of the country and its care-free life which we are inclined to imagine has only been heard since the rise of industrialism. To-day it is often as an almost physical necessity that this longing for clean air and open spaces seizes upon the town-dweller. To the Elizabethans it came as a spiritual nostalgia only ; like Horace escaping from the brilliant Court of Augustus to the quiet of his Sabine farm they envisaged the country as a refuge from the complexities and stress of a life that had even then assumed the guise of modernity. Of Elizabeth herself during her imprisonment at Woodstock in her sister's reign the saying is recorded : " That milkmaid's lot is better than mine, and her life merrier." So, too, Shakespeare makes his Henry VI dwell longingly upon the peace of the shepherd's life :

O God ! methinks it were a happy life,
To be no better than a homely swain. . . .
So many hours must I tend my flock ;
So many hours must I take my rest ;
So many hours must I contemplate ;
So many hours must I sport myself ;
So many days my ewes have been with young ;
So many weeks ere the poor fools will yean ;
So many days ere I shall shear the fleece :
So minutes, hours, days, weeks, months and years,
Pass'd over to the end they were created,
Would bring white hairs unto a quiet grave.
Ah ! what a life were this ! how sweet ! how lovely !

It is but to be expected, therefore, that Elizabethan

literature should give us a pleasant gallery of country portraits. From the shepherd at his meal of "homely curds," drinking out of his leathern bottle, and the milk-maid singing at her task, rousing the envy of kings and queens, to the good yeomen and country gentlefolk and great landowners, they come before us in many a pamphlet or play or poem, sometimes idealized but most often in fashion as they lived. Even in that most artificial of forms, the Pastoral, there are real rustics to be found now and again, standing out vividly from among the crowd of masquerading Dresden-china shepherds and nymphs. Phyllis and Corydon may have a monopoly of the lyric, but bluff country squires and their good ladies, Joan and Hobbinol, tinkers and pedlars live again for us in the pages of Shakespeare and many another author, known and unknown.

As befits his dignity we may begin with the country gentleman. In contemporary literature he occasionally suffers somewhat from the satirist, who is apt to make merry at his expense and depict him as a real "country cousin." Sir Thomas Overbury gives us one such unflattering portrait of the narrow-minded type of squire whose "travel is seldom farther than the next market town" where his only inquiry is the price of corn. He is a niggard too, for "he will go ten mile out of the way to a cousin's house" to save the expense of putting up at an inn, and he "rewards the servants by taking them by the hand when he departs."

But there were better types than this—sound, kindly men who did their part in building up the system of local government, who managed their estates wisely and wel:, and extended their benevolence and protection to all the poor of the neighbourhood. They had perhaps often enough the conservatism of idea that has always marked their class. They would be inclined, for example, to agree with the gentleman of a contemporary pamphlet who argues that the education of the children of their poorer tenants did more harm than good in the case of the unapt, "because there they continue so long, as a good mystery [1] or occupa-

---

[1] I.e. handicraft or trade.

tion might have been learned." They tended to keep to old customs, and to think that the ways of their fathers were good enough for them. Newfangled dishes found no favour at their tables ; a barrel of caviare, sent as a present by a great lady, was opened and tasted by one such honest gentleman, and sent back with the message, " Commend me to my good Lady and thank her honour, and tell her we have black soap enough already " ! [1]

Good worthy folk too were the franklins, the landowners of free but not noble birth, and in rank standing just below the gentry. Overbury is much more complimentary when dealing with the franklin than in his companion portrait of the gentleman. He is a peaceable, contented man, seeing to his estate in person and dealing kindly with his tenants. He loves honest pastime, and keeps all the old country festivals—" Rock Monday, and the wake in the summer, shrovings, the wakeful ketches on Christmas Eve, the hockey or seed cake." He keeps early hours, delights in simple food, and the best news one can bring him is that an aery of hawks has been found in his own lands, or that a colt of good strain has been foaled. Such a one is Nicholas Breton's countryman—in the dialogue from which quotation has already been made—who expresses his contentment with his lot and with his own simplicity : " This is all we go to school for—to read Common Prayers at Church, and set down common prices at markets ; write a letter, and make a bond ; set down the day of our births, our marriage day, and make our wills when we are sick, for the disposing of our goods when we are dead. . . . We can learn to plough and harrow, sow and reap, plant and prune, thrash and fan, winnow and grind, brew and bake, and all without book ; and these are our chief business in the country." He hastens to add that he is no contemner of learning, which he reverences in the parson of the parish and the schoolmaster, and above all in the justices of the peace ; but for himself and his kind, " If we live within the compass of the law, serve God and obey our King, and as good subjects ought to do, in our duties and our

[1] Breton : " The Court and the Country."

prayers daily remember him, what need we more learning ? "

Times, as we have seen in an earlier chapter, were
changing even before James I came to the throne ; but
there were still many good landlords who were the centre
of the life and activities of their particular neighbourhoods,
and who lived on the friendliest of terms with their tenants.
If one used them with due reverence, as Breton's countryman assures us, and paid one's rent at the proper time, they
would hold friendly talk with their tenants ; and on holidays when they kept open house one could " make many
a good meal's meat with them." On the bench at the
Quarter Sessions they would speak so wisely " that it
would do one's heart good to hear them." On holy-days
one could go with them hunting, hawking, coursing, or
fishing, " and sometimes, to continue good neighbourhood,
meet and make matches for shooting and bowling."

Good landlords seem to have set a delightful example
of neighbourly courtesy. It was acknowledged as the
" country custom " of the gentry to bid every man welcome
to their tables, and in their own way humbler folk practised
a similar openhandedness. The present of a cake would
infallibly bring back one of a pudding ; a " pottle of beer "
would call forth the thanks of a pint of wine. " When we
kill hogs," says the countryman, " we send our children to
our neighbours with these messages : ' My father and
mother have sent you a pudding and a chine, and desires you
when you kill your hogs you will send him as good again.' "

Hospitality was still a country virtue. A seventeenth
century character writer, lamenting its decay in his own
time, praises the older type of gentleman who practised it,
before " pride, puritans, coaches and covetousness " drove
it from England. Such a landlord " loved three things,
an open cellar, a full hall, and a sweating cook : he always
provided for three dinners, one for himself, another for his
servants, the third for the poor." Such was the charity of
these good country gentlemen that " the poor, the passenger, his tenants and servants " all prayed for him. " He
had his wine come to him by full butts, but this age keeps

her wine-cellar in little bottles. Lusty able men, well
maintained, were his delight, with whom he could be
familiar ; his tenants knew when they saw him, for he
kept the old fashion, good, commendable, plain ; the poor
about him wore him upon their backs, but now since his
death landlords wear and waste their tenants upon their
backs in French or Spanish fashions." [1]

Justice Shallow had his limitations, but he practised old-
fashioned hospitality in his Gloucestershire manor house,
amongst the Cotswold uplands. Sir John Falstaff shall not
away to London without first doing honour to a banquet.
Davy bustles off to " William cook " with orders for " some
pigeons, a couple of short-legg'd hens ; a joint of mutton ;
and any pretty little tiny kickshaws." Even as they sit
gossiping together in the orchard there must be refreshment
provided—apples and a dish of caraways ; while of the
quality and the quantity of the good wine consumed in
that pleasant arbour we are well able to judge from the
amazing volubility of Master Silence. No niggards either,
when they feasted their workers and friends, were those
prosperous country folk of lower standing like Perdita's
foster-father : " Three pounds of sugar, five of currants,
rice, mace, seven nutmegs, a race or two of ginger, four
pounds of prunes and as many of raisins of the sun " her
foster-brother was commissioned to buy for the sheep-
shearing feast ; saffron, too, he was told to remember, for
colouring the warden pies—a pleasant list, promising dainty
fare.

The household of a considerable landowner in Elizabethan times formed a more or less self-sufficing and self-
supporting community. Its numbers would often run to a
hundred or more. Besides the owner and his family and
perhaps some relatives, and a chaplain, and a tutor for the
children, most great houses contained an almost unbeliev-
able number of serving men of a superior kind, considerably
distinguished both by capacity and treatment from those
who performed the really menial offices of the household.
These serving men or retainers wore the livery of their

[1] Donald Lupton : " London and the Country Carbonadoed," 1632.

master, and attended him on his visits to his neighbours or to London, if required. Such a serving man was trained to carve and serve at table, knew how to " unlace a coney, to raise a capon, trompe a crane, and so likewise handle all other dishes." He was often an accomplished wrestler and a good runner ; frequently he was a master of archery, or of the handgun, and was invariably conversant with all kinds of country sport. In the absence of his equals the master of the house would think it in no way unbecoming to his dignity to converse with retainers such as these on the subject of hawks and hounds and horses. Besides these superior serving men there was always in any great country household a miscellaneous collection of falconers, huntsmen, and lackeys about the stables ; bakers, brewers, cooks, and scullions about the kitchens ; personal attendants for the owner and his wife ; laundresses, shepherds, hogherds, and dairymaids.

Situated, as a rule, in some remote country spot, far from any town, and often with not even a village nearby, a household of this kind was accustomed to supply nearly all its own wants. Food for man and beast would be grown upon the estate, fuel came from its woods. " All the corn we make our bread of," boasts the country gentleman, " groweth on our own demesne ground ; the flesh we eat is all (or the most part) of our own breeding ; our garments also, or much thereof, made within our house. Our own malt and water maketh our drink." The lady took entire charge of her dairy, the profits of which were her own. She thought it no shame to walk in the pastures to see how her cows and calves were getting on ; she would walk " a long mile " to the field where the reapers were at work. A gentlewoman too fine or delicate to care for the duties of her position was " misliked " amongst the neighbouring dames, and condemned as " a clean fingered girl." [1]

Thomas Tusser gives us the character of the good country huswife in his " Five Hundreth Points of Good Husbandry." Practice teaches her how to govern her house-

---

[1] See the present writer's " Social Background " in " Companion to Shakespeare Studies."
[2] " Civil and Uncivil Life (1579). See Hazlitt : " Inedited Tracts."

hold, and she keeps a firm hand on the reins. Servants are
allowed to take no liberties, and woe to any idler, for the
good huswife herself is everywhere at once, overseeing all
that is done, casting a sharp eye into unswept corners,
deciding even the times at which she deems it advisable for
her retinue to shift their linen !   She is up at cockcrow, for
late rising on the part of the mistress ruins even a good
servant.   At once she sets all to their tasks—some to peel
hemp, some to peel rushes to be used as candle-wicks,
others to spin or to card or to seethe brine.[1]   Some are
sent out to the pastures to see to the cattle ; others grind
the malt ready for the brewing.   She herself serves at the
breakfast for men and maids, dealing out a mess of pottage
and a morsel of meat to each.   She believes in feeding her
servants well, though not daintily ; all who do their work
properly are sure of a good meal, and she likes to hear her
maids singing as they go about their tasks.

She does her own brewing, because it is better and more
economical, and she supervises very carefully the bread
baked for her establishment.   New bread is wasteful, and
bread which has been kept too long goes mouldy ; it is her
pride to achieve the golden mean between the two.   She
has no use for extravagant meals, even when guests arrive :
three dishes are enough to entertain a friend.   No scraps
are wasted ; with the bones they are thrown to the dogs
when the meal is over.

She makes her own candles, and saves feathers for the
beds and pillows.   She keeps a prudent eye on her cat, who
is excluded from the dairy, a mousetrap being employed
there instead.   She is careful, also, of open windows, not
only for fear of other people's cats, but also for fear of the
" wild cat with two legs "—the wandering rogue who is
the worse thief !   In the evening supper is not served until
she knows that the cattle are all housed or settled for the
night, and that no clothes put out to dry have been left in
the garden to be stolen by passing vagrants.[2]   She locks

---

[1] To boil salt water to extract the salt for household use.
[2] Luckily for Autolycus and his tribe, all Elizabethan matrons were not
such model huswives. He was able to make quite a good living by pur-
loining " the white sheet bleaching on the hedge."

up her dairy and her chest and puts her keys carefully away at bedtime. After supper all are dismissed to bed, and no candles are allowed in barn, hayloft, or shed.

> In winter at nine and in summer at ten
> To bed after supper both maidens and men.

Good huswives and masters alike maintained a strict discipline amongst their servants. As children suffered beating for even slight faults, so men and women domestics felt the rod on occasion. In some households the master would institute a system of rules and fines. Sir John Harington, when High Sheriff of Somerset in 1592, drew up such a series of orders for his household servants. Absence from morning or evening prayers " without lawful excuse " cost the delinquent 2d., and a careless oath was uttered " upon pain for every oath 1d. "! Another penny was exacted from the laggard whose bed was still unmade after eight o'clock in the morning ; and the price of a broken glass was stopped out of the breaker's wages. The cook was fined sixpence if the dinner was late, and the sloven who forgot to change his shirt on Sundays or neglected to replace any missing buttons on his doublet was mulcted a penny. These sums were deducted each quarter-day from the wages, and were then " bestowed on the poor, or other godly use."

Tusser's wise husbandman, on whom we may suppose many a good country squire or yeoman to have modelled himself, must have been as busy in his province as his wife in hers. Every season of the year brought its tasks, quite apart from the more obvious daily routine of the farm. In November the good husbandman remembers to have his chimneys swept in preparation for the winter. Tusser reminds him also to keep an eye on his thresher at work in the barns, otherwise he will steal something every day. In December when bad weather keeps the family indoors the husbandman grinds his tools and sends his bailiff to collect all yokes, forks, and farm implements, so that while he sits over the fire he can put them into good repair for the next year. And out of doors, when the frost comes, there are

the strawberries and the flower-beds to be covered with
straw for protection against the cold. There is kindling
wood, also, to be split with beetle and wedge—a task to
warm the blood on a cold winter morning. In January
there is ditching and hedging to be done as soon as the
frost breaks. Then in February he must needs remember
to send for the mole-catcher and set him to work in the
grass meadows. In March he must see to his sheep lest
they fall victims to prowling dogs—mastiffs and mongrels,
of whom, Tusser complains, there are a thousand too many
at large. In April it is time to put up the hop-poles that
were stacked carefully away after the last picking. Bark
must be sold to the tanner before timber is felled ; then the
careful husbandman will put aside elm and ash for carts
and ploughs, hazel for forks, sallow for rakes, and thorn
for flails. In May there is weeding to be done ; and children must be hired to pick up stones from the fallow land.
In June there is the washing and then the shearing of the
sheep. Then in July comes the hay harvest, when the
goodman keeps the field all day with his labourers in spite
of the heat. Food and drink is brought to them while
they work, for the hay must be got in as soon as possible.
And here honest Tusser has a piece of advice to give : pay
your tithes duly to God, he says, even though the curate
who receives them is a bad character, and the parson as
evil ! In August comes the corn harvest, when it behoves
the wary farmer to keep his eye on the loiterers. Being a
considerate and humane man he gives his reapers gloves to
protect their hands ; [1] and allows the poor to glean in his
fields after the corn has been carried. He is pleased also
to let all his folk have a jovial time in the hall while the
harvest continues, watches with satisfaction their merri-
ment as the black bowl goes round the tables, and enjoys
hearing their singing. Last of all, in September there is
the fruit to be gathered ; the wool from the summer shearing must be sold to the webster ; logs must be stacked for
the winter ; salt fish for Lent must be bought in the town

[1] In the Earl of Ancaster's MSS. (Bertie household accounts) threepence
is entered as the price of a pair of harvest gloves in 1561.

and laid up to dry. And thus the husbandman's year goes
by in a round of duties of this kind.

Thomas Churchyard in his poem of " The Spider and the
Gout " gives us a delightful sketch of a busy maidservant
in such a household. It is a quaint and realistic picture,
and he does not scruple to inform us that her lips though
pleasantly red were a little chapped, and that although she
had a good complexion her skin was so tender that her face
used to peel from exposure to sun and wind. She tripped
round the house, mincing in her walk " like Mistress
Grace " ; she was an excellent cook, and had the lightest
of hands with the pastry :

> As soon as flour came from the mill
> She made the goodliest cakes thereof,
> And baked as fair a household loaf
> As e'er was set on any board.

She rose with the " merry lark," and with her petticoat
tucked up, and a handkerchief tied over her glossy hair, she
was all over the house with her broom in the early hours.
Sometimes she would be up still earlier, carding or spinning
or sewing her smock by candlelight. Sweet and cleanly in
her attire, she swept and dusted the house thoroughly,
pushing her broom under every bench, shaking up the
cushions, tidying everything that was out of place. Her
mistress, knowing her trustworthiness, gave her charge of
the keys of the ale and beer for the household, and so day
in day out she worked away busily, having a holiday in
town only once a year, generally at Easter.

Of the poorer class of husbandmen the same writer gives
us an equally realistic portrait. His " poor but honest
husbandman " is " the veriest drudge in all the coast," not
worth five pounds in ready gold, but well esteemed in the
parish as a charitable and hard working fellow. His
appearance is vividly drawn :

> This grunting grub was short and thick,
> His face was red as any brick,
> Wherein there stood a bottle-nose ;
> A couple of corns upon his toes

> He had, which made him cut his shoe.
> He never put on garments new
> But when that to the Wakes he went,
> He was dressed up like Jack a Lent.

For working days he was apparelled like any other country lout ; but his wife, who was of gentle blood, insisted on better garments for church-going—a sleeveless jacket, a rather threadbare velvet nightcap, and a chamlet doublet trimmed with silk. His dwelling was a humble one, with whitewashed walls and a thatched roof, but it housed many children, and within it there were no idlers. " Fat bacon " hung from the rafters, the maids sang merrily at the spinning wheels—all were busy and happy within doors or without. Oxen champed in his stalls, pigs lay grunting in the styes, his hens laid plentifully, " the geese were gaggling on the green." For himself, the husbandman prospered, and kept his enemy, the gout, at bay, by the energetic life he led ; yoking his oxen to the plough, climbing the trees to shake down mast for the swine he was fattening to sell, folding his scattered sheep, his work kept him in the fields in all weathers, " in many a shower and bitter blast," fasting until noon.

His wife, despite her gentle breeding, must have had to turn her hand not only to the tasks with which the good ladies of the franklins and the gentry busied themselves, but to hard physical toil besides. In his " Book of Husbandry " Fitzherbert asserts that " it is a wives occupation to winnow all manner of corns, to make malt, wash and wring, to make hay, shear corn, and in time of need to help her husband to fill the muck wain or dung cart, drive the plough, to load hay, corn and such other." Not only like her wealthier sisters is she to take charge of all the dairy work, but she is also " to go or ride to the market to sell butter, cheese, milk, eggs, chickens, capons, hens, pigs, geese, and all manner of corn." Doubtless the muck wain was all in a day's work, and disturbed her no more than the daily milk-skimming. What probably came hardest upon this paragon of wives, however, was Fitzherbert's final demand that she should " make a true reckoning and accompt to her husband what she hath received and what she hath paid."

Of education for the children of tiny villages or great country establishments there was often little or nothing. One man would in most cases unite the functions of both parson and schoolmaster. Even "gentlemen in the country," unless their sons were to proceed in the study of Common Law, Divinity, or Physic, held them "learned enough if they can write and read English and construe Latin." Perdita's clownish foster-brother was able to read his marketing list, but he could not figure out the value of the wool from the shearing without the aid of counters. Those who were not able to write for themselves could appeal to the clerk of the church or the schoolmaster for help. While the majority of the poorest labourers must have been in this position the better sort could often fend for themselves. As Breton's Countryman says, the inditing of letters is a small enough matter. After some salutation one comes straight to the point, "either to borrow, or to pay, or to know the price of your cattle, or for a merry meeting, or I thank you for my good cheer." He can write the "fair idle words" of a love-letter ; and if the specimen he gives is typical, such epistles deserved to be well cherished by the recipients, as doubtless they were :

Sweetheart, I commend me unto you, and have been as good as my promise, and have sent you a pair of gloves by Meg, your brother's best beloved, and upon Friday (God willing) I will meet you at the market, and we will be merry, and talk further of the matter, and if you be as I am, say and hold, I know my portion, and when yours is put to it we shall live the better. And so, keeping your handkerchief near my heart : till I see you I rest

Yours during life in true love
W. T.

The poor folk of the tiny country villages lived a hard life in Elizabethan times. When forced to depend on their own exertions for every meal they ate and the very clothes on their backs, still more for the implements with which they cultivated the ground and the utensils in which they cooked their food, it is not surprising that men and women alike had generally little leisure in their long day, which began with the dawn and sometimes before it. Each village was self-supporting just as the great country household was. Village wives made their own thread from nettles ; they spun, wove, and dyed the cloth, which they then cut out and made up into clothing for their families. If any wore linen it was of her own making ; if a man wore a leather jerkin it was of his own tanning. A man had to make the yoke for his oxen before he could plough his field ; his wife had to malt her barley before she could brew her ale.

But if country folk worked hard they also knew how to amuse themselves, and to indulge in honest recreation at the end of a day's work, or when some village festival came round. Generally on a holy-day there would be dancing on the village green, or in the market house in bad weather. Breton gives us a charming picture of such a gathering : " The young folks, smiling, kiss at every turning " in the dance ; the old folks sit round, talking and laughing ; the children dance for a garland, or play at stoolball " for a tansy and a banquet of curds and cream." There is much drinking of " old nappy ale," much " casting of sheeps eyes " and plighting of troth between sweethearts, much exchanging between men and maidens of pairs of gloves or pretty handkerchiefs ; " and so merrily goes the day away " until it is time for the maids to hie them home to the milking.

Of all such scenes of rustic life and character which figure in Elizabethan literature none are more delightful than those of merrymaking which grace the " Winter's Tale." Shakespeare almost alone seems to have had the gift of creating a romantic atmosphere without sacrificing reality. Perdita is the king's daughter of the Pastoral, disguised as a shepherdess, but her adopted father and brother are genuine country fellows, and their sheep-shearing feast just such a one as Shakespeare himself may well have remembered from his youth, when there were four-and-twenty nosegays for the shearers, and when the good dame " welcom'd all, serv'd all ; would sing her song and dance her turn."

Always a welcome diversion in these out-of-the-way villages was the appearance of the pedlar with his pack. Whether he called his wares on the village green, or found his way to the servants' quarters of the great house, he was sure to be quickly surrounded by a bunch of eager country folk, ready to spend their pennies upon wonderful bargains, or, as often as not, to be fleeced by this persuasive Autolycus. With his topical new ballads of murders and monstrosities he brought them a magical glimpse of the outside world ; their credulity and simplicity made them the easy prey of his mountebank eloquence. But, indeed, if any of the tribe ever sang as sweetly and as merrily as Shakespeare's rogue while jogging on by " the footpath way " it is small wonder that the rustics flocked to buy. Never has cheap-jack cried his wares more alluringly than once that " snapper up of unconsidered trifles " cried them on the sea-coast of Bohemia :

> Lawn, as white as driven snow ;
> Cyprus, black as e'er was crow ;
> Gloves as sweet as damask roses ;
> Masks for faces, and for noses ;
> Bugle-bracelet, necklace-amber,
> Perfume for a lady's chamber :
> Golden quoifs and stomachers,
> For my lads to give their dears ;
> Pins and poking-sticks of steel,
> What maids lack from head to heel :
> Come buy of me, come ; come buy, come buy
> Buy lads or else your lasses cry.

But even if no earthly Warwickshire cheap-jack ever sang so tunefully, no doubt Autolycus' fellow sounded equally romantic to his simple village customers. With his tapes and his laces, his silks and his threads and his " ribands of all the colours i' the rainbow," he wheedled the pennies out of the pockets of the maids and their lovers. When he pulled out his bundle of new ballads they would flock round him again, listening with open-mouthed delight to the amazing tale, " to a very doleful tune," of " how a usurer's wife was brought to bed of twenty money bags at a burden, and how she longed to eat adders' heads and toads carbonadoed."

" Is it true, think you ? " asks Mopsa.

" Bless me from marrying a usurer ! " exclaims Dorcas in horrified dismay.

" Pray you now buy it," Mopsa urges her swain. " I love a ballad in print, a'-life ; for then we are very sure they are true."

Perhaps one day he would come chanting the London pedlar's cry : " What is't ye lack ? Fine wrought shirts or smocks. Perfumed waistcoats. Fine bone lace or edgings. Sweet gloves. Silk garters, very fine silk garters. Fine combs or glasses or a poking-stick with a silver handle." Then even the children of a dowager duchess could not resist him. A pedlar who called at Grimsthorpe in 1561 was surrounded by the children of the house clamouring for a glimpse of his treasures ; and the household accounts vouch for the fact that he went away at least two shillings the richer, as that is the sum entered as wheedled out of somebody—the duchess or the steward— by Master Peregrine and Mistress Susan " to buy them fairings of a pedlar at the gate." [1]

From amongst these rustic labourers, hedgers, ditchers, threshers, and reapers two picturesque individuals stand out and find their way into literature. These are the milk-maid and the shepherd, idealized alike by the Elizabethans themselves and by the character writers of the next century. Overbury's sketch of the former, indeed, charming as it is, savours too much of the pastoral convention, is idyllic rather than lifelike. Save for the admission that her hand is hard with labour, and that she spends her year's wages at the annual fair, she reminds us of some dainty Pastorella or Phœbe : " The golden ears of corn fall and kiss her feet when she reaps them, as if they wished to be bound and led prisoners by the same hand that felled them." Even his delightful touch, " She dares go alone and unfold sheep in

[1] Earl of Ancaster's MSS., p. 464.

the night, and fears no manner of ill, because she means none," is probably untrue.   A buxom country wench would have been as little afraid of man or beast then as now ; but if her grandmother's old tales of fairies and pixies had not made her " mortal skeered " of the good people—far too genuinely scared to venture out alone into the fields in the dark—then she was no true Elizabethan country girl.

Shakespeare's country lasses are much nearer to life. " Greasy Joan " stirs the pot of broth to cool it, Marian's nose looks red and raw—it is the English country in winter time, when " milk comes frozen home in pail " and when " ways be foul," when the keen wind nips the blood, and the coughing of the rustic congregation drowns the parson's best eloquence.   Touchstone's old love Jane Smile washed coarse linen, and the hands with which she milked the cow were chapped ; Audrey, to whom he transferred his affections in the Forest of Arden, was a real Warwickshire wench.   One and all they hail from the English counties Shakespeare knew and loved ; but Overbury's milkmaid comes from Arcadia.[1]

John Stephens' shepherd is also probably more literary and ideal than actual, but it is a pleasant portrait, nevertheless : " Give him fat lambs and fair weather, and he knows no happiness beyond them . . . the sweet fountain is his fairest ale house ; the sunny bank his best chamber . . . the next grove or thicket will defend him from a shower. . . . His flock affords him his whole raiment, outside and linings, cloth and leather." He is the true philosopher, " the pattern of a moderate wise man," " neither daunted with lightning and thunder, nor over-joyed with spring time and harvest." He delights in his daily task—" whether to mend his garments, cure a diseased sheep, instruct his dog, or change pastures." Perhaps, however, there was a touch of truth in it.   Shake-

---

[1] This is literally as well as figuratively true. H. Dugdale Sykes, in " Notes and Queries," Vol. XI, 1915 (April and May), shows in a most convincing manner that not only are some thirty-two of the characters in the 1615 edition of Overbury—amongst them the milkmaid—probably the work of the dramatist John Webster, but also that the writer, whether Overbury or Webster, borrowed both the idea and even much of the phrasing for his milkmaid from Sidney's " Arcadia."

speare's shepherd, Corin, speaks in much the same tones.
He describes himself as " a true labourer " : " I earn that
I eat, get that I wear, owe no man hate, envy no man's
happiness." Maybe the townsmen who thus pictured the
felicity of the countryman's lot would have found in his
hard-worked life only disillusion ; but it is surely not quite
without significance that so many in search of contentment
and peace of mind should turn to the country and see in
the lives of its typical figures that quietude which they
found lacking in their own. Dirt and drudgery, poverty
and vice showed the seamy side of village life ; but watching their flocks in the solitude of the downlands and hills
there must have been many a man who, like Wordsworth's
shepherd, Michael, developed an integrity of soul that
really lifted him above the stress of things, making him
such a one as Campion pictured :

> Whom hopes cannot delude,
> Nor sorrow discontent . . .
> Good thoughts his only friends,
> His wealth a well-spent age,
> The earth his sober inn
> And quiet pilgrimage.

To leave the last word to the countryman himself, however, here is his own version of the delights of the country.[1]
Admittedly he speaks as a prosperous man, but he need not
therefore be accounted the worse judge :

" For the delight of our eyes we have the May-painting
of the earth, with divers flowers of dainty colours and
delicate sweets ; we have the berries, the cherries, the peas
and the beans, the plums and the codlings in the month
of June ; in July the pears and the apples, the wheat, the
rye, the barley and the oats, the beauty of the wide fields,
and the labours with delight and mirth, and merry cheer at
the coming home of the harvest cart. We have again in
our woods the birds singing ; in the pastures the cow
lowing, the ewe bleating, and the foal neighing, which with
profit and pleasure make us better music than an idle note

[1] Breton : " The Court and Country."

and a worse ditty, though I highly do commend music, when it is in the right key.   Again we have young rabbits that in a sunny morning sit washing of their faces, while as I have heard beyond the seas there are certain old conies that in their beds sit painting of their faces ; we have besides tumblers for our conies and greyhounds for our courses, hounds for our chase, hawks of all kind for the field, and the river and the wood ; so that what can reason conceive, that nature can desire, but for the delight of both the country doth afford us ? "   Finally, with " hay in the barn, horses in the stable, oxen in the stall, sheep in the pen, hogs in the sty, corn in the garner, cheese in the loft, milk in the dairy, cream in the pot, butter in the dish, ale in the tub, and Aqua Vitæ in the bottle, beef in the brine, brawn in the souse, and bacon in the roof, herbs in the garden, and water at our doors, whole clothes to our backs, and some money in our coffers "—having all this, " if we serve God with all, what in God's name can we desire to have more ? "

CHAPTER IX

MASTER AND MAN AND MASTERLESS MEN

SOCIAL relations between master and man were pleasant enough in the ordinary Elizabethan home. The formality which environed the dinner-table of Anthony Viscount Montague [1] was more than compensated for in the house of the good London citizen by a freedom of speech and intercourse which had managed to survive from the more patriarchal family life of the Middle Ages. Hollyband's well-to-do merchant treats his servants not indeed as his equals, but in a free and easy and genuinely friendly manner. He is quite prepared to give a saucy lackey a box on the ear, but he is proud of his proficiency in singing, gives him a good drink of wine before he starts his song, and listens with complacency while he indulges in banter with one of the guests at the table. The reproof he delivers to the clumsy and forgetful William is the reproof of the parent who persists in " bringing up " his child, company or no company: " William, give here some bread . . . you will never learn to serve ; why do you not lead it with a trencher plate, and not with the hand ? I have told it to you above an hundred times." [2] William, we feel, is one of the family ; his master has not yet developed that particular form of class-consciousness which reserves this kind of rebuke for afterwards when the guests have departed. It is eloquent of an intimacy between master and man which we find reflected in so much contemporary literature—the intimacy which exists, for example, between the master-shoemaker and his men in Dekker's " Shoemaker's Holiday." Simon Eyre is proud of the skill of all his expert workers ; and behind their uncouth and outspoken behaviour lies a real affection for their eccentric master. Eyre enters the yard in front of his

---

[1] Cf. Chapter II. [2] Hollyband : " French Schoolemaister."

house, calling, " Where be these boys, these girls ? They
wallow in the fat brewiss of my bounty, and lick up the
crumbs of my table, yet will not rise to see my walks
cleansed. What, Nan, what Madge Mumblecrust. . . .
What Firk, I say ; what Hodge ! open my shop-windows."
Firk replies in kind : " O master, is't you that speak ban-
dog and Bedlam this morning ? I was in a dream and
mused what madman was got into the street so early."
The ordinary middle-class huswife, of whom Simon's wife
Margery is a typical example, was on equally informal
terms with her household, and even Erondell's dignified
Lady Ri-Mellaine [1] proves ready to gossip with her waiting
woman while having her hair brushed. It may not have
been pleasant for the waiting woman to be told that she
had a " coney's memory " simply because she had forgotten
to bring her mistress's farthingale, but it at least betokens
a human relationship between mistress and maid ; there is
nothing stand-offish about it !

Part and parcel of this attitude which included the hired
servant as one of the family was the natural tendency of
the ordinary master or mistress to regard their servants in
the way that they regarded their children—not, indeed, as
beings of a lower order, but as chattels and dependants. A
servant's time was wholly his employer's ; and the box on
the ear or the horsewhip—as in the case of children—were
the obvious and usual means for the correction of error.
Apart, however, from what would inevitably, in the
sixteenth century, have been the severe but quite normal
restrictions imposed upon them by any master, the hired
servant and the apprentice were also subject both to
municipal and State control, which effectively prevented
any crank amongst employers from setting his fellows an
unhealthy example of over-indulgence or undue regard of
individuality amongst his dependants. Wages were controlled, conditions of employment were controlled, hours of
work were controlled ; even clothing and amusements were
regulated. An employer who gave higher wages than those
fixed by the justices was liable to a five-pound fine and ten

[1] " French Garden."

days' imprisonment; the recipient of such unlawful gain was liable to twenty-one days' imprisonment. In a word, a strict control of labour and its conditions was enforced upon both parties to any contract of employment.

In London, for example, the city authorities kept a fatherly and censorious eye upon the recreations and the apparel of the young apprentice. Eustace's master,[1] who refused to let that merry fellow frequent a fencing school or learn the latest dance measures, was not an exceptional and curmudgeonly elder, but merely a law-abiding citizen, carrying out the regulations of the Lord Mayor and Aldermen and liable to get into trouble if he did not. The personal liberty of Eustace and his kind had been grievously curtailed in 1582 by these unfeeling authorities. So many of the London prentices were the children of gentlemen and " persons of good quality " that the numbers who " did affect to go in costly apparel and wear weapons and frequent schools of dancing, fencing and music " were continually increasing, until an order in Common Council dealt with the matter.[2] After this, not for Eustace the joy of indulging his Elizabethan taste for peach colour, or orange-tawny, or flame colour, even when off duty; the city—aided by his unsympathetic master—insisted on the dull uniformity of blue, russet, white, watchet, and sheep's colour. He might not pride himself on the smart cut of his breeches and doublet, and feel himself the equal of any proud swaggerer when he escaped from the shop; the unimaginative city fathers forbade " great breeches " with stuffing, and firmly refused to allow him a padded doublet. " A small plain slop " with no waste of good material, said the Common Council; and for stuffs he was restricted to fustian, canvas, sackcloth, leather, and wool. Silk stockings were forbidden, nor could he even console himself by using silk laces to tie his fustian doublet to his leather breeches—leather or thread were the only kind of points sanctioned by authority. Shirts with embroidery on them

[1] See Chapter IV
[2] Stow : " Survey," ed. Strype, 1720, Vol. II, pp. 328-9.

or ruffs at the neck and wrists were also forbidden, and as a last straw the authorities and his master clapped on top of his head the famous flat woollen cap [1] and forbade him to carry about him any offensive weapon save only a " convenient meat knife." Eustace might risk it, and have his fling, but if he were caught the punishment for a second offence in any of these kinds would be " open whipping " in the hall of his company. Perhaps a hint of the way in which some of the more daring spirits attempted to circumvent these unpleasant restrictions upon their liberty is to be found in another section of the order which forbids the prentice to keep a store of clothes anywhere except in his master's house. So perhaps Eustace occasionally strutted abroad in his great breeches and his peascod-bellied doublet in spite of the Lord Mayor and all his Aldermen.

Of equal stringency and greater seriousness was the control exercised over the person of the ordinary worker by the State. Early in the reign it had been enacted that every unmarried person between the ages of twelve and sixty, and every married person under thirty, who possessed less than forty shillings a year should work as a servant hired by the year. If unable to obtain employment in their own trade all such were compelled " to serve in hus-bandry," agriculture apparently having room for all the surplus. Their wages were fixed by the justices, and their work hours by the statute 5 Eliz., cap. 4. From March to September labourers and artificers were to work from five in the morning until seven or eight at night ; from September to March they were to work from dawn till dusk, and for every hour's work missed a penny was to be deducted from their wages. The employer was not to have things all his own way, however : the day's work might be a long one, but out of it, the Statute decreed, he was to allow his labourers two hours off for meals and " drinkings." The pleasantest touch of all is that of

---

[1] By 13 Eliz., cap. 19, every person of six years and upwards had to wear a woollen cap, made in England, on Sundays and holy-days, unless his rank excused him. The statutory fine for disobeying this order was 3s. 4d. for each offence.

section 9, where it is provided that from May to August the
labourer shall be entitled to an extra half hour for his midday nap, so that his " forty winks " may be said to be a
national institution.

The same statute provided that labourers and artificers
thus hired by the year were not to leave their employment
or be dismissed from it before their term was up, unless
two justices gave the necessary permission ; a master who
dismissed a servant without due cause shown and leave
obtained was liable to a forty shillings fine, and the servant
who was found " unduly departing " was imprisoned
until he or she undertook to finish his time. A servant
might not leave the place in which he had been working
without a testimonial from the city or the parish, " declar-
ing his lawful departure." If he was so unwise as to depart
thus without this " character " he was liable—if discovered
—to whipping or imprisonment, and his next employer
might find himself mulcted of five pounds for taking on an
uncertificated worker.

The basis of this domestic policy was the very sound
idea that those who were insufficiently endowed with this
world's goods must earn their living ; every one was to
work, unless he had other means of support. The State
was anxious that a trained worker should follow his own
trade ; if, however, his trade had no room for him he was
to find employment in husbandry ; and eventually it
was decreed that, if he could find no one to employ him in
any capacity whatsoever, then the parish was to provide
him with work and pay him for it. By the Act of 18 Eliz.,
cap. 3, in 1575 the justices were required to raise money
by taxation and with it to provide a common stock of
wool, hemp, flax, iron, etc., for the employment of the out-
of-work poor. They were to pay for the work done, and
any recipients of this State aid who spoiled their material
were to be sent to the house of correction provided in
each county. Thus, when normal employment failed, the
State took upon itself the task of seeing that the able-
bodied received sustenance, but only in return for work
done.

12

When regulating conditions of trade and labour Elizabeth's Government was guided primarily by its desire to ensure employment. In order that children should be properly trained they made seven years the statutory period of apprenticeship throughout the country. To guard, however, against the crowding out of the trained worker by the child-labour of apprentices, it was decreed that a reasonable proportion between the number of apprentices and journeymen employed by a master must be kept in every trade ; the clothmakers, tailors, fullers, shearmen, weavers, and shoemakers, for example, were allowed three apprentices to one journeyman in the first instance, but the acceptance of a fourth or fifth apprentice entailed in each case the employment of another journeyman. Finally, the justices and the overseers of the poor had to arrange for the apprenticing of orphans and of the children of vagrants, and to see that the poor themselves duly apprenticed their children when their schooling— if any—was done with. In so far as legal machinery could, statutes ensured firstly that the young should learn an honest trade, and secondly that having learnt one they should follow it.

Wages were undoubtedly low in Elizabeth's time. They had not gone up, under the Tudors, in proportion to the rise in prices ; the cost of wheat was quite four times as high as in the fifteenth century, but wages were hardly more than double what they had been. It seems almost impossible to arrive at any just idea of the average income and budget of the ordinary Elizabethan working man. Conditions and the prices of commodities varied so in different years and in different places that any generalization would probably give a hopelessly false impression. An income of forty shillings a year seems, however, to have raised its possessor above the lowest class of wage-earners. On this, apparently, a man who tilled the four acres attached to his cottage [1] and paid only a small and reasonable rent [2] could live and bring up his family. It was not

---

[1] 31 Eliz., cap. 7.
[2] Rent, like wages, had not risen everywhere in proportion to prices.

the bare "subsistence level," but it must have been perilously near it ; a bad year could easily reduce such families to complete destitution.

Wage-earners fell into several distinct categories. There were the household servants and others who were hired by the year, and who received, in addition to their wages, board and lodging and sometimes a certain allowance of clothing. Of the wages paid to such servants some account has already been given in Chapter VII. In another and more precarious position were the forty-shilling cottagers just described. Then in a slightly better position came those cottagers or smallholders who were also skilled workers, cultivating their own acres to provide themselves with the greater part of their food, and working also as day labourers for a certain portion of the year to earn the small income that was necessary for the purchase of such commodities as they did not themselves produce.

Records of wages paid are fairly easy to come by ; there is much information to be gleaned from household accounts, and there are also a number of the justices' annual assessments still extant. These annual assessments were made to preserve a reasonable proportion between wages and prices ; they were sanctioned by the Privy Council, and issued as royal proclamations, and we have apparently no reason to doubt that they were adhered to in the ordinary course of events.[1] London rates of wages being consistently higher than those in other parts of the country, assessments such as those for Chester or for the county of Lancashire are probably better examples of the ordinary scales of payment. Under the Lancashire assessment for 1595, for example, a master-mason or carpenter or joiner or thatcher received fourpence per day and also his food ; without meat and drink his pay was eightpence. The same rate obtained under the Chester assessments for 1591 and 1594 ; and under these a smith would receive twopence a day, a bricklayer twopence halfpenny, and a shoemaker twopence, in each case with food. The ordinary

[1] For satisfactory evidence that these assessments were regularly made see E. McArthur : "English Historical Review," XV, p. 445.

worker or journeyman received about half what a master-craftsman earned. A linen weaver under the Chester assessments received a penny a day, with food ; a master-carpenter fourpence and his food ; a joiner twopence.

If we take our master-carpenter as a definite example, and suppose him to work four days a week throughout the year, we find he earns £6 18s. 8d. Wheat in 1591 cost him 22s. 6d. per quarter, malt 20s., and oatmeal 38s. 8d.[1] Beef would cost him about 2d. a lb., butter 5d. ; or it is perhaps simpler to take it that the fourpence allowed, under the Lancashire assessment, for food represents the actual cost of feeding a man for one day. It is obvious, therefore, that such a man's earnings would not have kept himself and a family, unless he had been able to supply a very considerable portion of their food from his own ground. He would not expend much on clothing materials ; coarse frieze cloth, for example, could be bought for about 1s. 4d. a yard, and a pair of children's shoes would cost from 6d. to 1s. Nevertheless, without their acres the peasant and artizan—if figures are any evidence—could not have lived. As the population of the country survived it is obvious that the assessments are based not only upon the prices of food and clothing, but also upon the assumption that the average journeyman or master-craftsman produced a large proportion of his own food. Often enough it was a false assumption, and the position of those workers who had no land, and yet persisted in retaining their independence, must have been extraordinarily difficult. Unless, indeed, the whole family worked—the wife and children at spinning, weaving, and whatever other employment they could obtain, the husband and grown sons at their trades—they could not possibly have lived upon the wages paid. In the country, what with a scrap of land, commonable rights, perquisites, and employment by the day, the cottager was not too badly off : he could make ends meet, by thrift and frugality. In the towns, however, without any of the advantages enjoyed by the agricultural labourer, the lot of the ordinary worker was extremely

---

[1] According to Thorold Rogers.

hard. Men and women of this class in the towns became
only too easily the destitute but deserving poor.

So far as employment was concerned the policy of
Elizabeth's Government worked well. Labour was regulated, and in an age when humanitarian feeling for the
worker had not been heard of it is worth noticing that the
employé was not wholly disregarded by the law. But the
employment that existed was quite incapable of absorbing
all the potential employés, whether willing or unwilling.
The Tudor period saw the dawn of a new era of national
prosperity, but it also saw the beginning of a widespread
destitution previously unparalleled in this country.
Labourers, cottars, and expropriated smallholders, driven
from employment by the upheaval of the rural economy,
added their thousands to the ranks of the destitute ; discharged soldiers, the unemployed and the unemployable,
the diseased and the maimed, the aged and indigent, and
the rogues and vagabonds made up a veritable army of para-
sites, hurtful to the commonwealth, burdensome to the
worker, and a perpetual source of trouble and disquiet
to the authorities. The coincidence of the several causes
already noticed—the conversion of arable lands into grass,
the spread of enclosures, and the destruction of the monasteries—had brought the evil to such a pitch that by the
time Elizabeth came to the throne every one had realized
that legislation to cope with this new social problem was
an absolute necessity. The Government found itself compelled to assume as a national responsibility a charge that
had formerly been borne by the Church, working partly
through the monasteries and partly through the charity
which it had inculcated in the individual.

The Government began its work by reaffirming the enactments previously made under Edward VI and Mary, by
which collectors of alms were appointed throughout the
country to ensure that all who were able to do so should
contribute for the relief of the destitute. By raising charitable funds and by licensing certain poor folk to beg for
themselves it had been hoped, when the evil first became
apparent, to provide for all who needed help. Experience,

however, soon proved that such half measures were useless ; between the hardness of men's hearts and the rapid growth of destitution the method was overwhelmed. Voluntary charity was totally incapable of remedying such a state of affairs as already existed ; 1562 therefore saw the introduction of compulsory contribution ; the parson and his churchwardens were to " gently exhort " the parishioners, and if they failed, the bishop was to exercise his powers of persuasion ; if after the episcopal exhortation a man of means still remained " froward, wilful and obstinate " then the justices were to take the matter in hand, assess the niggard and levy the money, and imprison him if he did not yield the required sum when visited by the collector.

By 1572 (14 Eliz., cap. 5) the responsibility of each parish to provide for its aged, impotent, and sick poor had been affirmed by the statute which appointed overseers of the poor and empowered them to assess the parish in order to obtain the necessary funds. By 1601 parishioners became similarly charged with the relief and maintenance of disabled soldiers and sailors belonging by birth or residence to their parish (43 Eliz., cap. 3). To prevent unnecessary applications for relief the mutual liability of parents and children to support each other had already been established (39 Eliz., cap. 3) ; refusal of relief and maintenance from either, if possessed of any means, involved the offender in a fine of twenty shillings a month. Against exploitation by the " won't-works " the parish was further protected year by year by a series of enactments dealing with vagabondage.

The Act of 1572 found that all parts of the kingdom were " presently with rogues, vagabonds, and sturdy beggars exceedingly pestered, by means whereof daily happeneth horrible murders, thefts and other great outrages." To refuse to work for lawful wages was therefore made a punishable offence, and those who refused the work provided for them by the overseers of the parish were to be whipped and stocked to bring them to a better frame of mind. Begging and vagabondage were doomed, if legal measures could kill. All persons of fourteen years of age

.or more, if convicted of wandering, begging, and the
" roguish trade of life," were to be " grievously whipped
and burnt through the gristle of the right ear with a hot
iron of the compass of an inch about." Their only chance
of escape was if some good-hearted parishioner offered
them a year's employment, in which case the penalty was
abrogated. For a third offence in this kind the penalty
was death. " Masterless men " were not to be tolerated.

Here, apparently, were measures fitted to deal with the
army of sturdy beggars and rogues of whom the traveller
along any highway inevitably made the acquaintance.[1]
The " moon-men," for example, whom Dekker describes
in " O per se O," would be caught by the parish constable
and the overseers and made to forsake their roguish trade.
Roaming the country in bands of some half dozen, with their
morts and their kinchins,[2] and clothed in fantastic rags, they
would be brought to book and indicted before the justices
under 14 Eliz., cap. 5. To leave them no loophole, a twenty-
shilling fine was to be imposed on anyone found guilty of
harbouring such rogues, or of giving them alms, food, or
lodging. The penalties were excellently devised, but the
crux of the matter was—first catch your rogue, then whip
him. The moon-man and his like could live quite happily
on the poultry he stole, and the average farmer—knowing
the capacities of the village constable—was generally
readier to risk the twenty-shilling fine than the burning of
his thatch or his stores. Anyway, in 1612, if Dekker is
to be trusted, the moon-men were still able to terrorize
the farmers into letting them sleep in their barns, although
the Act had been on the statute book for forty years.
Acts and constables had not even then succeeded in driving
them into houses of correction or honest occupations,
though the constables' opinion of their own duties and
troubles is probably summed up adequately by one of their
kind, Ben Jonson's Toby Turfe, High Constable of Kentish
Town in the " Tale of a Tub " :

> . . . now by our Lady of Walsingham,
> I had rather be marked out Tom Scavenger

[1] See Chapter V.   [2] I.e. their wenches and their children.

> And with a shovel make clean the highways
> Than have this office of a constable.

Tom Scavenger's was no savoury job in the days when one's neighbours would cheerfully leave a dead pig to decay in the middle of the road in front of their houses, but it is easy to see that the troubles brought upon the constable by rogues and vagabonds and the necessity for their apprehension must have been the sorer trial. After his whipping and stocking—both the constable's duties—the convicted vagabond had to have his testimonial, recording his punishment, given to him, and be dispatched upon his homeward way, if he belonged to another parish. The Act of 1576 laid upon the constable the responsibility of handing him over to the constable of the next parish on the road, and so as the vagabond progressed towards his native house of correction each unfortunate Toby Turfe had to take charge of him until he had seen him safely out of his own confines.

Needless to say, vagabondage and roguery proved themselves extremely elastic terms. Begging was begging, but the rogue was a tougher problem. Rowlands, the satirist, in his " Dr. Merryman " has drawn two of these rascals :

> As perfect lousy as they both could crawl.
> Each had a hat and nightcap for the cold,
> And cloaks with patches. . . .
> Great satchel scrips that shut with leather flaps,
> And each a dog to eat his master's scraps.
> Their shoes were hob-nail proof, soundly bepegged,
> Wrapt well with clouts to keep them warmer legged.

A rogue of this kind was in love with vagabondage and the life of the roads; he was an expert pilferer, and he had many a colourable occupation to take him on his way. He did not want to be relieved or reformed. The only thing that frightened him was work, and, once the Government discovered this, the problem of the sturdy rogue was well on its way to a solution. The Privy Council did not begin to realize this until 1575, however, and in the meantime the rogues flourished. Diseases, as we have seen, were easy to counterfeit ; so were begging licences and passports. Palmists, tinkers, pedlars, bear-wards, fencers, players, minstrels, and the rest might or might not be genuine ; players, if attached to some great lord, would produce a licence from him whenever they came to a town or village where they intended to perform ; tinkers and pedlars had to have licences from two of the justices of the county in which they were travelling ; but many a rogue found one or other of these professions a handy cover for his vagabondage, and the puzzled village constable must often have been hard put to it to distinguish the true pedlar from the counterfeiting rogue who ought to be arrested.

But gradually, as the reign went on, local and central authorities began to realize the efficacy of work. One of the Somersetshire justices, Edward Hext, went to the root of the matter when he wrote that the vagabonds would " rather hazard their lives than work." [1] Rogues brought up before him in Somerset would plead to be sent to jail rather than to the house of correction, where they were put to some useful task. The London authorities showed in 1591 that they had learnt this lesson. They held a round up of the sturdy vagabonds, and set them to work upon the filthy city ditches, probably long overdue for a cleaning. They were paid at the rate of fourpence a day, and doubtless they earned their money. This kind of treatment, rather than the whippings and brandings, brought about a real diminution in their numbers. In the later years of the reign the evil undoubtedly began to abate : nevertheless, what it had been and could still be is very evident from Hext's letter to Burghley. Not only, at the height of their flourishing, did they carry on a campaign of petty rapine and theft " to the utter impover-ishment of the poor husbandman," but they would even mass themselves in large companies and deliberately waylay and rob the country folk on their way to market with their wares. Hext tells of a band of eighty who in

[1] 1596. Lansdowne MSS., 81 (62).

his own county of Somerset took a cartload of cheese from a man who was driving it to the fair, and divided it amongst themselves. He also quotes the case of three rogues who to his knowledge stayed at an ale-house for three weeks, during which time they consumed no less than twenty fat sheep, all of which they stole from neighbouring farmers.[1]

The financial aspect of the twin problems of roguery and poverty bore hardly upon the parish or the municipal purse. It cost money to build houses of correction for the vagabonds and to work the rogue-extirpating machinery ; it took yet more to provide for the sick, disabled, honest, and impotent poor. Hospitals had to be built and kept going, orphans had to be provided for, maimed soldiers and sailors had to have pensions. If one parish could not afford to cope with its own poor, as the statute demanded it should, then its richer neighbour had to assist. If an inadequacy in the existing machinery was revealed one year, it was remedied the next by another statute ; at all costs the Government had determined to deal with the whole social problem of employment, destitution, and vagrancy. In spite of every difficulty, it may safely be said that Elizabeth's reign saw the whole matter satisfactorily taken in hand. Solutions of each of its component problems could not, of course, be achieved in one reign—have not yet been achieved ; but the remedies put forward in these successive enactments known collectively as the Elizabethan Poor Laws were effective and far-sighted enough to check the evils against which they were directed and to form a satisfactory basis for modern legislation. Not so spectacular as some of its achievements, the way in which the Elizabethan age dealt with its social problem of poverty and labour must always be remembered as providing a sound basis for the vagrancy laws and the poor relief of the next two hundred years.

[1] If Hext were not such a sensible man we might be forgiven for wondering whether even Elizabethan rogues, who obviously did things on a generous scale, were really capable of devouring food at the rate of one sheep a day between three !

CHAPTER X

RELIGION

THE picturesque quality of the Elizabethan age is apt to divert our gaze from certain essentials, with the result that it is possible to pick up many books purporting to deal with the period which are yet silent regarding its religion, although nothing in the life of the age is in reality more fundamental or more necessary to our proper understanding of it. An individual might be definitely hostile to the State religion, as were the Roman Catholics, or fiercely critical of it, as the more advanced Reformers. Atheism, or a complete denial of religion, was not unknown ; the one attitude which cannot be found was indifference. It was an age in which religion mattered supremely, to the individual as to the nation.

The religious settlement achieved by the Queen and her ministers was admittedly a compromise. Satisfying the extremists on neither side, it had that characteristically English virtue of appealing to the large majority of moderate minded people, and of providing for all except the most fanatical a *modus vivendi* that involved the sacrifice neither of loyalty nor of faith. A glance backward over the preceding Tudor reigns will show simply enough how the compromise was arrived at.

Henry VIII, mainly from motives of policy, had assumed the title of Supreme Head of the Church in England. By so doing he had fostered the national feeling which for many reigns had been resentful of papal interference in English affairs, and had scored, if one may say so, a " patriotic " success on a political move, designed to facilitate his own divorce and to divert money into his own coffers. In order to accomplish this he had fallen back upon two very strong lines of defence : one, the instinct and desire for reform of the Church and its clergy which had been developing in England from the time of Wyclif, and the other the practical expedient of following the Lutheran example of setting up the authority of the Bible as the only supreme court of appeal in such a case of conscience.

Henry himself had little enough sympathy with the tenets of the continental reformers. It was not so many years since his own attack on Luther had earned him the bestowal by the Pope of the title of Defender of the Faith. As a result, his " reform " of the Church struck mainly at sources of revenue rather than at articles of belief. Monasteries were suppressed and their estates and revenues confiscated. To colour the matter, superstition was attacked by the destruction of images and the stripping of the shrines of the saints ; but very little onslaught was made upon the doctrines of the Church. The English translation of the Bible, the joint work of Tyndale and Coverdale, was put into every church, and that was about as far as Henry was prepared to go. Rash Protestants who were anxious to proceed further along the lines laid down by Geneva had their ardour severely checked by statute and persecution.

The Protector Somerset, however, was less wise and more fanatical. During his brief authority over his nephew, Edward VI, sweeping changes were introduced : the old services and the Book of Common Prayer were much modified ; vandalism was let loose upon the churches, where the remaining pictures and images which had escaped before were whitewashed and destroyed ; and the teaching of the older faith was attacked at various points, Archbishop Cranmer himself, for example, denying its doctrine of fasting by eating meat in Lent. Such wholesale inno‧ vation met very naturally with general resentment amongst the mass of the people, with the result that the succession of Mary was for the moment cordially welcomed.

Mary's immediate restoration of the old services was popular, and had she but followed her father's methods it would have been successful. But—fatally, as it proved, for her Church—Mary was the one member of her family purely and devotedly religious in spirit. To the restoration

of the papal domination the nation was not as a whole
strongly opposed, provided that no restitution of Church
property was required ; and this latter security had been
given by the legate, Cardinal Pole, when he absolved the
country and received it again into the Roman Communion.
Had the situation been allowed to remain as it was at
this juncture all might have been well.   National feeling
had, no doubt, been accumulating, and running strongly
counter to the idea of papal interference, for a long time ;
but national feeling was also equally cognizant of the need
for national unity, and therefore of the need for outward
religious conformity. Mary, however, must have more than
that : with all the intensity of her nature she was determined to save the souls of her people by the eradication
of heresy, no matter at what cost. Persecution was the
only method known to her age ; she and her council applied
it deliberately for four terrible years, on a scale unprece-
dented before in England.   It was the hair that turned the
balance.   The national consciousness had already been
alarmed and put on the defensive by the Queen's Spanish
marriage ; persecution now united in the national abhorrence Philip and the papacy, representing foreign domination.   Sixteenth century England may have been conser-
vatively attached to the old faith, but she would put herself
to the discomfort of forsaking it when by adhering to it
any longer she felt her national liberty endangered.   The
convictions which took the reign's three hundred victims
to the stake were religious ; the effect of their martyrdom
on their fellow-citizens was primarily a political one.   It
established in the minds of the majority of Englishmen,
not indeed that hatred of the faith and observances of
the Roman Church which animated those of the Reformed
persuasion, but a sturdy hatred of Rome and its methods,
which made alliance with its Church an impossibility for
that nation which in the Elizabethan age was to assert its
nationalism more vigorously than it had yet done in any
other period of its history.

Some of the Jesuit executions of Elizabeth's reign are
undoubtedly quite as unpleasant to an unprejudiced

modern as the Smithfield fires of her sister's. The execution of Campion, for instance, has called forth the execration of one of our most Protestant historians ; and the naïve records of the methods employed against his fellow-captives do not make edifying reading. Still, in spite of the modern tendency to whitewash the " Bloody Mary " of picturesque tradition, and to point out the judicial atrocities of Gloriana, the fact remains that the burnings of the one finally sickened the ordinary citizen of the Romish faith, while the hangings, drawings, quarterings of her sister were entirely in accord with popular sentiment.[1] The " Book of Martyrs " was the record of the burnings, not of the hangings. It ranked with the Bible, very nearly, in popular favour ; it was placed in all the churches by appointment. Its enemies may have derided it as " Foxe's Golden Legend," but for the ordinary man and woman it was an inspiring record of the heroism of gentle and simple, of the men and women of their own time, who had suffered in the cause of English freedom.

When Elizabeth came to the throne she and her counsellors and all clear-thinking men and women of that generation had had an opportunity of seeing for themselves the workings of three systems. What the Church needed more than anything else was settlement—a period of quiet in which the new ideas which had obviously come to stay could have a chance to settle down peaceably and become naturalized. What the country needed, if it were to be able to withstand the manifold dangers from abroad which threatened, was a rest from its religious preoccupations. All this Elizabeth and her advisers fully realized, and in consequence they dealt with the problem as statesmen first and churchmen only secondarily.

The obvious course was that of a compromise which would alienate the fewest possible members of the extremist parties on either side. The supremacy of the sovereign in ecclesiastical affairs was essential for stable government ; it was secured by the Crown being declared supreme " in all causes ecclesiastical as well as civil." [2] On the other

[1] See the present writer's " Queen Mary I " in " Great Tudors."
[2] 1 Eliz., cap. 1.

hand, the title of Supreme Head of the Church was directly offensive to Elizabeth's many Roman Catholic subjects. It would have been injudicious at the outset to have forced them to choose definitely between their religion and their country. Elizabeth therefore was well content to provide the necessary loophole for conscience by claiming the political substance but refusing the spiritual title. In effect the Pope was got rid of, but by a tactful jesuitry the fact was not stated as such. Refusal to conform to the doctrines of the established Church became therefore no longer heresy, but a refusal of loyalty to the State, the body politic.

From the political point of view, therefore, the compromise is simple enough to understand. It is when we turn to matters of dogma and ritual that the question becomes more difficult, as the essential nature of a compromise is its flexibility, its lack of rigid definition. The Church of England was to be neither Popish nor Puritan, neither in its tenets nor its services. " Calvin's religion was too lean, and the Catholic religion too fat, because the one had many ceremonies, the other none," as a seventeenth century pamphlet put it. The exact shade of belief held by the individual, however, might vary very widely ; a man could more or less think what he liked provided he had the discretion to preserve the necessary outward conformity enjoined by the law. Even the extremists could pursue their several ways to a considerable extent. It was Elizabeth's reign, after all, that saw the foundation of the Brownist sect ; and recusancy—as Roman Catholic opinions came to be termed—was possible at least during the first ten years of the reign, for the well-to-do, provided they paid their fines and made a monthly communion at their parish church. The arrival in England of Mary Queen of Scots in 1568 was the signal for the enforcement of penalties, but until then toleration of opinions and conformity of conduct had marked the relations of the State and its English Roman Catholic subjects.

The practical effect of the compromise upon the services of the Church and religious observances in general can be

easily seen by looking at the 1571 " Articles " drawn up
by Grindal and Sandys, then respectively Archbishop
of York and Bishop of London. It can also be seen in
the working in the account given by Harrison of the
ordinary routine of the parish, and an extremely interesting
account of it, as viewed from the Roman Catholic stand-
point, can be found in a rare pamphlet called " Tessaradelphus,"[1] written in 1616. This last, though somewhat
spiced with malice, is most vivid, and gives what is undoubtedly a reliable account of the scheme of things to
which the Elizabethan churchgoer had to adapt himself.
The writer describes the dress of the clergy as " something
priestlike, with a corner cap and a rochet " ; they " go
ordinarily in black," he continues, " but the most part of
them wear ruffs much like merchants, but not altogether
so large : as for jerkins, doublets, breeches and suchlike,
many of the ministers make them after the newest fashion
taken up, as the laymen do." Besides the services and
preachings on Sundays and holy days, " their Injunctions
appoint them to read something in the Church upon Wed-
nesdays, Fridays and upon vigils and evens, in manner of
an evensong : but that custom is little observed, and in
few places, as also their holy days grow out of use and are
little regarded." He mentions that " they have two sacraments, baptism and the supper, and the Bishops sometimes
do confirm after a new fashion, but account it only a ceremony and no sacrament, neither do they much urge it.
. . . They have besides many . . . observances taken from
Catholic religion, as in some churches, wearing of copes,
playing on organs, singing in the old Sarum tune and suchlike : they wed with a ring, and bury with solemnity,
the minister meeting the corpse readeth prayers and other
things." He comments, too, upon the general taste for
sermons : " All the reckoning is of a sermon, and ordinarily
they have two upon Sunday : as for their service, they say
it by pieces, omitting what they will, . . . before and after
the sermon they sing a section of a Geneva psalm turned

---

[1] " Tessaradelphus, Or the foure brothers," collected and translated by
Thos. Harrap, 1616.

into rhyme in the vulgar tongue. Here all sing, boys,
wenches, women and all sorts." We get finally an extraordinarily vivid glimpse of the way in which a state of
conflict of beliefs tyrannized over men even in their homes :
" Their laws bind them to celebrate and keep holy the days
of the Apostles, and of many other saints, as also to fast
Lent, on vigils, and to abstain from flesh on Fridays and
Saturdays, but few observe them or fast or abstain from
flesh any day. *If any do he is suspected to be a papist.*
Indeed great personages and such as be in high offices
and dignities will usually have their tables furnished with
fish and some dishes of flesh on such days, and every man
may eat what liketh him, but if he eat no flesh he is deemed
to be no sound Protestant."

From the " Articles " we learn that the black gown of
the Genevan minister was abjured as too puritanical ;
the elevation of the Host was similarly rejected as savouring
of papistry. " A comely surplice with sleeves " was
enjoined for wear at all services, and there had to be provided for the Holy Communion " a comely and decent
table standing on a frame . . . with a fair linen cloth."
The custom of walking the bounds of the parish on Rogation
days was retained, but no " wearing of surplices, carrying
of banners or handbells, or staying at crosses or other
such like popish ceremonies " was permitted. " As for
our churches themselves," writes Harrison in 1577, " bells
and times of morning and evening prayer remain as in
times past, saving that all images, shrines, tabernacles,
rood-lofts and monuments of idolatry are removed, taken
down and defaced." The coloured glass, however, was
left in the windows, to save expense, as Harrison naïvely
explains, being gradually replaced by plain white as it
decayed !

" Holy and festival days " were reduced in number from
over a hundred to twenty-seven in all, a change of which
Harrison approved. The reform of the priest's attire
was also a matter for congratulation in his eyes. He
considers it " more comely and decent than ever it was
in the popish church." The colour and pageantry of

the medieval service had quite departed ; formerly the priests " went either in diverse colours "—" like players," he interpolates sarcastically—" or in garments of light hue, as yellow, red, green, etc." Then over the luxury of the apparel of the " proud prelates " of former days he waxes denunciatory : " Their shoes piked, their hair crisped, their girdles armed with silver, their shoes, spurs, bridles, etc., buckled with like metal, their apparel (for the most part) of silk and richly furred, their caps laced and buttoned with gold, so that to meet a priest in those days was to behold a peacock that spreadeth his tail when he danceth before the hen."

The order of the services is fully outlined by Harrison. Morning prayer in the ordinary parish church would begin at seven o'clock, although in cathedrals and schools and colleges five was the usual hour in summer. After the psalms were read came the lessons, the first from the Old and the second from the New Testament. Then followed the Litany, of which Harrison himself thought very highly, " although many curious mindsick persons utterly condemn it as superstitious and savouring of con-juration and sorcery." At the end of morning prayer the communion was held, if any were present to receive ; if not, " the decalogue, epistle and gospel, with the Nicene creed," were read, followed by a homily or sermon with a psalm before and after it. When the service was over any infants brought to church were baptized. Harrap in " Tessaradelphus " says : " They baptize most commonly at the font in the church, with some ceremonies taken from the Catholic Church, as with the sign of the Cross, but that is most odious to the purer sort."

Afternoon service began at two o'clock, and consisted of psalms, lessons, and a sermon. Young people over six and under twenty were catechized for an hour. " Thus do we spend the Sabbath Day," writes Harrison, " in good and godly exercises, all done in our vulgar tongue, that each one present may hear and understand the same."

Compromising upon the ritual and dogma of two faiths, the Elizabethan settlement made no compromise at all in the matter of faith itself : that, by the law of the land, every loyal subject was required to avow. Shades of belief might vary, but " church discipline " was no empty phrase. The Church may have lacked something of piety, but it was admirably organized, and its control touched the individual at most points of his life.

Being both logical and far-sighted in its methods the Church began at the beginning, that is, with the child. The Elizabethan baby had to be baptized in his parish church before he was a month old, otherwise his parents were punished for the offence, one Yorkshire recusant being in the seventeenth century fined no less than £100. As soon as the child reached the age of six his father had to see that he went to church and learnt his catechism in readiness for the rite of Confirmation at the age of fourteen. From this year onwards he was required to receive the communion at Easter, and at least twice a year besides. Nor did the control of the church end there, for he was not allowed to be taught in his school unless the master had a licence from the diocesan to teach ; and even then the Church's paternal care still followed him, enjoining the use in lesson time of certain approved grammars and catechisms.

The State ordained that man, woman, and child should attend divine service on Sundays and festivals. A choice of church was not permitted, every one being required to repair to the one in his own parish. Morning service in itself was not enough. A good subject was expected to hear evening prayer as well, and was responsible—if the head of a household—for the attendance of his wife and children and all his servants and apprentices. Those who proved neglectful of this duty were " presented " in the ecclesiastical court, and a fine of twelvepence was exacted for every absence for which no sufficient excuse could be alleged.

No person ignorant of his or her catechism and the Ten Commandments was allowed to communicate. Three communions a year being, however, required by law, such a one had to attend at his own parish church, and there receive the necessary instruction. " By the laws," writes

Harrap, " they should minister their Communion in singing bread as Catholics use, but many will none of that but use common loaf bread instead thereof, and they have a silver cup wherein they give the wine : all by the law must receive kneeling." A man was liable to presentation if he married without having his banns published in his parish church. To his own church also he was required to resort for the marriage ceremony. Such, in brief, was the strict supervision of the individual exercised by the Church under the Elizabethan settlement.

The parish itself was equally well controlled, being organized upon a system of reciprocal responsibility. The officers of the church were responsible for the manners and morals of the parishioners ; the parishioners, represented by the churchwardens, were similarly responsible for the manners and morals of their vicar and his curate. The churchwardens had to break into inns and interrupt the roysterers and bring them to church ; they had also to see that the incumbent wore his surplice at services. They had to see that all prescribed books, such as Erasmus' " Paraphrases on the Gospels " and Bishop Jewel's " Apologia Ecclesiæ Anglicanæ " were provided for the church, and they had to report their incumbent to the ordinary if he failed to use the ring in marriage or the cross in baptism. Finally, if the churchwardens themselves neglected any of their manifold duties they were liable to be reported to the ordinary by their vicar.

This discipline could be enforced by the secular as well as the ecclesiastical courts, but it was mainly to the latter that religious offences of all kinds were referred. Their powers seem to us to-day to have been excessive and in many ways contrary to all our ideas of equity. The procedure of common law was not followed in an ecclesiastical court, nor was a jury summoned ; anyone with a grudge to work off against a fellow-parishioner might denounce his victim secretly to the churchwardens, so that a man might find himself haled before the court on an entirely false charge, and, even if his innocency was successfully established, forced to pay all the court fees and the costs of the formalities. Further, these ecclesiastical courts had power to administer the oath ex officio to any person charged before them. By this means the person presented was forced to disclose, on oath, the most private affairs of his life and to give evidence against himself. Facts and evidence were not regarded as they were in a court of common law; instead, the primitive system called " compurgation " was still used, by which, if the accused could get together three or more neighbours to come to the court and swear that they believed his oath, a man was acquitted when he swore to his innocence. Indeed, the whole system of these courts was one which laid itself open to the most flagrant abuse, and they were the object of continual complaint and execration until their abolition by the Long Parliament in 1641.

Harrison explains the constitution and operation of these courts without any comment upon their accompanying evils. The archdeacons, "which are termed in law the Bishop's eyes," he writes, " besides their ordinary courts which are holden by themselves or their officials once in a month at the least, do keep yearly two visitations . . . wherein they make diligent inquisition and search, as well for the doctrine and behaviour of the ministers, as the orderly dealing of the parishioners in resorting to their parish churches and conformity unto religion. They punish also with great severity all such trespassers, either in person or by the purse . . . as are presented unto them, or if the cause be of the more weight, as in cases of heresy, pertinacy, contempt, and such like, they refer them either to the bishop of the diocese, or his chancellor, or else to sundry grave persons set in authority, by virtue of a high commission directed unto them from the prince to that end, who in very courteous manner do see the offenders gently reformed or else severely punished, if necessity so inforce."

Apart from the ecclesiastical courts the organization ot the Church was, from the practical point of view, admirable. It secured both the necessary outward uniformity and the convenient amount of official blindness. As a result it gave the country its long-needed rest. Controversy, when

it broke out, was controlled controversy—a war of words
and not of weapons.   If its dimensions threatened at any
time to become dangerous to national unity it was put
down with a firm hand.   For religion itself, however, not
as an institution but as a spiritual force, it is doubtful
whether such organizing and compromising was altogether
healthy at the time.   From its very nature such a state of
affairs could not be calculated to inspire zeal—was indeed
almost bound to create lukewarmness.   As it was, the
troubled years between the death of Henry VIII and the
accession of Elizabeth had already told heavily upon the
Church.   When the orthodoxy of one reign was the heresy
of the next the general standard of piety was bound to
suffer ; and it was upon the clergy as a body that these
conditions had told most heavily of all ; even their numbers
had been so seriously depleted that not only were able men
scarce, but, as Latimer complained in one of his sermons, the
students who undertook the study of divinity at Cambridge
were barely sufficient to furnish the colleges themselves,
thus providing no supply at all for the country at large.

One of the reasons for this shortage of ministers in
Elizabeth's reign was undoubtedly the extreme poverty of
most of the smaller livings and the lack of funds—formerly
provided by the monasteries—for the training of poor
students at the universities.   A small living, according to
Harrison, was worth from ten to thirty pounds a year at
the most, and even then was so burdened with charges such
as first fruits and tenths, that it was " not able to maintain
a mean scholar much less a learned man."   " Of a benefice
of twenty pounds by the year," he continues, " the incumbent thinketh himself well acquitted if, all ordinary payments being discharged, he may reserve thirteen pounds,
six shillings and eight pence towards his own sustentation
and maintenance of his family."   Taxed as ecclesiastics,
taxed as laymen, burdened with subsidies, and deprived of
the old Church lands that originally paid these charges, it
is small wonder that the average country living was not
much of a lure to a learned and able preacher, or indeed
to any but those who had failed in other walks in life, and

had no resource left but to turn the village "Sir John."
"The greatest part of the more excellent wits," writes
Harrison, "choose rather to employ their studies unto
physic and the laws, utterly giving over the study of the
Scriptures for fear lest they should in time not get their
bread by the same."

With the main features of the religious settlement thus
indicated it becomes interesting at this point to turn to the
religious history of the reign and study the way in which
Elizabeth and her Government dealt with the two extreme
parties who were practically outside of the compromise,
the recusants and the nonconformists. The latter might
be a disturbing element, with their demands for sweeping
Genevan reform ; from the political point of view, however,
their loyalty to the Queen could be absolutely reckoned
upon. The real danger lay with the Roman Catholics, and
towards them Elizabeth's policy, though it may not have
been above reproach, was undoubtedly able. With the
cautiousness learnt in the hard school of her plot-ridden
youth she waited for other people to make the mistakes and
then profited by them.

The individual who made the greatest mistake of all was
Pope Pius V, who in 1570 issued against her a Bull of
excommunication and deposition. By so doing he was
simply playing into Elizabeth's hands, rousing both the
nation and its Parliament and virtually forcing English
Roman Catholics to choose between their religion and their
nationality. Hitherto it had been possible for men like
the Duke of Norfolk to conform as far as the law demanded
while still remaining a Roman Catholic. The Rising of the
North in 1569 was as largely political as religious in motive ;
and when it had actually come to a test of this kind a large
proportion of the English Roman Catholics had preferred
their loyalty to their faith. Things had been more or less
quiet for over ten years, and although Elizabeth allowed
some not very serious persecution of Roman Catholics to
be started after the revolt had been crushed, in all proba-
bility things would again have settled down peacefully in
a short time. Then came the Pope's ill-calculated move in

March, 1570, and in August, 1572, in France the massacre of St. Bartholomew. Anger, resentment, and fear dominated English minds. Severe legislation was secured against Roman Catholics. The stories of the Inquisition and of Alva's persecutions in the Low Countries stirred the already strongly Puritan House of Commons into a new violence against Papistry. There had been no execution either for treason or religion for the ten years of Elizabeth's reign. In 1570, however, John Felton, who had pinned the Pope's Bull to the door of the Bishop of London's palace, was executed for high treason. The denial of the royal supremacy and the possession of a papal Bull brought the seminary priest Cuthbert Mayne to the scaffold in 1577. Three years later came the second papal blunder, and the game was in Elizabeth's hands. By their own action her opponents were forced into the open, forced into a direct trial of strength, forced to fight to a decisive issue on a ground of Elizabeth's own choosing, with the odds all against them by reason of that initial mistake of the Bull of 1570, which had put its own party in an impossible position, and had been the original cause of the very strong and almost militant anti-Roman feeling in the country which had increased year by year.

The crisis which the Roman Catholics forced upon themselves in 1580 was begun by the Jesuit Mission to England. The success of Elizabeth's policy had alarmed the leaders of the Catholic party to such an extent that they felt the most vigorous methods were necessary to rekindle the zeal of the English Romanists. The continental seminaries of Rheims and Douay, founded for the education of missionary priests, accordingly sent forth a considerable company of Jesuits, under the leadership of Edmund Campion and Robert Parsons from the English College at Rome, for the purpose of winning back England to the old faith.

The initial success of the mission proved its eventual undoing, and the end of the papal hopes. The Government knew it had strong cards to play, but it was not yet so secure as to feel beyond alarm. For a few months the Jesuits, under various disguises, passed up and down the country, stirring up the English Romanists, winning back the waverers, confirming the stout-hearted. Fresh laws were passed against recusancy and the harbouring of Jesuits, and it was then that the full effect of the mistaken policy of the Pope began to be apparent.

Both by the original Bull of 1570 and by the instructions they were enjoined to give to the adherents of the Romish faith the Jesuit missionaries were laid open to the charge of treason. By special parliamentary provision it had been made treason to introduce into the country any " writings of the Bishop of Rome," and treason to accept any of the articles of the Bull. By the law of the land the instructions given by the Jesuit mission were undoubtedly of a treasonable character ; English Romanists were told that they might profess loyalty to Elizabeth, for the time being, but must be prepared to assist in her overthrow if and when called upon. Every Jesuit was thus by the simple fact of his calling converted into a political offender, technically a traitor to the State ; every Roman Catholic became equally automatically the object of governmental suspicion as a potential traitor ; and Elizabeth's course was thus made easy. After Mary's reign religious persecution stank in the nostrils of most Englishmen. The final rigour of the law applied to Romanists, as heretics, might have been injudicious. High treason, however, was another matter ; there were no popular scruples to be overcome if once an offender could be convicted of that. Here, then, was Elizabeth's weapon, put into her hand by her enemies themselves for their own destruction.

With her usual discrimination in choosing the right man for the business in hand, Elizabeth gave the conduct of the campaign against the Jesuits to Walsingham—of all her Council by far the most fanatical and remorseless of the Puritan section, imbued with the deepest hatred of the papacy, and prepared to go to any unscrupulous lengths in the employment of torture and secret service methods against its emissaries. Within a year Campion and many of his followers were captured, and Parsons, although he escaped, was driven from the country for ever.

Campion was a genuinely religious zealot who strove to
win back souls to his faith.   Nevertheless he had to suffer
for the political aims of his party and for the undoubted
political intriguing of such men as his colleague Parsons.
He was tried and condemned on the charge of treason—
judicially yet necessarily murdered, because his party left
the Government no other alternative.   With him suffered
some nine other seminary priests ; and although there were
other abortive Roman Catholic attempts made during the
reign, such as the Babington conspiracy for the murder of
the Queen in 1586, the real crisis was over.   The Babington
plot, indeed, was little more than a device engineered by
Walsingham for the final discrediting of Mary Queen of
Scots and the removal by her death of the one remaining
focus for Catholic disaffection in England.   With Mary
dead there was no fear of English Catholics rallying to
James VI of Scotland.   And if Philip of Spain had any
remaining hopes that they would revolt in his favour he
was terribly disillusioned by the uniting of Catholics and
Protestants two years later for the destruction of his
invincible Armada.   His plotting went on till the day of
his death, but to Elizabeth and her advisers it was no
longer the serious political matter of the early years—
perhaps little more than a tiresome habit.   The Catholic
exiles who favoured his pretensions had no following at
home ; the English Catholics who had remained loyal to
the Queen in 1588 put their country before their religion.

The Roman Catholics' undoing lay in the fact that the
State regarded them as what they were—a politically disruptive element, as well as a religious sect.   Identified as
they were with Spain and with abortive attempts to place
the Queen of Scots on the throne of England, they undoubtedly constituted a serious menace to the national safety.
With nonconformity the case was different ; its quarrel
with authority began entirely with the Church ; it was
theological and disciplinarian, and only in certain develop-
ments eventually political.

It is important at the outset to distinguish between the
different elements in the nonconformist party, incorporating

as it did so many different shades of opinion. It included first and foremost the Puritan section of the community— those who accepted the compromise and the whole method and organization of the State Church, but who were desirous of seeing its observances further reformed, purified, and simplified along Genevan lines. Puritanism, however, as the word itself indicates, was an attitude of mind and not a dogma ; what it desired was further reform along the lines already laid down by the Church itself. It was in no sense a disruptive element and its advocates suffered little beyond restraint and occasional fines.

Quite distinct from the Puritan section, however, was the Presbyterian party. It believed in a State Church but not in the Elizabethan State Church ; it not only pressed for a complete reformation of Church government, but it also disputed the supreme authority of the Crown. It became thus definitely subversive of the whole Tudor idea of government, and had therefore to be dealt with as a political danger.

There was, thirdly, an important nonconforming group outside the Church. This was the Independent or Separatist group, consisting of the Brownists or Congregationalists, the " Family of Love," and the Anabaptists—all of whom were definitely opposed to an all-inclusive State Church and to the whole organization of the Anglican settlement.

The nonconformity problem which was thus presented to Elizabeth's Government was therefore a very real one. On the one hand there were those zealous Puritans who could not be allowed to proceed on their way of reformation wholly unchecked, but who were yet entirely loyal both to the State and its Church and who as strong nationalists could not be too roughly handled. It did not do to confuse reforming tenets with Presbyterian disaffection ; but it was very necessary to be always on the watch for those nonconformists who crossed the border-line from theological dispute and found themselves in the territory of political offence. The rock upon which, for the nonconforming party, the Elizabethan compromise was really to split was episcopacy. Puritan, Presbyterian, and Brownist alike might argue at intolerable length about the surplice and other " rags of popery," to which they objected ; they might fulminate against the keeping of holy days and the use of the cross in baptism. As long as they all restricted themselves to such ceremonial and " vestarian " controversy authority could afford a certain degree of official unconsciousness. When, however, Cartwright and his followers began to demand the overthrow of the whole Episcopal system—to them one degree less abhorrent than the papacy itself—and then to demand the substitution of Presbyterianism, it became necessary for the State to adopt strong disciplinary measures. Here was definite disloyalty to the State, and the man chosen to deal with the situation was not, as in the matter of Roman Catholic troubles, a statesman, but the churchman Whitgift, who in 1583 was made Archbishop of Canterbury for this very purpose.

Whitgift was at heart a disciplinarian. Believing throughout his life in the doctrinal theories of Calvin, he was equally consistent in his abhorrence of Genevan methods of Church government, and throughout his tenure of the See of Canterbury was the most strenuous and thorough advocate of the necessity for uniformity. Under his rule all separatist tendencies were kept severely in check, so long as Elizabeth's reign lasted. It is true that his main instrument, the Court of High Commission, laid up much trouble for her Stuart successors, but its immediate use is obvious. It secured the Anglican settlement till it grew strong enough to fend for itself.

The rigour of Whitgift's administration practically extinguished separatism as a movement by 1593. In that year Greenwood and Barrow, the two Brownist leaders, were executed, and the greater number of those nonconformists who still held separatist opinions were driven either into compulsory or voluntary exile in the Netherlands and even in the New World. The persecution to which they were subjected was less bitter than that from which the recusants suffered. Nevertheless we are faced with the fact that, apart from the numbers of nonconformists who paid for their devotion to their belief by exile, deprivation,

imprisonment, and fine, there were also many who suffered
the extreme penalty. Such was the price of religious conformity, as a necessary element of national unity ; and if
we regard it as a blot on the history of the reign it is very
necessary to remember that between the intolerance of
Whitgift and the intolerance of the anti-episcopal leaders
there was nothing to choose ; and that whereas the former,
by his intolerance, secured the growth of an essentially
tolerant institution, the latter, had they had their way,
would have substituted that intolerant jurisdiction in
which " new presbyter is but old priest writ large."

The last ten years of Elizabeth's reign were almost as
peaceful as the first. A hundred and eighty-seven Roman
Catholics, Jesuits and priests, and a considerable number
of nonconformists, had suffered martyrdom for their faith
during the twenty years between ; many more had been
driven to seek other lands for the sake of their faith ; but
the bulk of the nation had grown into the ways of the
Anglican settlement. Persecution had relaxed somewhat,
and the whole situation was, apparently, less tense. But
whereas those first ten years had been years of peace after
turmoil, years of settlement and construction, and of more
moderate feeling on all sides, the last ten were like that
delusive calm that precedes the storm. Because the end
could not be long the reforming party was content to wait,
to husband its resources ; but its temporary subordination
of faith to loyalty was to be conterminous with the reign
of the Queen—its last tribute to the last of the Tudors.
Under no other dynasty, so far as nonconformity was to be
concerned, would mere policy be allowed to control religion.

The Spanish Ambassador, de Quadra, is reported to have
said that in Elizabeth's reign religion in England had
become merely a matter of politics. There was an element
of truth in his remark, but only in so far as it indicated that
Elizabeth's statesmen consistently dealt with religious
troubles from a strictly political point of view, and not as
fanatical or determined adherents of any religious party.
If militant violence is to be taken as the test of zeal it is
true that, in Elizabethan England, Catholic and Protestant

were not engaged in a fight to the death as they were in most other European countries. It is also true, however, that the religious spirit of the nation as a whole, though not fanatical, was as alive and vigorous as at any period of its history. The national energy was released for manifold purposes when Elizabeth relieved the nation of the responsibility of settling its religious affairs by taking matters out of its hands and settling them for it. The individual, however—follow the history of whatever sect we will—was still deeply concerned to make his personal adjustment to the living reality of the Divine. The strength and vitality of this preoccupation with religion can be gauged in various ways—largely by the popularity of the sermon, the amount of religious literature published, and the prevalence of private and family devotions, especially amongst the reformers. It can be gauged still more fully, perhaps, if we look forward to the troubles of the Stuart period, and are forced to realize what intensity of feeling there must previously have been, smouldering and accumulating beneath the surface quiet.

The Anglican settlement has received much criticism, and its lack, in this first difficult period of its existence, of noble and beautiful characters among its churchmen has been commented on by many besides Bishop Creighton. Nevertheless, before the reign was over, the compromise had firmly rooted itself. Elizabeth and her father had, between them, established something so appropriate, so congruent to English life and thought, that it was able to survive all the storms of the seventeenth century. They had had the opportunity, at a critical period in their country's history, not of making the Anglican faith, but of determining, in an era in which toleration of a diversity of religious opinions had not yet been envisaged, just how much Catholicism and how much Protestantism could be combined together to form a compromise suitable to the English temper. Elizabeth's amazing faculty for guessing right in any matters that concerned her people had worked triumphantly. In spite of every difficulty she established a solid foundation. Towards the beginning of her reign the zeal of many of the compromising clergy was admittedly not high. Able attack, however, creates able defence and advocacy. The deeply religious spirit which stirred and animated all sections of the reformers found vent in a continual criticism of the Anglican position ; and by the pressure thus brought to bear upon the settlement there was created before the end of the reign a body of men who believed in it, not because they would lose preferment if they failed to submit, but because they had grown up in its atmosphere and had come to regard it as the best way of faith. When Hooker's " Ecclesiastical Polity " appeared it proved conclusively that the Anglican settlement had already justified itself both on religious and philosophical grounds. It had shown that it could satisfy the man who to his simple and devout sincerity joined the high intellectual power which earned him the title of " the judicious Hooker." Its earliest advocates may have been in many cases mere time-servers ; its Hookers, Jewels, Bancrofts, and Parkers may not to-day stand in the first rank as religious teachers ; nevertheless the men of whom these four are representative were able to make their Church such that within a generation it was to command the allegiance and the spiritual fervour of a Donne, a Herbert, and a Jeremy Taylor.

Note.—For an introductory study of the effect of the Reformation on the everyday life of the people, see W. P. M. Kennedy, *Parish Life under Queen Elizabeth* (1914). For local documents, showing how the Elizabethan settlement worked in practice and how church discipline was investigated and the law administered, see the following : W. P. M. Kennedy, *Elizabethan Episcopal Administration,* 3 vols. Alcuin Club Collections (1924) : J. S. Leatherbarrow, *The Lancashire Elizabethan Recusants.* Chetham Soc. (1947) : J. S. Purvis, *Tudor Parish Documents of the Diocese of York* (1948). For self-analysis of the Puritan character and outlook, and a very useful select specialized bibliography, see *Two Elizabethan Puritan Diaries by Richard Rogers and Samuel Ward,* ed. M. M. Knappen (1933) ; also Knappen, *Tudor Puritanism* (1939). For an autobiographical account of the experiences of one of the Jesuit missionaries in England, see *John Gerard,* translated by Philip Caraman (1951).

CHAPTER XI

CHILDHOOD AND EDUCATION

CHILDREN in the Elizabethan age, as in the ages before it, were appreciated for their precocity rather than for the natural qualities of childhood. They were regarded by the normal parent as miniature but troublesome men and women ; the more nearly and the more quickly their mental growth and their behaviour approximated to the adult the more were they to be commended. Childhood, like the diseases incident to it, was a thing to be got over as quickly as possible. An inevitable but unsatisfactory state of being, it was early taken in hand with great thoroughness, both at home and at school. It is much easier to understand and to appreciate the precocious and witty little boys of Shakespeare's plays if this is realized. Child nature has not altered, but the circumstances in which it was then reared were very different, and its reactions differed accordingly. The methods adopted to deal with this unwanted immaturity were too often cruel and wrong, but the theory behind them was neither cruel nor unthinking ; it was the natural consequence of an ideal which envisaged happiness as the result of a fully developed use and realization of all the faculties proper to the adult man.

It is perhaps only natural, therefore, that of babies Elizabethan literature should have but little to say, although their advent was always the occasion of far greater festivity and celebration than it is to-day. We learn incidentally, however, from a curious poem on education written by a certain John Hake in 1574 that Elizabethan nurses were more up-to-date in their methods than we might have expected :

> . . . their child they never feed
> With all that comes to hand, but they
> Observe with careful heed
> Both what to give and how to give ;
> What quantity to use ;
> And eke to feed it leisurely.

Similarly, he tells us, they teach their charges to talk by
first " tattling forth their words "—" dad-dad " for father,
and " din " for drink—with the result that presently " the
baby speaketh plain." A later writer, Peter Erondell, in
a conversation manual published in 1605, gives us a pleasant
glimpse into the nursery in the morning. The mother
enters and asks the nurse how the baby has slept. The
nurse replies that he was " somewhat wayward " in the
night, and the mother suggests that this is because he is
cutting a tooth. The baby's " swaddling bands " are then
undone, and his nurse baths him to the accompaniment of
a constant stream of instruction and maternal admiration.
Afterwards he is dressed for the day, his mother telling the
nurse to put on " his biggin [i.e. baby's cap] and his little
band with an edge." " Give him his coat of changeable
taffeta and his satin sleeves," she continues. " Where is
his bib ? Where is his little petticoat ? Let him have
his gathered apron with strings, and hang a muckinder [i.e.
a child's bib] to it ; you need not yet to give him his coral
with the small golden chain, for I believe it is better to let
him sleep until the afternoon. . . . God send thee good
rest, my little Boykin."

Such pictures as these, however, are rare, and it is not
until we turn to the subject of schoolboy life and education
that the literature of the time has much to yield. Then
with one writer we can follow the new boy through his first
day at school ; with others we meet him in the class-room,
on his way to school, learning his lessons, playing truant ;
with yet others we can trace his studies during his schooldays and follow him afterwards to the university.

In an interesting school-book of the period, " The
Frenche Scholemaister," by Claudius Hollyband, there is
a delightful sketch of the schoolboy who dislikes early

14

rising.   He is evidently the son of a well-to-do London tradesman, and he is roused by Margaret the maid, whose duty it is to see that he gets dressed, has his breakfast, and sets off to school.   She warns him that it is past seven, and that he will be beaten if he does not hurry.   He calls lustily for his hose and his doublet, and Margaret, with aggravating inconsistency, then insists that he must put on a clean shirt and wait while she airs it, as it is still damp.   After kneeling for the paternal blessing he is finally dispatched to school, and sets off, " with his satchel and shining morning face."   If he is a zealous and obedient little boy, and has studied to good purpose the books which instruct him in manners and morals, he will have stowed away in that satchel his ink-horn and his quill pen, the knife with which he makes his pens, and some paper with which his father will have supplied him—paper at fourpence a quire was too expensive a commodity to be provided by the school :

> . . . thy satchel and thy books take,
> And to the school haste see thou make,
> But ere thou go, with thyself forthink,
> That thou take with thee pen, paper and ink.

And doubtless the reminder was well needed ; that tiresome business of " forethinking " is not likely to have come naturally to the Elizabethan schoolboy any more than it does to his fellow to-day.

On arrival at school his manners-book instructs him to salute his master, and go straight to his seat and take out his books quietly.   If a beginner, just learning to read and write, he would have a horn book [1] and also some copperplate " copies," and thus equipped he would be started upon the lengthy business of getting educated.   Here is a picture of him at work, drawn by Hezekiah Woodward, a

---

[1] The horn book was originally a wooden tablet with a handle, on which was pasted a written or printed sheet, giving the alphabet ; to preserve it, this was covered by a thin sheet of transparent horn—hence the name. The alphabet was printed first in small letters, then in capitals ; then came some thirty combinations of the vowels with b, c, and d, followed by the Lord's Prayer in English.   The small alphabet began with the mark of the cross, for which reason it was often known as the " Christ-cross-row " or simply " cross-row."   In later times the term horn book came to be applied to any primer which contained the alphabet.

grammarian of the Stuart period : " Poor child, he must to school to learn his mother tongue the very next Monday. And there we suppose he is, where the mistress helps to hold the book with one hand (and if it be as I have seen) a little twig in the other, which the child marks very earnestly, as we would have it do the lesson."

" Better unborn than untaught " was a favourite Elizabethan saying, and the ways by which the desired goal was reached were several and varied.   From Anglo-Saxon times right up to the Tudor period it was the custom in England for the sons of noblemen and gentry to be sent for their upbringing to the house of some great lord—Sir Thomas More, for example, being brought up in the household of Cardinal Morton.   Thus a social training in manners, morals, and accomplishments was provided for the ruling classes which only very gradually gave place to the public school system of education.   Roughly speaking, the reign of Elizabeth marks the beginning of the change ; it is a sign of the times that not only should the theorists be at pains to point out the superior advantages of a public school training, but that in the year 1564 two noble youths, such as Sir Philip Sidney and Fulke Greville, should have been sent to the recently refounded Shrewsbury School. William Kemp, a Plymouth schoolmaster, writing in 1588 on " The Education of Children in learning " puts both sides of the case very clearly : " Some here do counsel the Father to seek out a private Schoolmaster for his child, and we see that those which would be most exquisite herein do follow their counsel, because a private teacher hath leisure to use more diligence, and the learner under him is safer from taking hurt by infection of bad company ; but forasmuch as the correcting of a fault in one is the commending of virtue in another, the praise of virtue in one is the reproving of vice in another . . . we have greater cause to prefer a public Schoolmaster. . . . I speak nothing what help commeth to the Scholars by teaching one another, what by emulation and striving who may do best."

The older system, however, was by no means entirely superseded in Elizabethan times, and the various treatises on manners which were written for the instruction of these noble children enable us to form a vivid picture of the conditions under which they lived, and of the duties that devolved upon them. The most interesting is perhaps Hugh Rhodes' " Boke of Nurture, or Schoole of good maners," reprinted in 1577. The children are told to rise betimes and make their beds neatly, to say their prayers, clean their shoes, brush their clothes, comb their hair, and wash their hands and faces. Then come a number of warnings which suggest to our more squeamish notions that though of gentle birth these youthful nobles had not by nature the gentle manners we might have expected. They must not pare their nails at table, nor must they pick their teeth with a knife ; they must not sup their soup too loudly, nor dip their meat in the common salt-cellar ; they must not blow upon their soup to cool it, nor must they cram either their plates or their mouths too full ! They should also eat what is set before them, and not stare about nor lean their elbows on the table. It is indeed evident from these books, as well as from other sources of information, that although the liberal arts were regarded with admiration, the chief stress in an upbringing of this kind was laid upon manners, morals, and physical accomplishments.

Yet another alternative to the public school in Tudor times was the private tutor who educated both boys and girls in their own homes. The family of Sir Thomas More was brought up in this way ; and Lady Jane Grey spoke of the days of her tuition under Master Elmer as the happiest in her life.

To turn, however, to the method by which the greater number of Elizabeth's subjects were educated, there was in her reign no lack of schools for those of the middle classes who did not ape the ways of the rich and employ private tutors for their sons. In pre-Reformation times public education had been almost entirely in the hands of the Church, and had therefore suffered greatly at the dissolution of the monasteries. In spite of the efforts of Edward VI, education was at a low ebb when Elizabeth came to the throne, but in her reign a renascence was brought about, largely by the introduction of the lay element. New grammar schools were founded throughout the country, not only by corporations and other public bodies, but by wealthy individuals : Repton dates from 1559, Rugby from 1567, Uppingham from 1584, and Harrow from 1590.

At the basis of the Elizabethan school system was the conception that education should be free to every one. All the great schools founded at this time were in the main designed to educate the children of their particular locality, either for no cost at all or for some more or less nominal entrance fee. In various instances—Harrow amongst others—" foreigners " (that is, children from other parts of the country) could be educated in the school on payment being made to the master. Shrewsbury gave free education to all and sundry, upon payment of an admission fee—ten shillings for a lord's son, six and eightpence for a knight's son, and so by varying sums down to the fourpence for which a burgess of the town could procure for his child the same education as that which Sir Henry Sidney chose for his son Philip.

The " free scholars " at Harrow were limited to forty, and might be rich or poor, provided they dwelt in the neighbourhood, preference being given to the latter. At the Merchant Taylors' a hundred free places were allotted to the sons of poor people, fifty places were kept for those whose parents could afford two shillings and sixpence a quarter towards their maintenance, and a hundred more were open to the sons of the rich or others who could pay five shillings a quarter.

Elementary education in reading and writing might be obtained in several ways. The larger grammar schools insisted that such knowledge should be acquired before the pupil was admitted. The statutes of the St. Albans Grammar School, drawn up in 1570 by Sir Nicholas Bacon, the essayist's father, require that " none shall be received into the school but such as have learned their accidences without book, and can write indifferently." In such cases a boy would probably learn to satisfy this requirement at what was called a " petties' school," that is, a preparatory school for small children (i.e. from the French *petit*). The petty school might be either a little private school, or else an offshoot of the grammar school proper. The former kind was frequently a dame school, such teaching being generally left to " the meanest and therefore the worst," because good scholars would not undertake it. That these poor old dames were often nearly as ignorant as their charges may be inferred from the complaint of the well-known schoolmaster Hoole, who asserts that they were sometimes " poor women or others whose necessities compel them to undertake it as a mere shelter from beggary."

Although the elementary education of the age was in this unsatisfactory condition there were many who both wished and worked for its improvement. At least one great schoolmaster, namely, Richard Mulcaster, thought that " the first grounding should be undertaken by the best teacher." But then, as now, Mulcaster was ahead of the times, and his complaints give us the actual condition of affairs : " Too often we grammar school masters can hardly make any progress, can scarcely even tell how to place raw boys in any particular form with any hope of steady advance, so rotten is the groundwork of their preparation."

The smaller grammar schools were not able to make such stringent regulations as those which governed admission to most of the larger kind, and so were burdened with the grounding of the " petties " in reading and writing. Masters complained that this extra instruction took up more than half their time, and resulted in the neglect of their " grammar-scholars " ; and although for many there was no remedy, in some schools an additional teacher was provided, and in others some of the elder pupils were pressed into service. At Christ's Hospital, for example, two masters were provided for the " petties," but at Bungay School in Suffolk it was arranged that " some of the highest form shall weekly, by course instruct the first form, both in their accidence, and also in giving them copies to write."

The methods by which reading and writing were taught were crude and simple enough. The child began by learning his alphabet, and putting together vowels and conso-

nants—*ag, eg, ig, og, ug* ; then he went on to diphthongs
and longer combinations of letters, gradually picking up
the art in the dullest and most mechanical way possible.
For writing he would be provided with some carefully
written " copies "—tied to his paper to prevent loss.   The
teacher, if proud of his or her own penmanship, would
make the copies : otherwise they would be written by a
good scrivener.   In some of the country grammar schools
an " honest and skilful Penman " would be engaged each
year for a month or six weeks to teach every one to write
legibly.

There was yet another kind of school in existence of
which no authoritative modern account has been written,
but of which we know something from the literature of the
time.   This was the kind run by an individual for his own
profit.   It seems to have developed either from the private
petty school, or from a school for the teaching of modern
languages, into a school which combined both these functions with the ordinary grammar school course.   We get
what is probably a typical account of one of these hybrids
from the conversation-manuals of the already quoted
Claudius Hollyband, a Huguenot refugee who set up a
school first in Lewisham and then in Paul's Churchyard in
Elizabeth's reign.   In one of his dialogues he gives us a
conversation between himself and the parent of a prospec-
tive pupil.   The father wishes the boy to learn to read and
write and also to speak French.   He inquires about the
fees, and Hollyband replies that his charges are " A shilling
a week, a crown a month, a real [1] a quarter, forty shillings
a year."   To this the father returns, " It is too much ; you
are too dear " ; but Hollyband convinces him that if the
boy makes good progress it cannot be too much to pay.
Eventually the boy is left at the school, and as the father
goes away to buy him the necessary satchel, ink-horn,
quills, paper, and penknife, his parting injunction is :
" Master Hollyband, take a little pain with my son ; he is
somewhat hard of wit . . . he is shamefast, wicked, liar,
stubborn unto father and mother ; correct, chasten, amend

[1] I.e. the ryal, also known as the rose-noble, worth about fifteen shillings,

all these faults and I will recompense you." Then as a final touch this ideal parent is made to add: " Hold, I will pay you the quarter beforehand."

The new boy thus begins his first day at school, and Hollyband inquires his age. He replies, " I cannot tell, master ; my father hath put in writing the day of my nativity in our Bible which is at home." He also admits that he cannot read very well, and is then sent to his place, and admonished to " learn well to the end that you may be a good man, and that you may do better service unto your Prince, your country, unto the commonwealth, help your parents, yourself, and all yours."

In studying the Elizabethan school we find plenty of material to enlighten us as to what was taught and how it was taught. We are also fortunate in the possession of the theoretical views on education held by such eminent teachers as Roger Ascham, at one time tutor to Queen Elizabeth, and Richard Mulcaster, first head master of the Merchant Taylors' school for twenty-five years, and afterwards head of St. Paul's. One thing is noticeable throughout, namely, the extreme divergence between the wise, humane, and often modern theories of a man like Ascham and the brutality and harsh discipline which seems to have been customary in the schools of the time. Ascham laments that the school which should be " ludus " or " play " is turned for children into a place of bondage and punishment—a veritable prison to the body, and cramping in its effect on the mind. While Ascham inveighs against the system of flogging which drove boys to run away from school, and which dulled their wits by fear of punishment and by physical brutality, those who remembered their own schooldays bore witness of their treatment much as Thomas Tusser does in his frequently quoted lines on Nicholas Udall, the " flogging head master " of Eton in the time of Henry VIII :

> From Pauls I went, to Eton sent,
> To earn straightways the Latin phrase,
> When fifty-three stripes given to me
> At once I had :

> For fault but small or none at all
> It came to pass thus beat I was.
> See, Udall, see the mercy of thee
> To me, poor lad !

An even more terrible picture is that drawn in Thomas Ingeland's " Disobedient Child," an interlude published about 1560. In it the Son, talking with his Father, says that a school is nothing but a prison ; he calls the school-master a brute, and says that the boys report that :

> Their tender bodies both night and day
> Are whipped and scourged, and beat like a stone
> That from top to toe the skin is away.

He also asserts that one boy was killed by the master's cruelty, being hung up by the heels and beaten, and having his head crushed against a wall. Whether or no any of Ingeland's statements may be taken at their face value, Ascham's commentary on this ferule-discipline, that boys " carry commonly from the school with them a hatred of their master and a continual contempt for learning," is quite sufficiently suggestive in itself.

In partial justification of the schoolmasters it may perhaps be urged that inordinate beatings, cuffings, and rough treatment were similarly meted out to their offspring by the average parent; humanitarian feeling on the subject of the treatment of schoolboys, lunatics, and criminals is a sentiment of comparatively recent growth. Ascham reports what Lady Jane Grey told him of the severity of her upbringing at home : " One of the greatest benefits that ever God gave me is, that he sent me so sharp and severe parents and so gentle a schoolmaster. For when I am in presence either of father or mother, whether I speak, keep silence, sit, stand, or go, eat, drink, be merry or sad, be sewing, playing, dancing, or doing anything else, I must do it, as it were, in such weight, measure and number, even so perfectly as God made the world, or else I am so sharply taunted, so cruelly threatened, yea presently sometimes with pinches, nips and bobs, and other ways which I will not name for the honour I bear them, so without measure misordered, that I think myself in hell, till time come that I must go to M. Elmer, who teacheth me so gently, so pleasantly, with such fair allurements to learning that I think all the time nothing, whiles I am with him."

Tudor parents believed that to spare the rod was to spoil the child, and exercised over the unfortunate boy or girl an absolute authority which, however it may have been rebelled against by its victims, as a right was questioned by no one. When Sir Peter Carew, afterwards famous as a soldier, ran away in his boyhood from Exeter Grammar School, and climbed one of the turrets of the city wall, threatening to leap from it if the master came after him, his father, on hearing of the escapade, had him coupled to a hound, led back to his home, and chained in a dog-kennel. He records that he was left there, not until he repented, but until he managed to escape. In view of examples such as these it is perhaps small wonder that the Elizabethan schoolmaster regarded as a matter of course, sanctioned by home treatment, punishments which we to-day consider barbarous.

Such a system of punishment, however, is perhaps even more thoroughly accounted for when we consider the school hours and the schoolboy's course of study. The medieval curriculum in school and university had consisted of the seven liberal arts : grammar, logic, and rhetoric, known collectively as the *trivium* ; and arithmetic, geometry, astronomy, and music, known as the *quadrivium*. The intellectual training provided by these was made to serve equally for the preliminary equipment of the doctor, the lawyer, or the theologian. The best thing to be said for the *trivium* is that it was thoroughly utilitarian, producing able latinists in an age when Latin was still the international language, as well as the language of all records and of officialdom. Its worst point is that it almost entirely neglected the teaching of literature. It was not until the time of the Renaissance that the reading of the best authors became an educational ideal. Then, from the Reformation onwards, grammar as a means of enabling the student to read the finest literature of the classics may be said to have shared the time-table with one other subject of primary importance, namely, religious instruction.

The Elizabethan curriculum, though derived from the medieval, was definitely humanistic in its modifications, in so far as it insisted on the study of good literature. Its aims, however, were still severely practical ; literature was to be studied not primarily for its matter, but for its manner ; to be regarded not as an end in itself, Professor Foster Watson points out, so much as " the store house of adequate and eloquent expression." Logic, the third subject of the *trivium*, gradually slipped out of the school course, and rhetoric tended to become simply a branch of the study of Latin, both being pursued, however, at the university.

In spite of able advocates such as Cheke, and Ascham who avowed that it was his first love, Greek was but little cultivated in Tudor and Stuart times. At Westminster, it is true, the Elizabethan scheme of studies included such authors as Xenophon, Demosthenes, and Homer ; at Shrewsbury and Harrow, Greek books were prescribed ; and Eton proceeded as far as the Greek grammar. In the ordinary grammar schools, however, the teaching of Greek was very rare. In Latin the pupil as a rule began with some simple dialogue-book, such as the " Colloquies " of Erasmus, or Vives or Corderius. Starting with simple questions and answers on everyday subjects these dialogue-books accustomed the Elizabethan schoolboy from his first entrance upon the study to regard Latin not as a dead language but as the language of conversation ; and when he achieved his first remove in most schools he would probably find himself in a form where Latin speaking was compulsory both at work and at play, and where unfeeling monitors would report him for punishment if he lapsed into his native tongue. Having worked through such a text-book he would then be promoted to a selected edition of Cicero's " Epistles," from which he would eventually turn to the study of Terence—always regarded as one of the finest models of a pure latinity. In the lower forms he would also use such books as Ovid's " Metamorphoses,"

Æsop's " Fables," and Virgil ; not as a rule, however, Cæsar, as would his present-day descendant. Afterwards he would proceed to Sallust, Juvenal, Martial, Persius, and Horace.

From his reading in these authors the schoolboy was expected to cull apt and witty phrases, choice epithets, and well-turned ideas, which he entered in his notebook, for use in the writing of original Latin themes. In prose composition—which at Harrow, for example, was begun in the Second Form—he would be encouraged to imitate Cicero ; for Latin verse—begun at Harrow in the Third—Ovid and Virgil were the approved models : " As Tully for prose, so Ovid and Virgil for verse," writes John Brinsley in his " Ludus Literarius," an account of the grammar school and its methods. Even in a private school like Hollyband's much the same course was followed.

Although rhetoric was studied mainly in order that the schoolboy might learn to speak good Latin, and so may be said to have constituted not a separate subject but only a part of the classical training, it deserves special notice for the influence it undoubtedly exercised over the vernacular literature of the sixteenth and seventeenth centuries. Such a training in the effective use of all the devices of style was undoubtedly a prime cause of some of the most striking characteristics of English literature in this period—its rich and copious imagery, its sonorous and stately rhythms both in prose and verse, its interest and experimenting in literary forms, its desire to use the vernacular in the most effective and varied ways possible. If largely responsible for the exaggeration and the artificiality which characterize much Elizabethan writing, it was also responsible for that deliberate cultivation of the technique of literary expression which is essential to any renaissance of letters.

Dean Colet's provision for religious instruction directed that the boys of his school of St. Paul's were to be taught the catechism, the articles of the faith, and the Ten Commandments in English. In times such as those of Elizabeth religious instruction was a matter of necessity in the schools. Professor Foster Watson puts the case succinctly :

" The Elizabethan fathers and mothers, with their rigour of
family prayers, and readiness of mind and soul for long
services and sermons, would have insisted on school
religious exercises, even if the ecclesiastical and civil
authorities had not just as determinedly prescribed them."
Daily prayers were the rule in schools of every kind,[1] and
the boys in company with their masters were required to be
present in church on all holy days as well as Sundays.
Sermon time was a serious matter to the Tudor schoolboy ;
not for him the stolen delights of unobtrusive games in the
corner of a pew.   Next morning he was expected to give
chapter and verse, and to repeat the substance of the
preacher's discourse, and woe to the unfortunate who had
failed to commit at any rate a goodly portion of it to
memory.   In Corderius' book of dialogues, as translated by
Brinsley for school use, we get a realistic picture of such a
" black Monday " morning :

Master.   Wast thou present at the sermon ?
Pupil.   I was present.   [He calls some of his schoolfellows
to witness to the fact.]
Master.   At what o'clock began the preacher ?
Pupil.   At seven of the clock.
Master.   From whence took he his text ?
Pupil.   Out of the Epistle of Paul to the Romans.
Master.   What chapter ?
Pupil.   The eighth.
Master.   Thou hast answered well hitherto, now let us see
what followeth.   Hast thou committed anything to memory ?

Then begins his downfall.   He remembers " nothing which
he can rehearse," which finally becomes, on pressure being
applied, " nothing at all—not a word."   Rebukes follow,
and he is told that his negligence is due to deliberate lack
of care, not to any lack of capacity.   To this he makes
rueful assent, and admits that he slept when he ought to
have been attending, and " thought of a thousand follies,
as boys are wont."   He admits that he " deserves stripes "
for his scandalous behaviour, and is only let off at the last
minute on promise of future amendment.

[1] Three times a day at the Merchant Taylors' !

Modern subjects were practically unknown in the ordinary grammar school. History, geography, and modern languages were taught, indeed, in Elizabethan England, but not by the schools ; they were regarded both in theory and practice as part of the necessary education of a gentleman of high birth, but not in any way as essential to the masses, for whom in the main the schools were supposed to cater. Music and the other subjects of the *quadrivium* naturally attracted the interest of the youths of the nobility, and by them they were cultivated. When, however, these same subjects also attracted the grammar school boy he was required to pay for them as " extras." From the first the schools offered to the introduction of modern subjects that effective resistance of passivity which they have in some cases continued even within living memory.

Geography was not systematically taught in English schools as a whole until the eighteenth century. Such knowledge as was acquired by an Elizabethan schoolboy would be more justly described as cosmography—a miscellaneous collection of geographical, astronomical, and anthropological facts and fictions, intermixed with smatterings of natural philosophy and history, astrology and navigation. Maps and globes, however, were part of the equipment of some of the more progressive schools in Elizabethan times : and although the teaching was only incidental, we know that by 1621 at least one school— namely, Westminster—regarded geography as a distinct subject for the fourth and seventh forms. " After supper (in summer time) they were called to the Master's Chamber (specially those of the seventh form) and there instructed out of Hunter's " Cosmography " and practised to describe and find out cities and counties in the maps." [1]

History was not taught in the schools, which to the cynically-minded may help to explain the popularity of those dullest of dull plays, the chronicle histories. As

[1] " Memoir of Richard Busby," G. F. R. Barker. The quotation is taken from an account of the daily life of a Westminster schoolboy in the seventeenth century which is preserved among the State Papers in the Public Record Office (Domestic Papers : Charles I, clxxxi, 37).

imparted, however, by the chronicles and by such a compilation as Foxe's "Book of Martyrs" it was read with avidity by gentle and simple, men and women alike. It was considered by most theorists of the time to be an important subject for the training of noblemen, but, like geography, it was not deemed essential for the ordinary "grammar scholar," and any such knowledge as the latter might acquire during his schooldays would be incidental, arising, probably, as the subjects for Latin themes. Mathematics, again, was regarded as a "gentleman's study"—useful to a nobleman in the conduct of a war; and arithmetic, both in medieval and in Tudor times, was not taken as a school subject, even in the Stuart era being taught in the grammar schools only as an "extra." Modern languages were in much the same case; French and Italian were taught in noble families by private tutors, while schools such as Hollyband's catered for ordinary folk with ambitions to acquire foreign tongues. But in the grammar schools themselves up to the end of the Commonwealth there was, according to Professor Foster Watson, probably not a single case of the provision by school statutes for the teaching of a modern language.

The mother tongue was similarly neglected, in spite of the wise and spirited plea made for its cultivation by Mulcaster in his "Elementarie" in 1582. He considers that we only follow the dictates of reason and nature "in learning to read first that which we speak first, to take most care over that which we use most, and in beginning our studies where we have the best chance of good progress owing to our natural familiarity with our ordinary language." Avowed lover of the classics, he can yet exclaim, "I honor the Latin, but I worship the English," and there is no finer vindication than his of the worth of our language, no stronger appeal for its use and for the teaching of it to be found in Elizabethan literature. Nevertheless, until after the time of the Restoration the classical ideal still held undisputed sway in the grammar schools; if the reading and writing of English was taught as a subject it was taught only in the elementary stages of education.

Mulcaster was a practical teacher and also one of the most enlightened educationalists in the history of English pedagogy. He was a warm advocate of both drawing and music as necessary auxiliary subjects in elementary education. The former was not entirely neglected in the schools in Tudor and Stuart times ; the curves and flourishes of the writing books gave the learner a certain amount of practice, and map drawing was often taught with arithmetic. It never occupied the permanent place in the curriculum, however, which Mulcaster advocated. Christ's Hospital in 1692 was the first school to adopt his idea and establish a drawing department.

Music Mulcaster placed "among the most valuable means in the upbringing of the young," and writes eloquently and at length in its praise. He gave signal proof of his belief in its value by training the boys under him at the Merchant Taylors' in both singing and instrumental music—an unusual privilege of which we must suppose at least one of his pupils, namely, the poet Spenser, to have taken full advantage. It was not, however, seriously cultivated in the average school—a curious fact, when the widespread musical proficiency of the age is remembered. But it was a proficiency acquired outside the school by a nation of music lovers, and in both the sixteenth and the seventeenth centuries, being accounted a subject suitable for "the gentry" only, music began that career as an "extra" which to a large extent it still pursues to-day.

Brinsley gives us a full and interesting account of the school day, placidly describing a time-table which strikes horror to the heart of the modern educationalist. Seven or eight was the ordinary age at which a boy began to go to school, and in order to arrive in time the unfortunate infant would have to be roused soon after dawn, for "the school time should begin at six," writes Brinsley, "all who write Latin to make their exercises which were given over-night in that hour before seven." It is to be hoped that their parents took pity on them and gave them some food before they set out ; because so far as the school was concerned work went on until nine o'clock, when they had "a quarter of an hour at least, or more, for intermission, either for breakfast or else for the necessity of everyone, or their honest recreation, or to prepare their exercises against the master's coming in." They then worked again until eleven, " or somewhat after "—this latter proviso being intended, Brinsley explains, to " countervail " the time lost by the ironically named nine o'clock " intermission " !

But it is too soon yet to exclaim with dismay at the state of exhaustion, fidgeting, and naughtiness to which we would suppose the wretched children to have been reduced. As yet the day was only half over. A scamper home through the streets, a midday meal, and punctually at one o'clock they were all to be back in their places, to work until half-past three, when they had another of those so-called intermissions, which this time involved their staying on till half-past five to make up for it. Then they ended the day with prayers and the singing of two staves of a psalm, their " diligence, obedience and profiting " being rewarded every week by the indulgence of " one part of an afternoon for recreation," generally on Thursday.

A ten hours school day ! And yet, if we may judge from the pictures of it left us by contemporary writers such as Hollyband, schoolboy human nature was much the same then as now. Francis was an incorrigibly late riser ; John used to play in the streets so that he arrived late at school ; Martin used to talk during lessons ; Nicholas fought with William and pulled his hair ; and the sneak told tales of John Nothingworth who " swore by God, played by the way, sold his points, changed his book, stole a knife, lied twice, and lost his cap." If Sir Peter Carew was a typical schoolboy they must have been wild young colts, rougher than our roughest. To keep a mob of them in order, and at work for ten hours at an impossible curriculum, must inevitably have taken not only a strong character but a strong arm. Not inapplicable was the remark made to Erasmus by a Cambridge don when the former was looking for an under-master for his friend Colet's school : " Who would put up with the life of a schoolmaster who could get a living in any other way ? "

15

" Impossible " as a means of holding the schoolboy's
natural interest the curriculum undoubtedly was. Its
monotony would still have been deadly, even if the hours
had been more reasonable. As we have seen, there was
none of that pleasant diversity which nowadays revives the
flagging interests and energies every three-quarters of an
hour. Modern subjects were practically unknown ; the
arts were " extras " ; " manners " were persistently inculcated, largely by the reading of treatises somewhat similar
to those already mentioned which were written for the
benefit of the young nobles.. Entertaining as these doggerel
compilations may prove to the present-day reader, they
can hardly have been of enthralling interest to the average
schoolboy who was set down to study them. Seager's
" Schoole of Vertue," published in 1557, is typical. After
the usual instructions about getting up, washing, and
dressing, the schoolboy is reminded about the contents of
his satchel, and admonished to take off his cap politely
when he meets people on the way to school. When work
is over and he goes home he is not to " run in heaps " with
his schoolfellows, " like a swarm of bees," nor is he to shout
and whoop in the streets. Even in the pursuit of gram-
matical rules he was not allowed to escape from this continual sermonizing ; the first thing that would meet his
eye when he opened his Lily's grammar would be a long
Latin poem " De Moribus," which recapitulated all the
precepts about bed-making, hair-combing, and punctuality,
of which he must already have been wearied to distraction
by Seager and his tribe. In fine, Latin and religion,
with such stuff as Seager, was the dry fare provided for ten
hours daily to nourish the brave imaginings of a Shakespeare or a Raleigh, a Sidney or a Marlowe, in their boyhood. An advanced thinker like Mulcaster may advocate
a six hours day : " From 7 to 10 in the forenoon, and from
2 till almost 5 in the afternoon are the most fitting hours,
and quite enough for children to be learned." An individual school may admit music into its curriculum ; a
theorist like Ascham may denounce the brutality and un-
wisdom of the excessive corporal punishment employed ;

but if we are to take the average conditions of school life they will be found to be much as has been depicted.

Holidays were of the kind advocated every now and again in the silly season correspondence columns of the modern dailies. Sixteen days at Christmas and another twelve at Easter were, as a rule, the ordinary grammar school boys' only recreation ; although some of the bigger schools, such as Shrewsbury, allowed the comparatively magnificent extras of two more days at Christmas and nine at Whitsuntide. Fervently, indeed, must the average schoolboy have echoed the words of John Howson, Bishop of Oxford, who, preaching at Paul's Cross in 1597, exclaimed : " We suffer our childhood in the Grammar School, which Austin calls magnam tyrannidem et grave malum, and compares to the torments of martyrdom."

It would be foolish, however, to suggest that this system of education was either pernicious or without its alleviations. Boys then as now made the latter for themselves, and the escape from drudgery which could be achieved by one who could persuade his fellow to " prompt " him during lessons was no new discovery. R. Willis in his " Mount Tabor," published in 1639 when the author was in his seventy-fifth year, gives an account of what happened once to himself as a schoolboy at the free grammar school of Gloucester :

" Before Master Downhale came to be our Master in Christ-school, an ancient Citizen of no great learning was our schoolmaster ; whose manner was to give us out several lessons in the evening, by construing it to every form, and in the next morning to examine us thereupon. . . . Now when the two highest forms were dispatched some of them whom we called prompters would come to sit in our seats of the lower forms, and so being at our elbows would put into our mouths answers to our master's questions, as he walked up and down by us : and so by our prompters' help, we made shift to escape correction ; but understood little to profit by it." Willis, however, had the misfortune one day to quarrel with his prompter over " some boys' play abroad," with the result that the older boy " in his anger, to do me the greatest hurt he could (which then he thought to be to fall under the rod) he dealt with all the prompters that none of them should help me so (as he thought) I must necessarily be beaten." Nothing daunted, however, by this treachery, Willis "gathered all his wits together," listened very carefully to all the boys who were put on to construe before him, and getting by good luck an easy word to parse, made shift to escape that time. Discovering that the prompters meant to continue their boycott he was forced to attend to his lessons, and to learn how to parse, with the happy result that he soon became able to be a prompter himself.

There are signs, too, that the ability to speak Latin was appreciated by the schoolboys themselves, incredible as it may sound. T. F. Kirby in his " Annals of Winchester College " prints a very remarkable document, by which no less than eighteen of the scholars bound themselves of their own accord to speak only in Latin from the autumn of 1639 until the following Whitsuntide ! The rules made at Oundle and at Harrow directing that the boys must speak to each other in Latin, even when outside the school or at play, horrifying as their revival would be to the modern *alumni* of those famous schools, were perhaps not so intolerable to the Elizabethan boys for whom they were originally framed. Similarly, the acting of Latin plays, customary in English schools, as well as at the universities, must have helped to reconcile to his task the natural human boy who can enjoy most things as long as they do not involve his sitting still. Charles Hoole, as a result of his practical experience, recommends this method of teaching in glowing terms : " When you meet with an act or scene [of Terence] that is full of affection and action, you may cause some of your scholars—after they have learned it—to act it first in private amongst themselves, and afterwards in the open school before their fellows. Herein you must have a main care of their pronunciation and acting every gesture to the very life." In an age when English drama and English acting were admittedly the finest in Europe, the congeniality of such a method of teaching must have gone far to overcome the schoolboy's natural distaste of a tongue other than his native one.

Probably, too, this classical training was less narrow and one-sided than it appears. A historian such as Camden must have introduced much interesting and miscellaneous instruction into the Latin theme work of his scholars at Westminster. Sir Henry Wotton, poet, epigrammatist, traveller, and diplomat, can hardly have been a dull provost of Eton. Thomas Farnaby, friend of Ben Jonson, companion of Drake and Hawkins in their last voyage, soldier, author, editor, one of the most famous schoolmasters and classical scholars of his time, must surely have brought his pupils into touch with the vital deeds and living issues of the day, even if the language employed was one which we now call " dead."

We shall find, however, the fullest justification of this method of education if we refer ourselves again to the ideal towards which it was directed, and to the practical results of it, as seen in the deeds and lives of the men who made the age famous. It is likely, indeed, that the savage discipline and the monotonous scheme of study helped to account for the extreme wildness of behaviour in young manhood which characterized some of the most interesting personalities of that time ; undue restraint almost inevitably breeds the greater licence. But that aspect is, after all, only one side of the case ; it would be neither fair nor judicious to say that we have a Shakespeare, a Spenser, a Marlowe, and a Sidney not as a result of, but in spite of, their early training. It was a Spartan method, with no mercy for the unfit, but it was the day in England of a sturdy breed of men. Bearing in mind the results, it is surely impossible for us to-day to do more than deplore the wastage involved by such a system, while realizing at the same time that it served as no inadequate instrument to mould the characters of some of the greatest Englishmen of all ages.

CHAPTER XII

THE UNIVERSITY

SIR ANDREW AGUECHEEK, that accomplished dancer of jigs, once lamented to his friend Sir Toby Belch that he had never been sent to a university : " I would I had bestowed that time in the tongues that I have in fencing, dancing and bear-baiting. O ! had I but followed the arts ! " From contemporary criticisms it would appear, however, that only too many of Sir Andrew's quality flocked to Oxford and Cambridge in Tudor times. Founded originally for the benefit of poor scholars like Chaucer's Clerk of Oxenforde with no riches save his " library " of twenty books, which abstinence from gay clothes and musical instruments may have enabled him to buy, the universities had begun to attract the sons of the rich, who, according to Harrison, were inclined to " study little other than histories, tables,[1] dice and trifles," and bring the universities " into much slander," because, " standing upon their reputation and liberty, they ruffle and roist it out, exceeding in apparel and haunting riotous company . . . and for excuse, when they are charged with breach of all good order, think it sufficient to say that they be gentlemen." [2] He regrets, too, that the rich have so encroached upon the benefits originally intended for the needy that in his time even fellowships go by favour, and it is " an hard matter for a poor man's child to come by one . . . though he be never so good a scholar." We can imagine, though, that when faced with a " recommendation " from the Queen herself, even the most impartial and independent of colleges would have been hard put to it to insist on merit as the deciding factor in the election.

In general, however, Harrison, like most other writers, has

---

[1] Histories, i.e. stories ; tables, the invariable name for backgammon in the sixteenth century.

[2] " The Description of England," II, iii.

great praise for both Oxford and Cambridge as institutions. He dwells with approval on the college system, contrasting it with that of foreign universities, " where the students are enforced for want of such houses to dwell in common inns and taverns, without all order or discipline." Both Harrison and Paul Hentzner describe the college life as " almost monastic "; and Nicholas Fitzherbert, who entered Exeter College about the year 1568, adds the interesting piece of information that although the youth of the nobility could attend any of the sixteen colleges at Oxford, they and the sons of the rich mainly frequented eight extra halls where the discipline was decidedly less strict !

Harrison describes the colleges as " goodly houses, builded four square . . . of hard freestone or brick, with great number of lodgings and chambers in the same for students." Then, as now, they were famed for their beautiful gardens, and each one boasted a library, to which, Hentzner says, every student of " any considerable standing " possessed a key. Harrison, an M.A. of both universities, is impartial in his comparison of Oxford and Cambridge. He praises the Oxford colleges as " much more stately, magnificent and commodious," but adds that with the exception of the Divinity School at Oxford the " common schools " of Cambridge are " far more beautiful." And the two places, he declares, are alike in the habits of their townsfolk, who delight to " match and annoy " the students, and to charge them excessive prices !

The age for leaving school varied, but Brinsley considered that no boy should be sent to the university until he was at least fifteen, as a younger child could scarcely be expected to have " good discretion how to govern himself there and moderate his expenses." Fifteen was also the age prescribed by the university statutes at the time Brinsley wrote ; but in Tudor days students—especially noblemen's sons—were often admitted much younger. Robert Devereux Earl of Essex, was sent to Trinity College, Cambridge, at the age of ten, although he did not matriculate until two years later. Bacon was only twelve when

he also went to Trinity, and fourteen when he passed on to
Gray's Inn ;   Sir Philip Sidney was fourteen when admitted
to Christ Church ; and Edward de Vere, seventeenth Earl
of Oxford, matriculated as a fellow-commoner of Queen's,
Cambridge, at the age of eight, taking his M.A. at fourteen !
Essex was another of these fourteen-year-old M.A's.[1]

Naturally such children were not left entirely to their
own devices, but were put in the care of a private tutor,
who not only supervised their studies, but took entire
charge of their manners and morals, their clothes and their
money. A comparatively mature student of fifteen
years or more would probably be committed to the care
of his college tutor, who would then stand to him *in loco
parentis*, be to a certain extent his companion, see to his
expenditure, and instruct him in his work. It took the
student seven years to become a Master of Arts. During
this period he would habitually reside at his college, both
in term time and in vacations ; and after becoming an
M.A. could proceed to further degrees in Medicine, Law,
and Theology if he chose. At both universities, however,
important personages and noblemen were frequently granted
their M.A. without having fulfilled these conditions. Payment, itself statutory, helped to overcome the statutory
difficulty—ten shillings, for example, enabling the son of a
Lord of Parliament to become an Oxford B.A. before the
end of his fourth year. Recommendations from high places
would also serve to incline the universities to overlook the
breach of some of their regulations. Mr. Hotson's recent
discovery of the documents relating to the death of Marlowe
has also brought to light the fact that the poet experienced
some difficulty, by reason of absence from Cambridge,
in extracting his degree from the authorities in 1587. A
letter from the Privy Council, however, signed by Whitgift,
the Archbishop of Canterbury, and by the Treasurer,
Burghley, the university's own Chancellor, setting forth
his services to the Queen during his absence secured the
necessary compliance, and Marlowe took his M.A. without
further hindrance.

---

[1] See Venn : " Alumni Cantabrigienses," I, p. 250 ; and II, p. 38.

The chief facts concerning the curriculum can be put very briefly. For the undergraduate rhetoric was the main branch of study; for the graduate ambitious of his mastership, theology. Mathematics and medicine were in their infancy: Galen and Hippocrates were still the textbooks for the latter. The canon law was unpopular, and civil law was not much read at either university, partly because the lawyers of the Inns of Court were as a body strongly opposed to this lay study of the law. In spite of the revival of interest in Greek under such men as Cheke and Ascham, and in spite of the existence of chairs of Greek and Hebrew, these languages were greatly neglected. History as a serious study was hardly yet in existence; and degrees in music, even in this age of musicians, were very rare. Examination was still by public disputation, as in the Middle Ages. Teaching, however, had become quite definitely the function of the colleges. The professors of the university gave their lectures as formerly, but the individual colleges had their own lecturers also: Brasenose, for example, gave one theology and two logic lectures each week, and in 1572 the college decreed that if its Greek lecturer failed to deliver any of his lectures he should be mulcted twelve pence for each offence.

With the accession of Elizabeth both the universities entered upon a period of reorganization and reform after a decade of trouble and unrest. Burghley became Chancellor of Cambridge in 1560, and Leicester Chancellor of Oxford in 1564. The rule of the latter has been severely criticized, but Sir Charles Mallet shows very clearly that his disciplinary measures and his care for the university's interests were of real benefit. During his chancellorship new statutes were promulgated, which not only paid detailed attention to such minor irregularities as " excess in apparel," but also reorganized the curriculum and brought the undergraduate under better control. Seniors and juniors alike were forbidden openly to wear " any doublet of any light colour, as white, green, yellow, etc." [1] The unattached student had to betake himself for residence

[1] Wood : " Annals," II, 153.

to a college or a hall, and there he would have to subscribe to the Thirty-Nine Articles, the Queen's Supremacy, and the Prayer Book. Popery was thereby discouraged, and conformity to the Anglican way forwarded. The remodelled curriculum for the arts student enjoined two terms of grammar, four of rhetoric, five of dialectic, three of arithmetic, and two of music for the Bachelor's degree. Astronomy, geometry, natural and moral philosophy, and metaphysics occupied the three remaining years during which the B.A. prepared himself to proceed Master of Arts. Leicester was unsparing, too, in his criticism of any " negligence and slackness " on the part of both students and teachers ; and absence from lectures, after the new statutes were accepted, involved the delinquent in a fine which was really exacted.

Life at either university, as in town or country, was more comfortable than it had been. College fellows fared well, and a lord's son would find himself well-housed and able to equip his apartments with the luxuries that his own pretty fancy dictated and his purse allowed. The Earl of Essex, who seems to have been but poorly supplied with money during his college career, had glass put in his chamber windows, and paid sixteen shillings for hangings of painted cloth for his study ; he spent a shilling to have shelves put up, and another five on decorations. Rushes and " dressing of the chamber " cost him four shillings, and the table at which he worked another three and fourpence.[1] The panelling which was everywhere becoming fashionable for chamber-walls found its way also to the universities ; and such amenities of life as feather beds and chests for linen and clothing were introduced by all who could afford them.

It is difficult to estimate the cost of a university education in Elizabethan times. The majority of the students were still poor men's sons—" ragged clerks', weavers' and butchers' sons," the " Pilgrimage to Parnassus " describes them in 1602.[2] Lack of means compelled many of them

---

[1] See Ellis : " Original Letters," Ser. 2, Vol. III, p. 72 ff.
[2] III, ii.

to do without any breakfast, as well as to " fag " for their better-off companions. Room rent was a considerable item : at Brasenose, for example, in 1596 the price of the " best room " was twenty shillings a year, a smaller one costing ten. At St. John's College, Oxford, senior fellows were allowed three pence for both dinner and supper ; a B.A. received twopence halfpenny, as did the undergraduate. Bread and drink, however, was served as an equal portion to all. These allowances give us perhaps some idea of the average expenditure on food necessarily incurred by the undergraduate who was not a scholar. Meals were taken together in the college halls at three separate tables. To the first or Fellows' Table were admitted earls, barons, gentlemen, doctors, and a few masters of arts. This table was naturally more expensively and plentifully served than the others, the second of which accommodated the M.A.'s and B.A.'s, gentlemen and eminent citizens, the third being for " people of low condition." It is doubtless the fare of this last table that Thomas Cogan in his " Haven of Health " describes in 1596 : " At Oxford in my time they used commonly at dinner boiled beef with pottage, bread and beer and no more." He adds the information that each man was allowed a halfpenny worth of beer, and elsewhere in his book tells us that on festival days the students by way of an extra delicacy " are wont to eat crevices (crayfish) last, after flesh." [1] Eleven o'clock in Cogan's time was the hour for dinner ; supper was at five. During the meal a student would read aloud from the Bible, and after grace had been said every one was free to retire to his own chamber. Here, however, especially in the winter season, the poorer student cannot have found much comfort, scantily furnished and generally fireless as these rooms were. Further, the colleges in Elizabeth's reign were very crowded ; so that although a Fellow would be allotted a room to himself, and special

[1] Even a Gaude dinner in 1597 (at Brasenose) was not a sumptuous affair, in comparison with an ordinary Elizabethan feast—cabbage 2d., beef 1s., leg of pork 1s. 6d., 2 couple of rabbits 2s. 8d., quart of wine and sugar 1s. 1d., ale, apples, and cheese 10d., table cloth and napkins 6d. (See " Brasenose Quatercentenary Monographs," II, i, 10).

privileges would be given to the sons of nobles, the ordinary student was compelled to share one room with three or four companions.

The discipline at both universities was strict, and as such a large proportion of the students were mere boys it is not surprising that the pains and penalties inflicted upon the erring savour more of the Elizabethan school than of the modern university. To be " scanted of sizes," or deprived of their allowance of bread and drink from the buttery, was a common punishment at Cambridge. The frequenting of plays brought down dire wrath on the heads of offenders, an Oxford statute of 1584 providing that any master, bachelor, or scholar of more than eighteen years of age who was caught attending a public performance should be imprisoned, while for the undergraduate of less than eighteen the penalty was " open punishment " in St. Mary's Church. Those found haunting inns and taverns, or shops where tobacco was sold, were adjudged a public flogging ; and the same penalty was inflicted upon those who were rash enough to play football within the university precincts or in the city streets ; while if a minister or deacon so far forgot himself he was promptly expelled. Cambridge however, recognized football, along with archery and quoits, as a " legitimate " game. The undergraduate of sporting proclivities found himself kept in hand at Oxford by what he doubtless regarded as tiresome and grandmotherly legislation : the only dog he was allowed to keep was a " spannell," and then only provided he could obtain the Vice-Chancellor's licence for it ; guns, hawks, and ferrets were all strictly forbidden. The statutes of the individual colleges were equally strict concerning the students' behaviour and appearance ; one such forbids the under-graduate " to encourage an inordinate growth of hair " under penalty of a fourpenny fine ; [1] another enacts " that no one shall prevent his fellows from studying or sleeping

---

[1] Institutions, in Tudor times, seem to have been extremely particular about such details. At Lincoln's Inn, for example, in 1550, no one was allowed to wear a beard of more than fourteen days' growth under penalty of expulsion for the third offence ; and in 1553 those who wore beards had to pay a 12d. fine every time they dined in Hall in that condition.

by singing, making a noise, shouting, or discharging guns, or by any other kind of uproar or din." Most of the colleges, too, seem to have been concerned that the under-graduate should not take his walks abroad unaccompanied. Some colleges birched even their twenty-year-old students for certain breaches of discipline, and in cases where an offence brought the doer within the danger of the law of the land the full operation and savagery of the legal code was given its way. A libel on the Vice-Chancellor, for example, cost an unlucky Merton youth not only a whipping but the loss of his ears.[1]

Even with the vagaries of fashionable undergraduate attire Elizabethan Oxford and Cambridge attempted to cope, though apparently with little success. Silks and satins and " excessive ruffs " called forth periodical denunciations from the authorities ; and much complaint was made at Cambridge in 1578 of the wearing of " hoses of unseemly greatness or disguised fashion." This extrava-gance of apparel, however, can have prevailed only among the richer and more idle section ; those sizars and poor scholars who in return for more or less regulated " tips " were prepared to act as valets to their wealthier fellows—rousing them for morning chapel, cleaning their boots, and running their errands—cannot have had much to spare for expenditure on dress. Even the monied graduate with sartorial ambitions must have thought twice about walking through the streets of Cambridge without his " gown reaching to the ankles " and his proper hood when faced with the alternative of a six and eightpenny fine for each offence.

It takes us a long way from the daily routine of life and the ordinary round of disputations, lectures, and study in either university, but even such a brief account as this can hardly omit all mention either of the yearly festivities that graced the Christmas season or of the memorable occasions on which the Queen honoured both Oxford and Cambridge with ceremonial visits. Cambridge was first favoured in 1564 ; Oxford's turn came in 1566. In each

[1] See Chamberlain's " Letters," Camden Soc. Publ., p. 179.

case the procedure was more or less the same, involving the usual addresses of welcome and parting, and an edifying if wearisome round of academic exercises, preachings, and plays. The Queen appears to have been indefatigable both in attendance and attention. At Oxford, for example, where she was lodged in Christ Church, she passed four hours listening to philosophical disputations in Latin ; the next day she spent the whole afternoon listening to yet more debates, this time on Civil Law ; the day after, Medicine and Divinity took the field, and she attended disputations upon the power of the medical art to prolong life, and the right of subjects to take up arms against a tyrannical ruler. As Sir Charles Mallet puts it, " To see Oxford it was essential to hear Oxford men dispute," and Elizabeth listened to all their eloquence with unflagging zeal, professing herself at the conclusion of these exercises delighted with all she had seen and heard. As a Cambridge spectator had written of her behaviour at the Latin play on the occasion of her visit to the sister university, while many " bore with difficulty the loss of so many hours, she remained of peaceful aspect until the last round of applause and did not show in her face even the slightest sign of being bored." [1]

Not least among the lighter amusements provided by both universities were the Latin plays acted by the students. At Cambridge Elizabeth saw the " Aulularia " of Plautus ; at Oxford Edwards' " Palamon and Arcyte " and a tragedy called " Progne " were presented for her delectation. Plays in the vernacular and common players might be banned at the universities as corrupters of youth, but to acquit himself well in a Latin play was no disgrace to the most sober or virtuous scholar. As in the schools, Latin plays were still regarded almost as an item in the educational curriculum. They were frequently performed on Sunday as well as Saturday evenings, by which their diversional and educational value is well indicated ; and the work of the students themselves was produced alongside that of the ancient writers.

[1] Latin account by Robinson ; see Nichols' " Progresses," III, 59.

At Christmas time the students made holiday for some twelve days. The majority of ordinary scholars found a return to their homes beyond their slender means, but their more or less enforced residence did not stifle the desire for merrymaking, and the usual strict discipline, the lectures, and the exercises were suspended while the old traditional licence of mummery and playacting engrossed every one's energies. A "Christmas Prince" or a Lord of Misrule would preside over the festivities until Twelfth Night concluded his brief reign, and then lectures and disputations were again resumed. Such, with the few legitimate games and exercises, were the relaxations of the sixteenth century student.

Types that are still familiar at the universities abounded in Elizabethan days. Overbury gives us an acid sketch of "the mere scholar" who persistently upholds the antiquity of his own university, and also the supreme excellence of his own college—"though but for a match at football." [1] Earle has a companion picture of the rich young idler who comes to the university in order to wear a gown and boast of his education. "His father sent him thither, because he heard there were the best fencing and dancing schools; from these he has his education, from his tutor the oversight." [2] The only marks of seniority ever to be observed in such an one are the worn velvet of his gown and his proficiency at tennis: "When he can once play a set he is a freshman no more." He has fine books on the handsome shelves of his study, which he occasionally takes down to while away a wet afternoon, and he is known as a haunter of taverns.

Students destined to rise to eminence in their several callings, however, were also to be found in considerable numbers at both universities. Burghley at St. John's, Cambridge, and Jewel of Merton and Corpus, for example, were reputed tireless workers, rising at four in the morning to begin their studies and continuing till late at night. The former is said to have given at the age of sixteen a

[1] Overbury: "Characters," 1614–16.
[2] Earle: "Microcosmographie," 1628.

lecture on sophistry and three years later one on Greek, though at this time " there were but few who were masters of Greek either in that College or the University." [1]

Even if too many youths like Robert Greene the play-wright lighted in the university " amongst wags as lewd as themselves with whom they consumed the flower of their youth," there is ample evidence that at this period Oxford and Cambridge, both in point of intellectual culture and disciplinary conduct, could challenge favourable comparison with the most famous continental universities. They had their drawbacks, seen only too clearly by con-temporaries such as Bacon ; [2] but as the centres of national learning and a training ground for all servants of the public they were reverenced by the majority of Englishmen, and together with the Court were described as " the com-pendium of all England."

---

[1] Peck's " Desiderata Curiosa."
[2] See especially his " Advancement of Learning."

Note.—The intellectual, educational and social importance of the four Inns of Court made them a notable feature of Elizabethan life. Together with the nine smaller Inns of Chancery, the schools of theology, Gresham's College, the College of Physicians, and various other teaching institutions, they justified Sir George Buck's description of London as " the Third Universitie of England " (see his account in Stow's *Annales*, 1613). Many an eldest son, heir to broad acres, was sent to Gray's Inn or Lincoln's Inn, or the Middle or Inner Temple, as his father before him, not because he was to follow the law but so that he might learn enough of it to see the more shrewdly to the management of his estates and be the better equipped to take his place as J.P. in his own county. At no time have these four great Inns been more highly regarded as a proper training ground for young " gentlemen of blood ". Their buildings, their institutions, their mode of life, their social activities made them a collegiate centre, which drew thither young men, " gently bred, country bred ", from every part of England. Their association with the growth of the drama is typical of the part they played in the intellectual life of the day. *Twelfth Night* and *The Comedy of Errors* were given what appear to be their first performances at the Middle Temple and Gray's Inn ; and it was for the annual Christmas revels of the Inner Temple, in 1561, that *Gorboduc*, the first English tragedy, was written by Thomas Sackville and Thomas Norton, both members of that Inn. To remember Sidney, Raleigh, Bacon as Inns of Court men is to realize the justice of G. M. Young's description of this society in his delightful *Shakespeare and the Termers* (British Academy Annual Shakespeare Lecture, 1947). The Court only excepted, it was " the liveliest, most intelligent and most influential in England."

CHAPTER XIII

" YOUNG AND OLD COME FORTH TO PLAY "

THE Elizabethan worked hard, and when he took a holiday he took it whole-heartedly, stretched his limbs and his lungs, feasted himself and entertained himself on a generous scale. He loved the riot and noise of Bartholomew Fair or its country equivalent, with its side shows, its monsters, its fat women, its ballad-mongers, its gilt gingerbread, its hobby-horses, and its roast pig. He loved to gape at pasteboard and finery and fireworks ; pageantry of all kinds delighted him, and he indulged at every opportunity in trials of strength and skill. He seized upon any excuse for a junketing : when his child was born he feasted his neighbours as lavishly as his means allowed ; when the parish needed to raise funds for some particular purpose he brewed a noble quantity of good ale, and then retailed it to the surrounding villages. He danced at weddings, and ate heartily of the baked meats at a funeral ; and, above all, whatever the occasion, he was ready to sing and make music with a zest and a mastery that his nation has never since been able to recapture. He had lost the holidays of the Roman Catholic calendar, but he had not lost the spirit of merry-making and his delight in festivals and foolish old customs. May Days and Church Ales, Cotswold Games and Lord Mayors' Shows still called him out into the open and relieved the tedium of the long work hours. High spirits had to find some outlet, and they found an extremely good one in the outdoor sports and pastimes of the age.

Games, as one would suppose, were inclined to be of a rough and strenuous description. The only thing to be urged in extenuation of the delight men took in the extremely brutal sports of bull- and bear-baiting and cock-fighting is the equal delight they took in breaking each other's bones in wrestling matches, and their heads at cudgel-play. Their cruelty to beasts does not appear excessive when compared, for instance, with the practical jokes they were accustomed to play upon their friends. The average Elizabethan was not sensitive to the spectacle of physical suffering, either in human beings or in animals; spiritually he was well developed in some directions, and hardly at all in others. Contemporary descriptions of such a game as football make it quite plain why James I refused to class it amongst those sports which he held to be commendable. Even Mulcaster, who believed that if properly played it would be conducive both to health and strength, has not (in 1581) a good word to say for it " as it is now commonly used "—" with bursting of shins and breaking of legs, it be neither civil, neither worthy the name of any train to health." [1] Stubbes calls it " a friendly kind of fight . . . a bloody and murdering practice," [2] and describes what he had evidently seen for himself. His dislike is obviously increased by the fact that the game was often played upon Sundays. Even so, however, his account leaves us in no doubt of its extraordinarily rough and hazardous nature, and it is easy to see why the university authorities at Oxford banned it so firmly. " Doth not everyone lie in wait for his adversary," asks Stubbes, " seeking to overthrow him, and to pitch him on the nose, though it be upon hard stones, in ditch or dale, in valley or hill, or what place soever it be, he careth not, so he have him down ? And he that can serve the most of this fashion, he is counted the only fellow . . . so that by this means sometimes their necks are broken, sometimes their backs, sometime their legs, sometime their arms; sometime one part thrust out of joint, sometime another; sometime the noses gush out with blood, sometime their eyes start out. . . . But whosoever scapeth away the best goeth not scot free, but is either sore wounded, crazed [3] and bruised, so that he dieth of it, or else scapeth very hardly; and no marvel, for they have the sleights to meet one betwixt

[1] " Positions," 1581, chap. 27.   [2] " Anatomy of Abuses."
[3] Broken by concussion.

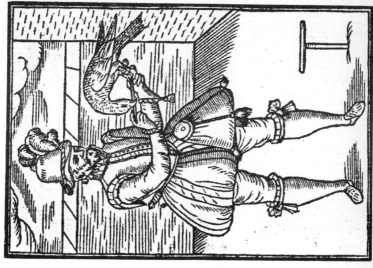

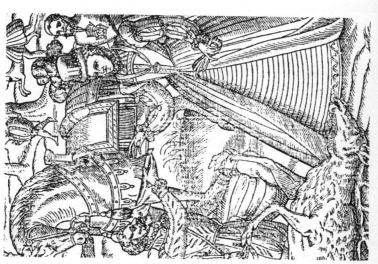

ELIZABETHAN COSTUMES (earlier part of reign)

(*From Turberville's books on Hunting and Hawking*)

two, to dash him against the heart with their elbows, to hit him under the short ribs with their griped fists, and with their knees to catch him upon the hip, and to pitch him on his neck, with a hundred such murdering devices."

If football was hazardous in the extreme when played in this rough-and-tumble fashion, cudgel-play, wrestling, and broadsword encounters were equally likely to send their players home with bloody heads and broken limbs. The object in cudgel-play has always been to draw your antagonist's blood with a sharp rap on the head : the red streak down the face was the sign of the winning hit. Of the breaking of ribs in wrestling Touchstone bears witness when he comments on the sport as one not suited, as a spectacle, for ladies. Even Spenser's Calidore, the model of courtesy, when he engaged in a wrestling bout, " almost brake " his opponent's neck. In all these games, however, the skill and strength displayed were of no mean order. The roughness of the play would be more in evidence at a village gathering or a match at a fair ; as practised, however, by such noble youths as Philip Sidney—who excelled at wrestling, running, shooting, swimming, and leaping—these games, though strenuous and at times dangerous, were not the least valuable side of the education of an Elizabethan gentleman. Even the timorous King James considered that running, jumping, wrestling, and fencing were sports suitable for princes, and groups them with hunting, archery, riding, and tennis as " honourable and recommendable." All of these, with such milder exercises as bowling, quoit-throwing, pall-mall, and skittles were popular throughout the reign—bowls, pall-mall, and fishing, in particular, being amusements practised also by ladies. Upon such country games as leap-frog, blindman's buff, prisoners' base, and barley break there is no need to comment ; with many such others they were exactly the same as the games known by those names and still played by children throughout the country.

If the weather kept him indoors when he was disposed to amuse himself the Elizabethan was much more likely to turn to some indoor game than to a book. There were not

only various table and card games and dice, but a great
number of forfeit games, guessing games, and parlour
games of all kinds, many of which are still played by
children. Chess was extremely popular, and more familiar
to the average man and woman than it is to-day. Of card
games, primero was easily the favourite : it was the chief
gambling game, at Court or in a tavern. Backgammon
was very popular, and is always spoken of as " tables."
Shovel board, draughts, and billiards were also played ; [1]
and simple country folk amused themselves with such
childish trifles as hot cockles, ninepins, shuttlecock, and
handy-dandy.

Dancing was popular with all classes : the great danced
in their long galleries and their stately dining halls, and
the villagers danced upon the green. The Queen herself
seems to have been extremely fond of the pastime. The
most curious picture of her that we possess is the painting
at Penshurst which shows her executing the lavolta [2]
in a dance with the Earl of Leicester. But the dances that
Elizabeth delighted to watch at Court were not at all the
same as the simple country dances in which the greater
number of her subjects rejoiced. At Whitehall and
Greenwich and Hampton Court they " trod a measure,"
or stepped the pavane, the galliard, and the coranto—
stately dances, well suited to the stiff and cumbrous
fashions of the day. But out of doors on the green, and
when the country folk or the serving men and maids
disported themselves in their master's hall, there was dancing of another kind—jigs, hornpipes, rounds, the morris
dance, and the hay, which was rather like a reel.[3]

In Elizabeth's time there were still a considerable number
of popular festivals, some of them regularly kept up all
over the country, others only in certain localities. Shrove

---

[1] The last of these was not so much played as the others until about the
middle of the seventeenth century. Sir Thomas Kitson, however, had a
billiard table in " the gallery in the tower " at Hengrave Hall : " Itm. one
billiard board, with two staves to it of bone, and two of wood, and four
balls." (1603 Inventory : see Gage's *History of Hengrave*, p. 34. 1822).
[2] The high spring into the air from which the dance—a form of the
galliard—took its name.
[3] See De Banke, *Shakespearian Stage Production*, for dance steps and
music.

Tuesday afforded occasion to all and sundry for a final
indulgence before the rigours of the Lenten season : pan-
cake tossing, football, masquing, cock-fighting and feasting
enlivened the day for all save the Puritan. Easter was
celebrated by sports of all kinds, and in some parts of the
country, especially at Reading and Coventry, Hock Monday and Hock Tuesday were still observed—on the former
day the men of the town would capture all the women
and hold them to ransom, on the latter the women did the
same to the men. The money thus collected went into
the churchwardens' funds for charitable use.

On May Day town and country alike went a-maying—a
custom for which Stubbes has no approval. " All the
young men and maids, old men and wives run gadding
over night to the woods, groves, hills and mountains, where
they spend all the night in pleasant pastimes : and in the
morning they return, bringing with them birch and branches
of trees to deck their assemblies withall." To Stubbes it
was just an opportunity for licentiousness, but Stow, who
was undeniably a serious man, suggests that there was
another side to the old custom : " On May morning in
the morning every man . . . would walk into the street,
meadows and green woods, there to rejoice their spirits
with the beauty and savour of sweet flowers, praising God
in their kind." The chief ceremony of the day was the
planting of the maypole. " They have twenty or forty
yoke of oxen," says Stubbes, " every ox having a sweet
nosegay of flowers placed on the tip of his horns ; and these
oxen draw home this maypole (this stinking idol rather),
which is covered all over with flowers and herbs, bound
round about with strings from the top to the bottom, and
sometime painted with variable colours, with two or three
hundred men, women and children following it with great
devotion. And thus being reared up, with handkerchiefs
and flags hovering on the top, they strew the ground round
about, bind green boughs about it, set up summer halls,
bowers and arbours hard by it, and then fall they to dance
about it."

There were others beside Stubbes who regarded the whole

affair as heathenish and immoral. At Shrewsbury, for
example, where it had always been the custom to erect
the maypole in front of the Shearmen's Hall, the May Day
revels excited so much Puritan displeasure in 1588 that
they were denounced by the public preacher of the town
and forbidden by the bailiffs. Popular feeling, however,
was still strongly attached to its old customs, and in 1591
a compromise was arrived at : the maypole might be
erected again, it was decreed, " so that it be done soberly
and in good order, without broils or contention." [1]   If
the sobriety was indeed observed there must have been
seen on May 1, 1591, at Shrewsbury some early specimens
of that famous figure—the Englishman taking his pleasures
sadly.   In most towns and villages, however, the morris
dancers and the hobby-horse enlivened the proceedings,
and continued to do so throughout the next two reigns,
" May games " being amongst those pastimes stamped
with the royal approval of both the first James and the
first Charles.

Church Ales were as abhorrent to Stubbes as May
games.   When a parish wanted to raise funds for the repair
of the church or the purchase of service books, or to meet
some extraordinary charge, it would purchase or obtain
by gift half a score or twenty quarters of malt which was
then brewed into a very strong ale and sold to all comers,
often enough in the church itself. " Then when . . . this
Huff cap . . . is set abroach, well is he that can get the
soonest to it and spend the most at it : for he that sitteth
the closest to it and spends the most at it, he is counted the
godliest man of all the rest."   It is not necessary to suppose
that the whole village and all the neighbouring hamlets
went home reeling drunk every night so long as the ale
lasted.   Many an Ale must have been a pleasant enough
merrymaking, the young folks dancing on the green, the
older people playing at bowls or watching while the
more energetic ones disported themselves.   Nevertheless
it is easy to sympathize with Stubbes' objection to financing

[1] " Transactions of the Shropshire Archæological and Natural History
Society," Vol. VI. 1883, p. 189.

the national religion in this dubious manner ; and the fact
that towards the end of the reign the law began to suppress
all Church Ales suggests that only too often they must have
been the cause of a disgusting amount of drunkenness and
of broils and troubles of all kinds.

Whit-Sunday in many parishes gave occasion for a Church
Ale, and the following Tuesday was for some years associated
in the west country with " Captain " Robert Dover's
famous " Cotswold Games." Of Elizabethan origin, they
lapsed towards the end of the reign and were revived by
Dover after James' accession. The descriptions in
" Annalia Dubrensia " give us a vivid idea of what such
gatherings were like ; there were coursing matches for
greyhounds, running matches, cudgel-play, and

> Abroad to jolly shepherds, bagpipes play,
> Of whom, some leap, some wrastle for the day,
> Some throw the sledge, and others spurn the bar.

August brought the harvest, and the end of the husbandman's year. To Nicholas Breton [1] it is a " merry time,
wherein honest neighbours make good cheer," and he gives
us a delightful picture of the country-side in this harvest
month :

" The sun . . . dries up the standing ponds . . . now
begin the gleaners to follow the corn-cart, and a little bread
to a great deal of drink makes the traveller's dinner :
the melon and the cucumber is now in request : and oil
and vinegar give attendance on the sallet herbs . . . the
pipe and the tabor is now lustily set on work, and the lad
and the lass will have no lead on their heels : the new wheat
makes the gossips' cake, and the bride-cup is carried above
the heads of the whole parish : the furmenty pot
welcomes home the harvest cart, and the garland of
flowers crowns the captain of the reapers." Hentzner,
too, gives us a pleasant glimpse of the "harvest home."
As he and his companions were returning to their inn
at Windsor, he tells us, " We happened to meet some
country people celebrating their harvest home ; their last

---

[1] " Fantasticks," 1626.

load of corn they crown with flowers . . . men and women, men and maidservants, riding through the streets in the cart, shout as loud as they can till they arrive at the barn."

September and October, when in the country " the hogs are turned into the cornfields " and " the flail and the fan fall to work in the barn," brought no festivity to the farmer or his men ; but in November there was Hallowe'en with its seed cake, its ducking for apples, and other games for the countryman ; and in London there was the Lord Mayor's Show, with all its elaborate pageantry, to delight the citizen and his prentice. The procession which still forms a part of the ceremonies pertaining to the installation of the Lord Mayor took place, as a rule, partly on land and partly on the Thames. The pageant " Metropolis Coronata " put together by the dramatist Anthony Munday the year before Shakespeare's death gives a good idea of what the show was like in Elizabethan times. In the morning the Lord Mayor-elect was rowed in his barge to Westminster, and was welcomed on the water by the first part of the pageant, consisting of a ship representing the " Argo," in which were Jason and Medea with the golden fleece,[1] and a sea " chariot " shaped like a whale in which was the " shade " of Sir Henry Fitz-Alwine, reputed the first Lord Mayor of London. Peals of ordnance and long speeches came next on the programme ; and when the procession had transferred itself to land it took its way through the streets to St. Paul's, accompanied by Neptune mounted upon a pellited lion, Father Thames upon a sea-horse, and a ram escorted by a carload of " housewifly virgins sitting seriously employed in carding and spinning wool for cloth." The " Argo," in the meanwhile, had been beached and equipped with a wheeled trolley ; it followed the ram, and was itself followed by " the chariot of man's life," and London and her twelve daughters —the twelve great livery companies of the city. Last of all came a " show " of Robin Hood and his green-clad huntsmen with their bows and arrows, carrying a newly-slain deer. The proceedings ended at night with a torch-

[1] The pageant was in honour of a Worshipful Draper.

light procession to escort the Lord Mayor to his own house. Then everybody went home to bed, the " Argo " and the chariots and the fancy dresses were put away until the next year, and the city went back to work, until Christmas with its Lord of Misrule brought to both town and country another opportunity for dressing up and holding revel.

Philip Stubbes looked grimly upon all popular festivities because he was a Puritan in the truest as well as in the ordinary sense of the word—that is to say, he was farther on in his spiritual development than the average Elizabethan citizen. He was not unique—Shakespeare abhorred cruelty to animals just as strongly, and has incidentally made it quite evident—but Stubbes was utterly single-minded in his detestation of the stupidity and insensitiveness of the average human being of his own day ; and as a result his style is lively and vigorous with his scorn, and he has registered for us some of the most vivid pictures we possess of his countrymen at their popular amusements. To him a " Lord of Misrule " is almost the devil incarnate, and in consequence every stroke tells when he describes the revels of the lusty villagers :

" First of all the wild-heads of the parish . . . choose them a grand-captain of all mischief whom they enoble with the title of my 'lord of Misrule ' . . . he chooseth forth twenty, forty, threescore or a hundred lusty guts like to himself . . . then every one of these his men he investeth with his liveries of green, yellow or some other light wanton colour ; and as though that were not (bawdy) gawdy enough . . . they bedeck themselves with scarves, ribbons and laces, hanged all over with gold rings, precious stones and other jewels : this done, they tie about either leg twenty or forty bells, with rich handkerchiefs in their hands, and sometimes laid across over their shoulders and necks. . . . Thus all things set in order then have they their hobbyhorses, dragons and other antics, together with their bawdy pipers and thundering drummers to strike up the devil's dance withal. Then march these heathen company towards the church and churchyard, their pipers piping, their drummers thundering, their stumps dancing, their bells jingling, their handkerchiefs swinging about their heads like mad-men, their hobby-horses and other monsters skirmishing amongst the rout." He has caught the very spirit and motion of the tireless, excited, dancing mob ; its drums and its bells echo through the sentences, which have the insistent throb of the dance in their rhythm.

Such, then, were some of the pastimes and the festivals of the period, and they bring us at last, at the end of the year, to Christmas—Elizabethan England's only " holiday season "—when, for about a fortnight work was more or less suspended both in town and country, and all classes held high festival. Hospitality and entertainment were the order of the day. At Court, plays, masques, and banquets succeeded one another until Twelfth Night ; there was merry-making and feasting in every great house ; and in the country the farm workers expected to be allowed to enjoy themselves until Plough Monday, when after a final orgy they went back to hard work and simple fare for another year :

> When Christmastide comes in like a Bride
>   With Holly and Ivy clad ;
> Twelve days in the year much mirth and good cheer
>   In every household is had.

Country " housekeeping " was decaying, and great men were beginning to hold their Christmas celebrations in London, but according to one of the popular ballads the country had still the greater reputation for its Christmasing :

> The Court in all state, Now opens her gate,
>   And bids a free welcome to most ;
> The City likewise, though somewhat precise,
>   Doth willingly part with her cost ;
> And yet by report, from City and Court,
>   The Country gets the day ;
> More liquor is spent, and better content,
>   To drive the cold winter away.[1]

At Court the Master of the Revels was busy for weeks beforehand seeing performances by the different companies

[1] Roxburghe Ballads.

of players in order to select those who were to perform plays before the Queen during the festivities. It must have required upon his part the exercise of some discretion ; the plays had to be carefully " perused," and then if necessary " reformed," anything " not convenient to be showen before her Majesty " being deleted. Elaborate rehearsals were given, that the master might form a considered opinion, and then the selected companies proceeded with still further rehearsals of their amended plays. Other responsibilities, too, rested upon the shoulders of the Master and his subordinates : Court entertainments took place at night and would last till one in the morning ; the Revels' office had to see to the hanging of enormous candelabra to light the hall ; then the players' slender stocks of properties and apparel had to be eked out with assistance from the Revels' wardrobe, and anything of an elaborate nature had to be designed and manufactured. Meanwhile the Office of Works was busy with the seating arrangements and the erection of a stage ; and the Revels after seeing to such diverse matters as the censoring of the performances and the provision of thousands of candles, had—probably at the last moment, and in the person of some harassed subordinate—to remember to provide gloves for all the players. So the preparations for the Queen's Christmas went forward.

Plays, however, were not the only dramatic entertainment : for the Christmas season the masque was in considerable demand. This pleasant, social affair—a mixture of dance, song, disguising and " dressing up," speech making, and spectacle—had been peculiarly attached to the Christmas pleasures since the Middle Ages, although naturally enough it was also extremely popular for any festive occasion such as a wedding. The informality and the brilliance of the spectacle were its chief attractions ; in the dance the guests mingled with the disguised performers during the larger part of the proceedings, and all the time the lights carried by their torch-bearing attendants gleamed and glanced upon the gay apparel, the satins and the spangles, of their elaborate and costly dresses. Cloth of gold or silver, and the finest fabrics, jewels, and glowing colour all helped to make of the masque the most spectacular of the courtly revelries.

In the country great lords out of favour at Court, or those who preferred the older fashion of life, might still see at Christmas time the crude folk maskings and mummings from which the gorgeous shows of the Court had originally taken their rise :

> To mask and to mum kind neighbours will come
> With wassails of nut brown ale ;
> To drink and carouse to all in this house,
> As merry as bucks in the pale ;
> Where cake, bread and cheese is brought for your fees
> To make you the longer stay.

" Now capons and hens, besides turkeys, geese and ducks, besides beef and mutton, must all die for the great feast," exclaims Breton ; " music must now be in tune or else never, the youth must dance and sing and the aged sit by the fire." Cards and dice were everybody's game during the twelve days of Christmas. Even the children were included : Peregrine and Susan Bertie were given five shillings for " play " on Christmas Day, 1561,[1] when they were, respectively, six and seven years old. And after supper there was dancing for every one :

> . . . the youth must needs go dance,
> First galliards ; then larousse ; and heidegy ;
> " Old lusty gallant " ; " all flowers of the bloom "
> And then " A hall ! " for dancers must have room,
> And to it then ; with set and turn about,
> Change sides and cross, and mince it like a hawk ;
> Backwards and forwards, take hands then, in and out, . . .
> And thus forsooth our dancing held us on
> Till midnight full.[2]

New Year's Day had its special ceremony of present giving, observed both by rich and poor.[3] At Court every one had a gift for the Queen, from great lords like Leicester to such humble officials as " Smyth, Dustman." On one

[1] Ancaster MSS., p. 469.   [2] Breton, ed. Grosart : II " Gleanings," p. 8.
[3] For a lively, documented account of how the Queen and a cross-section of her subjects kept Christmas, see *Elizabethan Christmas* in *An Elizabethan Garland* by A. L. Rowse (1953).

occasion the former presented her with " very fair jewel of gold, being a clock fully furnished with small diamonds and rubies : about the same are six bigger diamonds pointed, and a pendant of gold, diamonds and rubies, very small ; and upon each side a lozenge diamond and an apple of gold enamelled green and russet." [1]   In return the givers were presented by the Queen with a proportionate amount of gilt plate : Leicester had a hundred ounces every year, " Smyth " in return for his " two bolts of cambric " had twenty and one-eighth ounces ! This exchange of gifts was observed by every one : the country lass had a blue neckerchief for her sweetheart, and Peregrine and Susan Bertie received ten shillings each from their father.[2]   So the New Year was propitiously begun.

Having thus seen something of both the good and the bad aspects of Elizabethan amusements and holidays, it will be pleasant to conclude with some account of the part played in people's lives by all kinds of music.   Until recently we have been apt, as a nation, to depreciate our own taste and skill in music, and to assume that our musical history is a blank.   As a result of the work done by modern scholars upon Tudor music we are now just beginning to realize that in the sixteenth century we led the world ; that in this art we were without peers, sent our teachers to Italy to impart their skill and their methods, and were looked to by the whole of Europe as the most musical of civilized nations.   Our Elizabethan music, both vocal and instrumental, printed and in manuscript, is an enormous body of work that should be one of our proudest possessions, but that we are only just beginning to discover and appreciate.   As Sir Henry Hadow [3] has put it : " It is not too much to say that our music in the sixteenth century was of as great account as our literature : Palestrina is like Dante, Byrd is like Shakespeare, and he had round him a company of wit and genius not inferior to that which foregathered at the Mermaid."

[1] Nichols : " Progresses," IV, 99 ; II, 78.
[2] This was in 1561 (p. 463) ; by the following year it had gone up to 20s. each (p. 466).
[3] " Music," Home University Library, 1924.

Ordinary Elizabethan men and women felt ashamed if they could not take their part in the singing of a madrigal or accompany their songs upon the lute. Musical instruments and books of music were left lying about the room to solace the waiting guest much as the dentist to-day leaves " Punch " upon the table of his ante-room. An Elizabethan expected his visitor to pick up a music book and read an elaborate part-song for four or five voices and sing his part at sight ; when the dinner was over he called for his music books, and he and his guests and his children and his servants sang then as probably no such haphazard gathering of ordinary folk has ever been able to sing since. The scene which closes the good citizen's dinner-party in Hollyband's " French Schoolemaister " is typical ; it is a scene in which he himself must frequently have taken part in the houses of the parents of his pupils :

" Roland, shall we have a song ? " says the master of the house. " Yea, Sir," replies Roland, " where be your books of music, for they be the best corrected." " They be in my chest," the master rejoins. " Katherine, take the key of my closet ; you shall find them in a little till at the left hand." In a few moments, Katherine returns with " fair songs at four parts," and then with David taking the bass, John the tenor, and James the treble the quartet sing a song by " Master Edwards, master of the children of the Queen's Chapel . . . a man of a good wit, and a good poet."

The lute was undoubtedly the most popular instrument, and children began their lessons upon it at an early age. One was bought for Peregrine and Susan Bertie, at a cost of forty-six shillings and eightpence, when they were only six and seven years old respectively.[1] A lute was part of the furniture of a barber's shop ; with it his waiting clients beguiled themselves, and entertained the lathered occupant of the chair. To the lute the gallant warbled his love-songs, and for it such musicians as John Dowland and Campion wrote their delightful " Ayres." Four lutes figure amongst the instruments included in the inventory

[1] *Op. cit.*, p. 461.

of Sir Thomas Kitson's goods at Hengrave Hall, and
amongst his dance music and his songs there are " two
luting books covered with leather." The list of Kitson's
instruments throws considerable light, indeed, on the part
taken by music in a gentleman's household—what Nerissa
calls " the music of the house " : six viols, six violins, seven
recorders, four cornets, a bandora, a cittern, two sackbuts,
three hautboys, a curtall and a lysarden,[1] two flutes, three
virginals, and an organ made a remarkably full equipment
for family music. Over fifty books of part-songs and
dances are also included in the inventory, and it is interesting to find amongst the pavins, galliards, and measures
a set of country dances. And while mention is being made
of Kitson as a typical Elizabethan music lover it must not
be forgotten that he showed his devotion to the art in yet
another fashion characteristic of the time—that was, by
supporting in his service no less a composer than John
Wilbye, who stands in the very front rank of English
madrigal writers, inferior only to the two greatest masters,
William Byrd and Orlando Gibbons. The Elizabethan
may not have been above reproach in his choice of certain
pastimes, but he undoubtedly had " music in his soul."

---

[1] The curtal resembles the bassoon : the lysarden is the " serpent ",
a deep-toned bass wind instrument, about 8 ft. long, with three U-shaped
bends.

[2] I see no reason to accept the contention recently made that the singing
of part-songs was not a normal Elizabethan accomplishment. We need
only refer to R. Steele's *Earliest English Music Printing* to realize that a
very considerable number of part-song and madrigal books were published
between 1570 and 1600, and that this supply is obviously indicative of
demand, which, in its turn, indicates facility. In 1575 letters patent were
granted to Tallis and Birde to print music for " any and so many as they
will of set song or songs in parts, either in English, Latin, French, Italian
or other tongues that may serve for music in Church or chamber or otherwise to be played or sung." In 1587 we find William Bathe boasting in his
Brief Introduction to the Skill of Song that he habitually teaches people in
less than a month. He is even prouder of having taught a child of eight in
a month " to sing a good number of songs, difficult crabbed songs, to sing
at the first sight, to be so indifferent for all parts, alterations, cleves, flats
and sharps, that he could sing a part of that kind, of which he never
learned any song." Most convincing of all, however, is Thomas Morley, in
his *Plaine and Easie Introduction to Practical Music* (1597) : " Supper
being ended and the Music books, according to the custom, being brought
to the table : the mistress of the house presented me with a part, earnestly
requesting me to sing. But when after many excuses, I protested that I
could not : every one began to wonder. Yea, some whispered to others,
demanding how I was brought up "

CHAPTER XIV

THE THEATRE

THIS chapter is concerned with the Elizabethan theatre, not with the Elizabethan drama—with that multifarious life which we sum up in the phrase " the world of the theatre " and not with what is properly an aspect of the history of literature. It is, further, with the theatre as an institution rather than with the niceties of its structure as a building that we must concern ourselves ; fortunately the plan of this book precludes any necessity for the usual systematic account of the evolution of the drama and the conformation of the stage and its buildings.[1] In the history of drama the theatre is a separable accident ; it does not exist, for example, when we come to study the medieval English stage. In the Elizabethan age, however, it becomes all-important ; if we study the drama of the period as a whole we must study it as something removed by the fact of the theatre's existence from the realm of pure literature. We can all of us approach Shakespeare directly ; but as soon as we attempt the work of the lesser men we need to understand the significance of that joint activity of audience, actor, and playwright, organized upon a commercial basis, which for convenience' sake we are accustomed to call " the theatre." Drama is the creation of the artist, but the theatre is an activity of the social organism, and is here studied simply as such.

It is perhaps curious that the English theatrical world should ante-date the English theatre, but the actors were an organized profession long before anyone saw the commercial possibilities of erecting special buildings for them. The recognized " players of the King's Interludes " date back to the time of Henry VII ; Leicester is known to have

---

[1] The bare facts concerning the latter can be found, if required for reference, in Appendix IV.

given his patronage to a company of players as early as
1559.   When not required by their lord for private entertainments or for service at Court, these companies, whether
playing in London or touring in the provinces, had to take,
as a rule, any such haphazard inn yard accommodation as
they could get, set up a temporary stage, and take it down
again and pack up their properties when the show was
over.   It was not until 1576 that someone realized that a
theatre building would be a sound financial proposition.
James Burbage, then an actor, originally a joiner, was not
so famous on the stage as his son Richard, but he was a
good man of business.   He saw that London was determined at all costs to have a drama, was even ready to pay
for it.   He estimated the future of the drama as such a
certain thing that he risked the borrowing of several
hundred pounds in order to build a playhouse in Shoreditch.
In 1576 he erected the first English theatre—a wooden
building, partly inspired by a recollection of the inn yards
in which he had played, partly by the bull- and bear-baiting
rings on the south side of the river.   It had a platform
stage which projected into the middle of the auditorium, so
that the audience surrounded it on three sides ; it had no
roof, except over the galleries where the audience sat ;
and it had neither front curtain to its stage nor artificial
light.   Burbage's financial instinct proved perfectly sound ;
he had to pay heavy interest on his loan, but even so he
made a handsome profit out of " The Theatre " from the
first.   Rivals were not slow to follow his example.   Within
a year he had a near neighbour in " The Curtain " ; and
within less than a decade several playhouses had sprung
up on the Bankside.   It meant that for good or ill the
commercial theatre in England was launched on its career ;
it means that in surveying the Elizabethan theatrical world
one of the important things to be taken into account is that
eternal bogey of the literary man—the box-office point of
view.
     Notwithstanding its success, however, the commercial
theatre began its career under a severe handicap.   The
sites it was forced to choose for its buildings were not the

sites its business men would have selected had they possessed any freedom of choice. Finsbury Fields and the Bankside, it is true, had long been frequented by the Londoner for his recreation ; in the former archery, cock-fighting, football and other athletic festivities had always been practised ; on the Surrey side there were bull- and bear-baiting rings, Paris garden with the royal dogs and bears, and butts in St. George's Fields for the archers In summer the suburbs served the players' needs well enough, but in the autumn or winter months miry ways through the fields might well deter an audience—a good fire and a pack of cards would be a strong counter-attraction. South-wark and the northern suburbs, however, were the only alternatives open to the players, because the city fathers set their faces resolutely against any theatre building within their liberties. Luckily for the drama, the sway of the Lord Mayor and his aldermen ended in the middle of London Bridge and at the northern gates—beyond those limits theatres on the north and the south came, respec-tively, within the jurisdiction of the justices of the peace for Middlesex and Surrey. In the circumstances the situa-tions chosen were the best possible, but they give one reason why the disrepute attached to certain of the suburbs attached itself as well to the theatres, and they also explain why it was that up till the very end of the reign the players still made use of the inn yards, in spite of their obvious drawbacks and the equally obvious advantages of the real theatres.

The two main forces in the business world of the Eliza-bethan theatre were the Burbage family and a certain Philip Henslowe, who speculated in it with equal success. Minor ventures came and went, but the Burbage and Henslowe enterprises survived, mainly because they had identified themselves throughout with the acting and play-writing interests, and were never purely commercial. At the end of the century the lease of the ground where Burbage had built " The Theatre " ran out. Naturally his sons and inheritors, Cuthbert and Richard, wished to renew it, and continue their profitable enterprise, and so made overtures to their landlord. This latter personage, however, a certain Giles Allen, who had two objects in his mind, felt that his opportunity had come at last. As a God-fearing citizen—urged probably by the God-fearing city fathers—he wished to put an end to " The Theatre's " existence ; as a business man and landowner he was naturally not averse to making some profit for himself, even out of such a damnable enterprise. He therefore offered his tenants a few years' lease at an increased rental, with the proviso that the building should pass into his possession when the lease was up—terms neatly designed to serve both God and Mammon. Naturally, the Burbages refused them, and with an audacity and an enterprise worthy of their father's sons, they quietly gathered together a number of good fellows, and setting to work with a will they dismantled London's first playhouse, removed every piece of timber that was worth preserving, and transferred all the material bodily to the south side of the river, where it was presently incorporated in the fabric of that most famous of all Elizabethan theatres, " The Globe," associated for all time with Shakespeare and some of his greatest plays. Of the doubtful legality [1] of their proceedings they appear to have had more than a suspicion, as their equipment indicates. " Swords, daggers, bills and axes " aided them to enforce what was perhaps a moral if not a legal right, in what the irritated landlord described as " a very riotous, outrageous and forcible manner." Legal or not, Giles Allen was successfully tricked, and " The Globe " was successfully erected on the Bankside by 1599.

The theatrical world in general must have chuckled over the Burbages' exploit, although one or two individuals may have been slightly perturbed thereby. Hitherto Henslowe, in partnership with his son-in-law Edward Alleyn the actor, had had a practical monopoly of the theatrical profits on the south side of the river. His pleasantly named " Rose " and his unnamed playhouse at Newington Butts had never been seriously rivalled by the only other theatre in the

---

[1] The original lease contained a clause permitting them to remove the building at the end of their tenancy. This lease, however, had expired although their tenancy continued.

neighbourhood—a short-lived venture known as " The Swan," which ceased to be used for plays after 1598.[1] Now he found his monopoly seriously threatened by the successful man from the north. Henslowe and Alleyn, however, had their own share of business acumen ; with " The Theatre " gone, and only " The Curtain " left to cater for the northern audiences there was an opportunity for a move into the territory formerly occupied by their rival. By 1600 they had erected in Golden Lane, Cripplegate, a fine new playhouse which they called " The Fortune." From that date " The Globe " and " The Fortune "[2] became London's leading theatres, and the two rival companies, Burbage's and Alleyn's, became more or less permanently associated with them. Such, in brief, was the history of the establishment of the theatre as a commercial enterprise. It is worth while, at the outset, to realize this aspect of its existence, so as to grasp the fact that the theatre is yet another product of the commercial and organizing genius of the age. It reminds us that the generation which could produce a Shakespeare was also the generation which began to regard land as a profitable investment and ait as something that could be exploited commercially. Once the Burbages and Henslowe had dis covered its possibilities we were committed to the modern theatrical situation at which the theatre's best lovers to-day find themselves continually chafing.

With the fact of the Elizabethan theatre thus established, we may turn to its relation to the life of the community, and see what it meant to its contemporaries. Here, inevitably, we shall meet many contradictory or divergent points of view ; only by considering these separately shall we be able to form an idea of how the theatre impinged upon London life. If we begin by regarding it from the point of view of the tiring-house, or of the actors themselves, it appears a delightfully practical affair—a matter of wigs and beards and properties, parts and cues, " noises off,"

---

[1] Until 1611, when it was again used for plays for four years.
[2] " The Globe " was burnt down in 1613, rebuilt a few years later, and finally dismantled in 1644. "The Fortune" was burnt in 1621, rebuilt two years later, dismantled in 1649, and pulled down in 1661.

dresses and prompt books. It is easy enough to find one's way " behind the scenes "; it has amused several of the dramatists to conduct us there in person, and what is more, the most important document in the history of the Elizabethan stage happens to interest itself very largely in just these points. The document in question is Henslowe's " Diary," with which are generally grouped the " Henslowe Papers "; together they give us an invaluable record of all the details relating to the running of an Elizabethan playhouse. Philip Henslowe was neither actor, author, nor literary man ; he was, as we have seen, the father-in-law of the actor Edward Alleyn ; he was part-owner, with Alleyn, of two theatres, " The Rose " on the Bankside and " The Fortune " in Cripplegate ; and he was a sufficient capitalist to enable him to become a theatrical financier. When a company played at his theatre he managed their finances and most of the business transactions for them, taking care to make a substantial profit out of their tenancy. Luckily for us he was the kind of man who put everything on paper ; providentially, also, fortune sent him in Alleyn a surviving son-in-law and partner who hoarded anything in the nature of a document—hence the preservation amongst the archives of Alleyn's College of God's Gift at Dulwich of this unique and priceless record, the famous " Diary."

In the " Diary " and the " Papers " Henslowe jotted down, in the most execrable spelling, notes of all kinds of monetary transactions, theatre receipts, agreements, loans to needy playwrights, lists of properties, and apparel. Without Henslowe we should probably not have guessed that Tamburlaine strutted through his part in crimson velvet breeches and a coat trimmed with copper lace— quaint attire for the world conqueror ! Nor should we have known that if an actor happened " to be overcome with drink at the time when he ought to play " the Henslowe management would certainly mulct him ten shillings. But for Alleyn's delight in hoarding papers we should not possess an Elizabethan actor's individual part ; there at Dulwich is Alleyn's own part of Orlando Furioso in Greene's play of that name—a manuscript text, complete with cues, written on small sheets of paper which have been pasted together to form a long roll.

When a company procured a new play the manuscript copy supplied by the author was turned over to the stage-manager, who added to it all such necessary prompt directions as the author would not have been likely to insert—such as the cues for alarms and noises. Then each actor had to have his own part prepared. Snug's anxiety, when his character has been assigned him, to know whether Quince has " the lion's part written," so that he might begin conning it at once, was probably shared by other actors who were also " slow of study." Meanwhile the stage-manager would be busy about two other items essential to the equipment of the play. He would, like Quince, draw up " a bill of properties such as the play wants," and he would also prepare what was known as a " plot "—a skeleton outline of the play in the form of an entrance and exit list, with notes of the noises, music, and properties required, to hang beside the prompter, where both he and the actors might consult it at need. Here again Alleyn has preserved invaluable specimens for us.

If the play required new costumes these would be the most expensive item of the production. The Elizabethan stage made up in part for its lack of scenery by the gorgeousness of its costume. A play was not very expensive to buy ; £5 or £6 was the sum ordinarily paid by the companies who played at Henslowe's theatre, improving to something nearer £10 about the beginning of the next reign. But a fine cloak might cost as much as £20, and the materials—silk, damask, satin, and velvet—used for many of the gowns and doublets, even when not of the finest quality, were all extremely costly. With their cloth of gold and silver and their finery of every brilliant colour —orange-tawny, blue, peach-colour, carnation, and crimson—the players had heavy bills to foot when it came to a reckoning with Henslowe for the money expended by him in advance on their behalf. That they played ordinarily in contemporary costume would not reduce their expenses ;

display was essential, even if on closer inspection the gold
should turn out to be tinsel. And although distant times
counted for little upon the Elizabethan stage, and the con-
spirators met to plot the death of Cæsar clad in doublet
and hose, with " their hats plucked about their ears, and
half their faces buried in their cloaks," nevertheless the
strange and the marvellous had to lend diversity to the
actor's attire. A " fire-drake's suit " for some unknown
play is entered in one of Henslowe's lists ; and we come
frequently across such items as pierrots' suits, green coats
for Robin Hood and his merry men, coats for shepherds,
gowns and hoods for friars, and a cardinal's hat, all helping
us to visualize for ourselves the degree of realism in cos-
tuming attainable upon the public stage.

The lack of scenery in the public theatres is an historical
commonplace :

> When Burbage played, the stage was bare
> Of fount and temple, tower and stair ;
> Two backswords eked a battle out ;
> Two supers made a rabble rout ;
> The throne of Denmark was a chair.

In the same way the most casual modern reader of Shakespeare generally realizes that when the playwright wishes to
make his audience picture to themselves the surroundings
amidst which his characters move he accomplishes his aim
by description. Unfortunately, both these commonplaces
have led from the correct assumption of a lack of painted
scenes to the incorrect deduction of a complete lack of
realism and of attempts at scenic illusion. Nothing could
be more fundamentally misleading, and it is a mistake
which the most rudimentary acquaintance with the psychology of actors and audiences in all ages should have made
impossible. The first instinct of both is to demand an
illusion of reality, and it is absurd to let ourselves imagine
that the poetry of the plays was used in lieu of anything
except paint. It created " atmosphere," and we rightly
admire these set-pieces of exquisite description, and, incidentally, the audience which had the good taste and

appreciation to listen to them ; but for all that, the thing seen and the thing done were all-important on the Elizabethan stage.   Expense made it impossible for the actors in the public playhouses to attempt to rival the wonderful painted scenes used in the Court masques ; poetry was the only substitute their means could purchase, luckily for posterity.   Nevertheless, the popular audience of Shakespeare's day was not so different from our own that the actor could rely on poetry and poetry alone ; " realism " of a certain kind was as much a necessity then as it is now. The Elizabethan professional may not have been able to pay for the paint and the carpentry lavished upon a Court production, but he had at his disposal just those scenic resources which the impecunious but ingenious amateur of to-day has, namely, dresses and properties.   He knew how to attain the illusion of royal state by his property throne, his glass-jewelled crowns and sceptres, his gay and glittering robes.   He could not give his audience the very trees of that wood near Athens as a modern producer can, if he so pleases ; but he could grace Titania's bower with a mossy bank and some greenery, and Bottom had his ass head then as now.   A bedchamber is, after all, essentially indicated by its bed ; a tavern by its trestles and settles, its flagons and tankards ; a battle-field by the broadsword combats of armed men and alarums of drums and trumpets. There was no background of flaming cities and falling towers to set off the triumphal march of Tamburlaine, but he had a chariot to ride in, and a bridle [1] for those " pampered jades of Asia," the unfortunate monarchs who were condemned to draw it.

An Elizabethan stage-manager could not darken the stage of his open theatre to add a greater terror to the murder of Edward II in that foul vault of Berkeley Castle, but he could equip his murderers with lanterns just as he equipped the revellers in " The Merchant of Venice " or in " Romeo and Juliet " with flaring torches, which would of themselves be a sufficient indication of the night season, even to a modern audience.   He had rocks and tombs and

---

[1] Henslowe, as usual, records these items.

" Hell-mouth " itself to lend verisimilitude to his scene ;
the Admiral's men—Alleyn's company—while acting at
" The Rose " possessed, amongst other properties, a pair
(i.e. flight) of stairs, two steeples, a beacon, an assortment
of " dead limbs," a bay tree, two mossy banks, a snake, a
tree of golden apples, a rainbow, two coffins, a dragon, and
the cauldron designed by the Jew of Malta for the boiling
of his enemies, into which he was himself most unfortunately precipitated at the conclusion of the play. Skulls
and bones lent local colour to every stage graveyard, and
for " poles and workmanship for to hang Absalom "
Henslowe expended one shilling and twopence in 1602.

Realism, indeed, was carried just as far as was humanly
possible on the Elizabethan stage, and a good deal farther
than some of us would altogether appreciate to-day. One
good example is possibly sufficiently lurid to carry final
conviction on this point. We realize that somehow or
other an illusion that Absolom was " hanged " was contrived upon the stage ; we know that in " King Lear "
Gloucester was blinded upon the stage ; from Peele's
" Battle of Alcazar " those of us who are of a sluggish
imagination may learn what incidents of this kind really
looked like, when presented by an Elizabethan company.
In this play there is a dumb show at the beginning of the
third act, in which three of the characters are slaughtered.
A marginal note in the prompter's " plot " [1] states that at
this juncture " 3 violls of blood and a sheep's gather " are
the properties required. As a " gather " consists of the
animal's heart, liver, and lungs, it is not difficult to visualize
the gory realism with which one of these organs was torn
out of the breast of each of the victims. [2] That was
" realism " as it was understanded of Burbage and Alleyn
and their contemporaries.

Here, then, is sufficient indication to the curious that the
grease-paint and rehearsal aspect of the Elizabethan theatre
is in no way buried in obscurity. There are many glimpses
too of the actors and authors and theatre-goers which

---

[1] Cf. page 230. Generally spelled " plat " or " platte ".
[2] W. W. Greg: " Two Elizabethan Stage Abridgements."

hardly seem three hundred years old. Stage-struck gallants could not write sonnets to their favourite " actresses " when all female parts were played by boy-players, but they delighted to entertain players to supper in a tavern.[1] Players were human enough to delight to wear their splendid costumes to impress the friends and acquaintances with whom they dined or supped, so that Henslowe was forced to institute a system of fines to prevent undue wear and tear of the company's stock. Foolish fellows whose great delight was to call attention to themselves waited to take their places till the Prologue-speaker was ready to begin the play. For a final example, before leaving the tiring-house, here is the author as he sometimes appeared to the player, " officiously befriending " everybody behind the scenes, anxiously watching the progress of his play and standing ready " to prompt us aloud, stamp at the book holder [i.e. the prompter], swear for our properties, curse the poor tireman, rail the music out of time, and sweat for every venial trespass we commit." [2]

The theatre thus meant a practical day's work to the actor, but it meant something very different to the city authorities and the Master of the Revels—to mention but two sets of people who were vitally affected by its existence. To the former it was always a thorn in the flesh ; to the latter it meant a source of income and a test of his perspicacity. All plays had to be submitted to him, and receive his licence before they could be performed ; and for each play read he received from the company producing it a fee of seven shillings, which was gradually increased as time went on.[3] As the official licenser of plays it was his business not to watch over the morals of the community but to take care that nothing detrimental to the preservation of peace and authority should be spoken upon the stage. Shakespeare and his fellows were free to disturb men's social consciences as much as they pleased, and to probe as deeply as they wanted into the rottenness of current morality ; but they were emphatically not free to

---

[1] Jonson : " Everyman out of his Humour."
[2] " Cynthia's Revels."
[3] " Henslowe's Diary," ed. Greg, II, 115.

make remarks calculated to upset people's religious ideas, nor to touch upon topics of current politics. Meddling in matters of statecraft was not tolerated, and anything calculated to create a disturbance in the theatre or in the City had to be cut out. The theatre was subject to a strict censorship, but not of a destructive kind ; the censor who for political reasons forbids topical allusions is, albeit unwittingly, the drama's permanent benefactor—he encourages a healthy universality.

To the Privy Council the theatre meant a perfectly legitimate amusement for Court and City, which to themselves, as Privy Councillors, was nevertheless a constant source of trouble. The Queen wanted plays at Court at Christmas and other festive seasons, so there was no question but that players had to be tolerated and allowed to exercise their craft. The players, further, had protectors in the great noblemen who were their avowed patrons ; a powerful and an angry earl might have to be reckoned with when summary restrictions were imposed upon his men. On the other hand, there was the City, avowedly hostile to plays and players, and in a strong position to deal with both. Charged by the Privy Council with the duty of preserving law and order within their bounds, and of taking all precautions necessary to the public health, the Lord Mayor and Aldermen had a strong card to play whenever plague broke out or at any time when the political situation made unruly gatherings inadvisable. The theatre therefore kept the Privy Council busy, endeavouring to keep the peace between warring interests and demands ; it meant long, tactful letters to obtain privileges which the City had no desire to yield if it could possibly help it, and it meant at times letters in which the tact had worn very thin indeed, and in which relations between Crown and City were not all that might be desired.

To the City itself, as represented by the Lord Mayor and Aldermen, the theatre was an unmitigated nuisance. Quite apart from the growing feeling of protest amongst the Puritan section of the community—protest based on moral and religious grounds—the practical problems of plays and players made them only too anxious to banish both from their midst. Puritan feeling was strong in London, and the preachers of more extreme reforming tendencies were zealous in their denunciation of the stage. Time and again from their pulpits they thundered forth the wrath of God on the Sabbath breakers who left the churches empty and thronged to the play ; in every visitation of the plague they saw the hand of the Lord laid heavily upon the ungodly in punishment of their lewd delights, of which the stage was the first and worst. In sermon and pamphlet they and their adherents reiterated their charges ; the theatres were the haunts of immorality—inevitable from their situations ; the plays themselves gave incitement to evil passions in the young by their representations of murder, treason, loose living, adultery, and intrigue. Fervently they appealed to the magistracy in London to put an end to the whole bad business of plays and players. And the magistracy, harassed by the problem of the health of their city and by the danger of riotous assemblies, would have been only too glad to yield to the Puritan demand, had it not been for the Privy Council and the players' important patrons. The legislative measures, however, which classified players as rogues and vagabonds and threatened them with whipping in punishment of their " lewd manner of life " excepted all who were attached as his " servants " to any baron of the realm or other " honourable Personage of greater degree " (16 Eliz., cap. 5). Burbage's company, under the patronage of the Queen's cousin, Lord Hunsdon, a member of the Privy Council and Lord Chamberlain of England, was legally entitled to exercise its craft ; Alleyn's company, under the patronage of the Earl of Nottingham, Lord Admiral, was in an equally strong position ; the utmost the Lord Mayor and Aldermen could do was to regulate the places, hours, and seasons for playing and to issue strict inhibitions whenever an epidemic overtook their insanitary city. After years of struggle the whole matter settled down into a kind of workable compromise ; no public theatres could be erected within the city boundaries,

but on the other hand permission could be extorted by the
Privy Council for inn yard performances at such places as
the " Cross Keys " in Gracechurch Street ; plays were to
be allowed, but only on week-days ; they were to be banned
entirely during Lent and in time of plague. " For the good
government of the city, as for conscience sake, being persuaded . . . that neither in polity nor in religion " should
plays be suffered in a Christian Commonwealth' the Mayor
and Aldermen were " humble and earnest suitors " to the
Council that the plays and the theatres might be finally
suppressed, even as late as the year 1597.[1] Their protest
was unavailing ; the vitality of the drama itself, the
universality of its appeal, its influence, and the commercial
backing behind the theatres, were too strong for all the
city fathers. Before Elizabeth's reign was over the battle
was already fought and won, and the theatre had come to
stay.

We are left finally with the point of view of the person
who was very largely responsible for all this trouble about
plays and players, namely, the ordinary playgoer. Everything came back to one question—Was this individual to
have his theatre or not ? There was never any question
whether the Queen and the nobles were to have their
plays and players and the kind of drama that such an
audience would naturally evoke ; that had been settled in
Henry VIII's time, if not long before ; and the drama and
its exponents would have persisted if the man in the street
had been but barely aware of their existence. But the
thing that for good and ill made the Elizabethan drama
what it was and determined its whole character was the
fact that the ordinary citizen decided that what was good
for his betters was good for him also. The average Englishman discovered that the drama was as good an entertainment as bear-baiting ; and he was so convinced that this
was the way in which he wanted to spend his leisure hours
that he was prepared to pay for it. When its determina-
tion is put to and survives that test, the public gets what
it wants in the modern era ; and the Elizabethans,

[1] Letter from the Lord Mayor and Aldermen 28th July, 1597.

committed to the adventure of modernity, got their theatre. Like Dekker's gull, the ordinary man stepped upon the stage, " a teston [i.e. sixpence] mounted between a forefinger and a thumb," and forth came Burbage and Henslowe to provide him with his theatre, and then came Marlowe and Shakespeare to provide the theatre with its plays. That sixpence was at the root of all the trouble endured by the Privy Council and the Worshipful the Lord Mayor, and it was the man who was prepared to produce that sixpence and pay for his amusement who determined the character of the theatrical fare provided for him. It is nonsense to imagine that all Elizabethan drama is great literature ; once Shakespeare is excepted, the larger part of it simply caters for its paymaster, the great British public of 1595 and the succeeding decade.

Shakespeare was a happy accident, and " belongs to the ages " ; the commercial theatre may have given him his opportunity, influenced his technique, and determined his methods, but in essentials he has neither part nor lot in a discussion such as this. The average Elizabethan play, however, was written and chosen from the box-office point of view. Regarded from this angle the good play, then as now, is the play that fills the house. Box-office psychology is largely empirical—it is the practical man, with experience of the average audience, trying to estimate its tastes and reactions in advance. Fear of experiment and desire of novelty result in a succession of plays made from the same old ingredients but served up with a different sauce whenever possible. As a point of view it is not necessarily unintelligent ; it is simply the business man's attempt to cater in art, and the supply certainly bears some relation to the demand—the audience generally has something to do with the much-maligned result. The Elizabethan audience might differ in several respects from that of the present day ; the Elizabethan box-office might represent different interests ; but the relation between the two was undoubtedly the factor which determined the bent of the contemporary drama.

The Elizabethan box-office was, however, a more pleasantly co-operative affair than the modern ; practically, it was the company, or at any rate the chief members thereof. In Shakespeare's case it included the company's chief playwright. It was the normal thing for the authors and actors between them, and more particularly the latter, to make the practical reckoning ; the box-office was not in the hands of the business man from outside, speculating in plays, but in the hands of the artists who were forced into the position of being their own business men. It was the actor-manager's income, the hero's income, the villain's, the chief comedian's that suffered, if, between them, they failed to pick a play that would catch the public fancy. Salaries would be drawn by the hired men and boys then as now, whatever the fate of the play ; but some dozen members of the company would, in the average enterprise, be in the position of shareholders, looking for their portion of the takings : Shakespeare, for example, had a one-tenth share in the Globe Theatre. Such being the case we may expect a more happy union of art and interest than is usually possible to-day.

The audience upon whose patronage the actors depended and whose tastes they had to estimate was genuinely representative. The fanatical puritan—and consequently numbers of the well-to-do citizens—kept away : there was certainly a preponderance of men, and notably of young men ; but otherwise differences of sex and age, class and creed were immaterial. The drama was an Elizabethan national taste—like music. The theatre, as Dekker says, allows " a stool as well to the farmer's son as to your templar ", the Inns of Court gentleman : " your carman and tinker claim as strong a voice in their suffrage, and sit to give judgment on the play's life and death " as well as the professed critics and the courtiers and gallants.

The Elizabethan audience had its intellectuals who complained bitterly about the defects of the average play. Sidney and Jonson [1] speak for this minority, and incidentally give us the preferences of the ordinary theatre-goer. There was, for example, the gentleman " with more beard than brain " who liked a good old-fashioned play with no " humourous " nonsense about it, and who always swore

[1] See *Apology for Poetry, Everyman in his Humour, Cynthia's Revels.*

when he reluctantly attended Ben Jonson's latest effort "that the old Hieronimo, as it was first acted, was the only best and judiciously penned play of Europe." These good people who had found "The Spanish Tragedy" the play of the century formed a large part of the typical audience years after the drama itself had left that stage of its development behind. Ben Jonson might have the strength of mind to refuse them the "whining ghosts," the crude sensationalism, the half-dozen odd murders, the extravagant passions, and the noises and alarums of the earlier type, but the ordinary writer was much more concerned to please his audience than to educate it. It is even possible that, not being a Ben Jonson, the ordinary dramatist shared his audience's tastes, and wrote in all good faith. The dramatists had no theories of romantic art ; they were not rebels against the classical tradition ; they were too busy making practical experiments on the stage. They knew perfectly well from their own experience that their audiences did not in the least object to the marvellous and the improbable—that, in fact, they definitely preferred a certain admixture of the high astounding. Hence that complete disregard of time and place which so horrified the intelligentsia[1]—" Now ye shall have three ladies walk to gather flowers, and then we must believe the stage to be a garden. By and by we hear news of shipwreck in the same place, and then we are to blame if we accept it not for a rock. Upon the back of that comes out a hideous monster with fire and smoke, and then the miserable beholders are bound to take it for a cave." The audience took a positive delight in seeing

> a child, now swaddled, to proceed
> Man, and then shoot up, in one beard and weed,
> Past threescore years.

They delighted in a good skilful display of target-fighting, fencing, or broadsword ; they marvelled at stage thunder and lightning and at the rumbling of a storm counterfeited by drums behind the scenes, and naturally the dramatists

[1] See the present writer's *Shakespeare's Audience* in *Shakespeare and the Theatre* (1927).

gave these to them in good measure. As soon as audiences began to develop other tastes the dramatists altered their methods. When men began to be less interested in the fantastic and more interested in ordinary life we get at once, round about 1600, a sort of Jacobean Manchester School of domestic tragedy and comedy. Once we look at it from an angle other than the literary one, we cannot help realizing that because the Elizabethan theatre was the commercial theatre in embryo " the drama's laws the drama's patrons gave."

And so we finish up where we began—in the commercial theatre. The roots of our modern system go very deep, as deep as 1576. The Elizabethan state was essentially the modern state in its recognition of the importance of money ; it is entirely characteristic of the age that it should create the theatre—double harness for drama and commerce. That the result, from the point of view of literature, was not the degraded product that the drama can be in these circumstances we have to thank the Elizabethan audience, the peculiar quality of the national imagination, and the actors themselves. However much the idealist may deplore relations between art and commerce, the fact remains that it was the union of the two that gave us the Elizabethan drama. The Court demand for entertainment could never have evoked what the national demand did ; the people decided that drama was what they wanted, and thereby created the right atmosphere, favourable to the production of the dramatist's work. But it was the theatre that linked supply and demand, and gave the drama its chance to survive as a national drama. " Money talked " in the Elizabethan age. Burbage and Alleyn were respectable and prosperous, not to say wealthy, citizens ; and when the inhabitants of a certain district discovered that the erection of a playhouse in their midst would mean a substantial contribution to the poor rates, scruples faded away and all joined together to petition that the building should proceed forthwith.

The actors could have acted without theatres, but the theatre meant strength, obtained by organization and financial resources ; that the drama, in spite of all civic and Puritan opposition, was able to establish itself as a popular and national amusement, it may thank the commercial enterprise that we call the theatre. It is this popular and national character that gives the Elizabethan drama its vitality and its unique value. Elizabeth's pleasure may have been a convenient excuse for harassed authorities, driven to yield upon a point of principle ; but the real and happily worded reason for both the goodness and the badness and the existence of this body of work was simply expressed in 1574, in the special licence given by the Queen to James Burbage and four others to perform all kinds of plays throughout England—" as well for the recreation of our loving subjects as for our solace and pleasure."

Note 1.—Since 1944 G. R. Kernodle's " From Art to Theatre " has made us realize that the Elizabethan stage may have been a more decorative and less homely affair than has hitherto been generally supposed. Kernodle argues for a more elaborate and richly coloured architectural background, reminds us of the Fortune's carved columns and the Swan's stage pillars painted to imitate marble, and quotes Nashe's " Pierce Pennilesse " to witness that " Our scene is more stately furnished than ever it was in the time of Roscius ". For the suggestions made by J. Cranford Adams about structure and size see Appendix IV.

Note 2.—Since the third edition of this book an excellent study of " Shakespeare's Audience", by A. Harbage, has appeared. Mr. Harbage has investigated the size and make-up of the average theatre audience—not without a sense of humour, nor without warnings about statistics, his own included. To summarize a few of his findings does scant justice to the thoroughgoing ingenuity and pertinacity of the whole study. He accepts contemporary evidence as to the capacity of the Elizabethan theatres : as, for example, De Witt's statement that the Swan held 3,000, and Nashe's comment (in his " Pierce Pennilesse ") on how it would have joyed brave Talbot—" the terror of the French " in " Henry VI "—to have drawn the tears of " 10,000 spectators at least (at several times) ". He believes that the Rose held about 2,500 spectators, and the Fortune just over 2,300 ; and that the total audience for all the London theatres in 1595 works out at a daily average of 2,500 and a weekly average of 15,000. Relating audiences to the total population, he works out that in 1605 two persons in every fifteen went to the theatre every week. On a basis of 563 penny patrons, 594.4 twopenny patrons, and 91.6 threepennies, he reckons that an averagely good house at the Rose in 1595 took £8 9s. (cf. the £10 fee given for a Court performance). A popular " hit ", such as " The Wiseman of West Chester," taking £8 as its average, would therefore gross £256 with its 32 performances. This is an exciting book ; and not the least valuable of the points made is the stress laid on the predominance of *young* people in the audience, notably the student and apprentice elements.

CHAPTER XV

WONDER-BOOKS AND OLD WIVES' TALES

"DRAGONS there are in Ethiopia, ten fathoms long," read the Elizabethan child—and grown-up child too—in his Pliny ; and his mind, more happily attuned to the marvellous than ours, accepted it implicitly. The Middle Ages had passed away, but they had not taken with them all their superstition or their quality of soothfast-ness—that matter-of-fact acceptance of the impossible and the incredible which marked both their literature and their attitude to life. The Elizabethan child had a dull enough time in many ways, but he had easy access to wonder-books of all kinds. No one troubled to make any books specially for him, but what child would not prefer to take down surreptitiously from his father's bookshelf a genuine " grown up " book such as Pliny—" that excellent Natural Historiographer," as his translator calls him—and what child, turning over its pages, and coming upon that magical line, " Dragons there are in Ethiopia," would not be tempted to read on and discover for himself those marvels of beast-lore and travellers' tales in which his elders rejoiced ?

Setting out with Pliny to explore " The Secrets and Wonders of the World " the Elizabethan child learnt many things " right rare and strange." Every page yielded its full measure of marvels. There were wild dogs that had " hands and feet almost like men," and there was a won-drous tale—suggestive in its incomprehensibility—of some marvellous swift beasts of the northern regions " which have the upper lip so long that when they will feed they go backward." Then there was the lion, whose character as delineated by Pliny, is most gentlemanly : he is " full of nobleness and clemency and will sooner assail men than women, and never young children unless it be for great famine." Equally exemplary is the conduct of the panther who is also full of clemency : " We read that if a female meet a man strayed or lost in the woods, that fleeth for fear of her, she will compass him moving with her tail, showing unto him a sign of amity and love, and that after he is assured, she will lead him into a cave or hole wherein are fallen her young ones by misfortune, which the man pulleth out, and then she tumbleth and played before him to give him thanks." The section devoted to the sea-beasts, however, is perhaps even more amazing. From it the Elizabethan child learnt that " in the night there cometh many fishes out of the sea, that will eat the corn in the fields and after return again." Best of all, though, is the description of the Dolphin. Beginning soberly, it works up to an inimitable climax : " The dolphin is the most swiftest fish in the sea . . . above the nature of other fishes they love young children, and the sound of instruments, they live three hundred years . . . they rejoice when one calleth them Simon, and they love human voice." If only an illustrator had been employed to perpetuate in lively image the Dolphin rejoicing in his merry little heart when apostrophized as Simon ! It is only equalled by the information, vouchsafed suddenly in the midst of the " Book of the Little Beasts "—apropos of nothing at all— that " Zoroastes lived twenty years with cheese without feeling age."

And if Pliny disappointingly refused to follow up the subject of the Ethiopian dragons others were ready with any amount of information, for as Edward Topsell in his " Historie of Serpents " remarked, " Among all the kinds of serpents there is none comparable to the Dragon." He estimates the length of the Ethiopian variety at thirty yards, and provides his readers with a complete description of everything pertaining to the different species, from the tame Epidaurian kind with yellow-golden skins to the extra-fierce mountain dragons whose eyelids rattle with a sound like the tinkling of brass. It must have been delightful to be an Elizabethan child and to know that if only you had been born in Macedonia you could have had a tame dragon

of your own. " The most tameable dragons," you would
have learnt from Topsell, have very small mouths, and in
Macedonia the children play with them, " riding upon them
and pinching them as they would with dogs, without any
harm, and sleeping with them in their beds."

The question of the proper diet for dragons is also gone
into in great detail. They grow fat by eating eggs, and
their method of consuming them is highly diverting. A
grown-up dragon would swallow the egg whole, and then
roll about on the ground until it was crushed to pieces
inside him ; " but if it be a young dragon, as if it were a
dragon's whelp, he taketh the egg within the spire [i.e.
spiral coil] of his tail, and so crusheth it hard, and holdeth
it fast until his scales open the shell like a knife, then
sucketh he out of the place opened all the meat of the egg."
Was it, one is compelled to wonder, the youthful dragon
rather than the youthful human who originally gave rise
to the popular saying ? While eggs are agreeable to the
constitution of dragons, however, apples are poison, Topsell
assures us. Nothing so quickly upsets a dragon's digestion
as an apple ; and if a dragon determines to eat apples in
spite of his knowledge that they are bad for him, he always
takes the precaution—" so Aristotle affirmeth "—of eating
wild lettuce first, which acts as a remedy and " greatly
preserves his health."

The " moral value " of the dragon appears to be the old
one of all beast-lore—a good turn will always tame a good
dragon. Topsell has many dragon anecdotes to drive this
truth home, as well as others which illustrate their good
nature. After reading the story of the charming dragon
who loved the Thessalian neatherd because he had such
beautiful golden hair, and who always brought his friend
each day a gift " such as his nature and kind could lay hold
on," no Elizabethan child need have felt any terror of this
much misrepresented creature. Still more delightful is the
story of the dragon who loved Pindus. When Pindus was
killed the dragon kept watch over the dead body of his
friend, until he realized at last by the expressions on the
faces of the onlookers that they were afraid to approach.

As soon as this dawned upon him he immediately stood aside and " with an admirable courtesy of nature . . . gave them leave by his absence " to make all arrangements for the funeral. In fact, the only thing which appears seriously to reflect upon the character of dragons is their method of catching an elephant. On such an occasion they go hunting in packs, and when they come to a likely place they tie their tails together and stretch them across the path, so that when the poor elephant comes along he trips over them and stumbles, and in a moment the whole pack is upon him.

One looks in vain for a flicker of the eyelid. Topsell is absolutely serious. His books were intended to profit and delight the gentle reader. They were books into which a man might " look on the Holiest days (not omitting prayer and the public service of God) and pass away the Sabbaths in heavenly meditations upon earthly creatures." They were dedicated to a Dean, and their author signs himself " your chaplain in the Church of Saint Botolph, Aldersgate." They were Sunday reading for good citizens and good children, and Topsell would never have connived at the hoodwinking either of them or of the Dean.

The remote, as always, was matter for wonder, but so in those days was actuality. The pamphlet and ballad literature of the time abounded in marvels, stories of monsters, tempests, devils, and enchantments, generally attested by half a dozen excellent witnesses. One might not have the fortune to be present at the " strange and terrible wonder wrought very late in the parish church of Bungay near Norwich," but one could at least read a most circumstantial account of the terrible tempest which shook the church while the congregation were at their prayers between nine and ten in the morning, and of the black dog —who was, undoubtedly, the devil—that entered the building in the midst of the uproar. It wrung the necks of two of the kneeling worshippers so that they dropped down dead in their places, and then it clawed another man's back so that his skin shrivelled up " like leather scorched in a hot fire " ! One's own corner of the country might be quiet enough, but at Ditchet, in Somersetshire, rare things had happened, and there they were, plainly set down in print with the truth vouched for by seven respectable friends and relations. When produced from the chapman's bag its title must have lured many to buy ; nor would the purchaser have been disappointed by the contents of this " True and most dreadful discourse of a woman possessed with the devil ; who in the likeness of a headless bear [*a portrait is given below*] fetched her out of her bed and in the presence of seven persons most strangely rolled her through three chambers and down a high pair of stairs on the 4 and 20 of May last 1584 at Ditchet in Somersetshire."

Other counties, too, had their marvels, which sooner or later found their way into ballads, broadsides, or pamphlets. " Newes out of Cheshire " would tell of a wonderful healing spring, and the miraculous cures wrought upon those who had bathed in its waters. One's own village was a respectable God-fearing place ; nothing happened out of the ordinary in a twelvemonth. But at Hampstead a " monstrous pig " had been born in 1562, and in the same year yet another at Charing Cross with a head like a dolphin and forefeet like hands. There were the pictures of them, clear evidence to convince any sceptic. Yet more portentous and horrible were the accounts one might purchase from the pedlar of the monstrous children who were born, one near Colchester in Essex, another at Freshwater in the Isle of Wight, others at Mitcham in Surrey, Chichester, Maidstone, and Taunton. It was obvious, of course, why such unnatural happenings occurred ; they were a sure sign and token of God's wrath at England's wickedness, the direct and awful punishment of evil-doers, and a warning to all to mend their ways. Wicked folk indeed they must have been in these strange parts ; incredibly different from one's own law-abiding fellows . . . and those terrible storms of hail and thunder and lightning, that blazing star, the gales and the floods that travellers told of—were they not also the visitation of a justly incensed Heaven ? Indeed it behoved all men to look to their souls. Such marvels were not in the course of nature ; they had their meanings and there could be little doubt in the heart of any honest man what those meanings were. The day of miracles was not yet done. Travellers reported that near St. Neots in Cornwall there were seven upright stones set in the ground, and that the inhabitants called them " The Hurlers," believing that " they had been men sometimes transformed into stones for prophaning the Lord's Day with hurling the ball." [1]

For simple folk the marvellous lay all around them. There was an omen in the most apparently insignificant happening, generally a bad one. " It was not for nothing," Lancelot Gobbo asserts, " that my nose fell a-bleeding on Black Monday last at six o'clock in the morning." A swallow nesting in the eaves brought luck to the house ; but the hooting of the owl boded ill, and the raven presaged misfortune to all who heard its dismal note. Dogs howling in the night were held by many to be a portent of death ; so was a cow in the garden. One's own body gave many a warning : " By the pricking of my thumbs, something wicked this way comes." Dreams were meant to be interpreted, were warnings sent by God : " I dreamed mine eye tooth was loose and that I thrust it out with my tongue," says a character in one of Lyly's plays ; " it foretelleth the loss of a friend." The Elizabethan absorbed such old wives' superstitions as readily as his meat and drink. Why should he disbelieve them ? They were not tales for children, patently absurd to the adult intelligence —they were matters of general credit and anyone could furnish you with a dozen " modern instances " to uphold this granddam's wisdom.

One of the most marvellous aspects of life in those days must undoubtedly have been the " medicinal virtues " which appear to have been attached to anything of no obvious use or value. Quite apart from the difficulty of first catching your dragon one would have thought that the head of the beast could have been of little use to anyone ; but Topsell assures us that " the head of a dragon keepeth one from looking a squint and if set up at the gates and doors it hath been thought in ancient times to be very

[1] Camden : " Britania."

fortunate to the sincere worshippers of God." Even the eyes out of the head, "being kept till they be stale and afterwards beat into an oil with honey and made into an ointment keep any one that useth it from the terror of night visions and apparitions"; while the fat of a dragon dried in the sun is of great efficacy against creeping ulcers, or, if mingled with honey and oil, very helpful for dimness of the eyes.

We may be certain that no one suffered from these particular remedies, but from others of an equally curious nature there was less chance of escape. The sufferer from deafness may have avoided that very sovereign cure compounded from the bone taken from the tail of an armadillo, but it must have been much more difficult for the country lad whose hands were covered with warts to avoid his grandmother's prescription of "a mouse divided and laid upon them," or for his sister, when suffering from the toothache, to resist the good dames who wanted her to eat a mouse "flayed and beaten."

The *sorex*, which Topsell delightfully Englished as "the vulgar little mouse," figures in many an old wife's prescription. Regarded while alive as a domestic pest its corpse was immediately translated into a sphere of medicinal and cosmetic utility. One might cut a mouse in twain and lay it to the legs if afflicted with the gout; urged by vanity a fashionable dame might try the remedy of "young mice beaten into small pieces and mixed with old wine and so boiled," which "will very easily procure hair to grow upon the eyelids"; and the heads of mice, burnt, were said to make "an excellent powder for the scouring and cleansing of the teeth called tooth soap," spikenard being added to the mixture for the benefit of the squeamish.

Dead moles appear to have been almost as efficacious as pounded mouse in cases of toothache and baldness; and the left foot and claws of a hyæna, bound up in a linen bag and fastened to a man's right arm, had the excellent property of ensuring that the wearer should "never forget whatsoever he hath heard or knoweth." The blood of an elephant mingled with the ashes of a weasel made a sovereign cure for leprosy ; a piece of an elk's hoof, worn in a ring, would keep the owner from the falling evil, cramp, and fits ; for the cramp, again, a lynx's claw set in silver might be profitably worn. Only the rhinoceros, amidst this multifarious assemblage, appears doomed to inglorious uselessness, " for there is none of the ancient Grecians that have ever observed any medicines in the Rhinocerot."

John Aubrey, the seventeenth century anecdotist, who was curious in such matters gives, in his " Miscellanies " (1696), various charms and remedies he had come across. For toothache he has two cures which if no more convincing than the foregoing are decidedly less unpleasant and are of a kind that was equally prevalent in Elizabethan times. In one of them the sufferer has to " take a new nail and make the gum bleed with it, and then drive it into an oak." This, he avers, " did cure William Neal, . . . a very stout gentleman, when he was almost mad with the pain, and had a mind to have pistolled himself." The other remedy he gives on the authority of that Oxonian benefactor and antiquary, his friend Elias Ashmole, who " saw it experimented and the party immediately cured." It was little more than an old-fashioned charm with the pagan and Roman Catholic strata quite distinct :

> Mars, hur, abursa, aburse,
> Jesu Christ for Mary's sake,
> Take away this toothache.

This the sufferer had to write out on three separate pieces of paper ; he had then to burn them one by one, and the toothache would vanish.

With ghost lore and fairy stories the Elizabethan child had its mind filled from the time it could listen to a " winter's tale," told by the fireside by nurse or grandmother while the wind howled out of doors and the shadows flickered on the wall. " When I was a child," writes Aubrey, " the fashion was for old women and maids to tell fabulous stories nighttimes of sprights and walking of ghosts. This was derived down from mother to daughter.

. . . When the wars came, and with them liberty of conscience and liberty of inquisition the phantoms vanished.
Now children fear no such things having heard not of them,
and are not checked with such fears." Whether, indeed,
this oral literature can ever die out we may well question.
Pertinent to the matter in hand, however, is Aubrey's
assurance that the Elizabethan child drank its fill of such
marvels, whatever may have been the lot of his Restoration
grandson.

Fairies, witches, devils, ghosts, evil spirits, angels, and
monsters made up most of the matter of such tales. Outside in the meadow the little listener had seen the fairy
rings where the " good people " danced by night. He had
seen how the sheep, cropping the turf, moved away when
they neared the " sour ringlet," and then at night he
listened to his grandmother's cautionary tale of the boy
who went playing in a fairy ring, and was bewitched,
struck dumb, and stupid. He had watched the maid setting
aside a tiny bowl of cream for Hobgoblin Puck ; and when
he had come down in the morning and run to look he had
seen with his own eyes that the bowl was empty. With his
head full of old tales of Robin Goodfellow and his pranks,
what wonder that it never occurred to seven-year-old to
suspect the cat ? That ugly little baby in the village, that
puckered up its miserable tiny, wizened face and cried all
day—of course it was a fairy changeling. His nurse had
told him all about changelings, and how the little people
would always try to steal a beautiful human child out of
its cradle and put in its stead one of their own ailing, puking
brats—just like the baby in the village. He remembered
how when his little brother was born last year the midwife
had hung a knife from the canopy of the cradle, to keep
away fairies and witches :

> Let the superstitious wife
> Near the child's heart lay a knife ,
> Point be up and haft be down
> (While she gossips in the town)
> This 'mongst other mystic charms
> Keeps the sleeping child from harms.

Old Thomas Churchyard, in his " Handfull of Gladsome
Verses," gives us a pleasant doggerel summary of the tales
these old wives told ; of how

> . . oft in moonshine nights
> When each thing draws to rest
> Was seen dumb shows and ugly sights
> That feared every guest
> Which lodged in the house :
> And where good cheer was great
> Hodgepoke would come and drink carouse
> And munch up all the meat.
> But where foul sluts did dwell
> Who use to sit up late
> And would not scour their pewter well,
> There came a merry mate,
> To kitchen or to hall,
> Or place where sprites resort,
> Then down went dish and platters all
> To make the greater sport.

And so to bed—with a head full of " kit with the canstick,
dwarfs, giants, imps . . . the man in the oak, . . . the
fire drake, the puckle, Tom Thumb, Hobgoblin . . . and
other such bugs." [1]
   Witches were the most terrible of all these realities.
One might never have met the good people themselves, but
a witch was an old woman whom one might see with one's
own eyes :

> . . . poor, deformed and ignorant,
> And like a bow buckled and bent together.

A witch's black or white magic were real and potent arts.
A love charm could be purchased to win the regard of the
scornful ; and those who wanted a secret revenge could
surely compass an enemy's death if a wax figure were
moulded in his likeness, pierced as through the heart with
a needle, and put to melt by the fire.   As the little image
wasted, so would the victim droop and die.   Witches
could blast the corn in the air, send snakes to suck dry the

[1] Scot : " Discovery of Witchcraft."

udders of the cows, bring cramps and agues upon their enemies, and " overlook " an unbaptized child.

The Middle Ages had gone, and a few of their superstitions and marvels with them, but in their stead had come the wonders of a new world to enthral the imaginations of the young and the adventurous. In the realm of sober fact the prospect of England in the medieval period was bounded by the European horizon : for the Elizabethan there stretched a vista of vast, unexplored territories to conquer, untold treasures of gold and precious stones to be discovered, even perhaps Cipango, or the lost cities of Atlantis to lure men forth on their wanderings. For the stay-at-home the romance and the wonders of exploration were to be enjoyed in many a travel-book : " A certain Caravel, sailing in the West Ocean about the coasts of Spain, had a forcible and continual wind from the east, whereby it was driven to a land unknown, and not described in any map or card of the sea. . . ." It is the beginning of all adventure, it is romance, and it was the true story of what men were doing in far-away oceans. Stories there are in all these travel-books of storm and shipwreck, death and fighting ; there are cannibals and monsters, venomous trees, regions of blackamoors, giants with feet almost as long as two ordinary feet ! One might even read how the Virgin Mary in her own person overcame the devil in these lands where all marvels were true—lands of " gold, liberty and idleness," lotus-lands, slave-lands, El Dorado.

There were, too, maps in these wonder-books—maps which had not yet shaken off a medieval delight in the pictorial, maps which showed that their makers still realized, like Robert Louis Stevenson, that to all properly constituted imaginations a map was an inexhaustible fund of interest, something full of " infinite eloquent suggestion." There was the wonderful " Theatrum Orbis Terrarum " of Ortelius which, as Miss E. Seaton has recently shown, was the map that Marlowe used when he planned his Tamburlaine's world-conquering march. Not only might one feast one's fancy upon the high resounding names that Marlowe was to make into ringing music, but in Ortelius' seas, as

Miss Seaton says, " Mermaids, dolphins and flying fish rise above the surface, the whale waits open-mouthed to swallow Jonah, caravels and galliasses scud before the wind, slaves ply the oar in ' pilling brigandines ' and galleons grapple with bursts of smoke and flame." [1]

The flourishes of Ortelius' imagination were no more fantastic than the flourishes of the travel-books. Sober histories these were, written by the voyagers themselves ; yet might one read in their pages of how Sir John Hawkins and his men on their second voyage saw in the river of Rio la Hacha crocodiles, " some as big as a boat," which beasts, the tale-teller reports, are supposed " to cry and sob like a Christian body " when they wish to catch their prey, so as to provoke their victims to come to them— hence " this proverb that is applied unto women when they weep, *lachrymæ crocodili*." One might learn from the same source that there were lions in Florida, because there were unicorns there, and " there is no beast but hath his enemy . . . insomuch that whereas the one is the other cannot be missing." And it was all true, for did not these very men who had spoken with a Frenchman who had seen " a serpent with three heads and four feet of the bigness of a great spaniel "—did not these very men come safely home to Padstow in Cornwall on September 20, 1565, " with loss of twenty persons in all the voyage, and with great profit to the venturers of the said voyage as also to the whole realm, in bringing home both gold, silver, pearls and other jewels great store." The actuality of the gold and silver and the loss of twenty persons stamps it all as true.

Most Elizabethan books were wonder-books to their readers. Tales of travel and adventure lay ready to hand, their marvels enhanced by the possibility of gazing upon the " Golden Hind " in Deptford Dock. Geography to an Elizabethan meant discovery of countries yet unknown. Political pamphlets meant not statistics or theories, but exciting revelations of treason and rebellion, circumstantial narratives of the captures of Jesuits run to earth at last

[1] " Essays and Studies," English Association, Vol. X, 1924.

in a " priest's hole," hair-raising accounts of the practices of the Pope and the Roman Catholics and the martyrdoms of good Protestants. Pamphlet upon plagiaristic pamphlet thrilled honest country folk and sober citizens with anatomies of roguery, the whole art of conny-catching, by which unsuspecting folk in a great city like London might be cozened of their wealth. And although this popular exploitation of the printing press had begun, it had not as yet been able to destroy the older art of story-telling. Hand in hand with the marvels of the modern world went the oldest of old things—the strange happenings and the quaint beliefs that for generation after generation have been handed down in a winter's tale.

Note.—For a modern selection from Topsell, with reproductions of some of the woodcuts, see the present writer's " Elizabethan Zoo " (1926). For the contemporary view of the supernatural see Lewis Lavater's " Of Ghostes and Spirites Walking by Night " (1572), ed. J. Dover Wilson and M. Yardley, 1929. For geographical study in its wider aspects see E. G. R. Taylor's " Tudor Geography " (1930) and " Late Tudor and Early Stuart Geography " (1934) ; and for a well-illustrated study of cartographical ornament see E. Lynam, *Ornament, Writing and Symbols on Maps, 1200–1800* (reprinted from *Geographical Magazine,* 1946).   For the struggle between science and superstition over the part played by witchcraft and demonology in medicine and in Christian thought, see Paul H. Kocher, *Science and Religion in Elizabethan England* (Huntington Library, Cali-. fornia, 1953).

CHAPTER XVI

AN ELIZABETHAN DAY

SO far literature and documents, side by side, have
given us our material, illustrating and reinforcing
each other's value. For a final picture of the Elizabethan day, however, we may turn to literature alone :
having tested its truth and accuracy for ourselves throughout the preceding chapters we may at last be permitted
to take them for granted, and content ourselves with something which stands in need neither of commentary nor
explanation. Nicholas Breton, Dekker, Hollyband, Erondell, and Barnaby Googe can give us between them a " book
of hours " ; and with the help of Lady Hoby, an Elizabethan diarist, the last touch is added. The diary, standing
midway between literature and document, and partaking
of the nature of both, is the final link in the chain. Dekkei
as we have already seen, gives us a day in the life of a
foolish young man about town ; Hollyband and Erondell
give us, respectively, the day of the good citizen and his
family, and the day of the grand lady and her friends ;
Breton, in his " Fantasticks " gives us clear little vignettes
of town and country from morning till night ; Lady Hoby,
living on her Yorkshire estates and keeping her diary from
1599 to 1605, tells us, finally, how an Elizabethan gentlewoman of a strongly religious turn of mind passed her
quiet but fully occupied days.[1]

[1] Lady Hoby is an interesting figure. She was married three times—
first to Walter Devereux, younger brother of the Earl of Essex ; then to
Thomas Sidney, Sir Philip's younger brother ; lastly to Sir Thomas
Posthumous Hoby, younger son of the Sir Thomas Hoby who translated
Castgilione's " Il Cortegiano." Her diary is in the British Museum,
Egerton MS. 2614. So far as the present writer is aware, its value has
not been fully exploited by any general history of the Elizabethan age ;
" Shakespeare's England " (Chap. II), for example, merely refers to one
aspect of it. It has been fully described by Miss E. Fox in *Transactions of
the Royal Historical Society*, 3rd series, Vol. II , p. 153, and used by Miss V.
Wilson in *Society Women of Shakespeare's Time* (Chap. IV). Since the
first edition of this book appeared it has been admirably edited, with an
introduction, by Mrs. D. M. Meads : *The Diary of Lady Margaret Hoby*
(1930).

From all of them one fundamental thing emerges—the undoubted seriousness of life. After reading Lady Hoby, Googe, and Erondell, it is impossible to underestimate the part played by religion in normal family life. It is equally obvious that without an underlying seriousness of outlook in Dekker, we should not have had his masterly anatomy of folly. Lady Hoby's reading, for instance, consisted entirely of religious works—the Bible, sermons, Foxe's " Book of Martyrs," and books of famous theologians. A " Herbal " seems to have been her only secular volume. The unfortunate Lady Mary Grey supplies us with yet another example of an Elizabethan lady's library, and her books are every whit as serious as Lady Hoby's—A Bible, Foxe's " Martyrs," Latimer's Sermons, works by Whitgift, Luther, Cartwright, and Knox ; " The Ship of Assured Safety " by D. Cradocke, Book of Common Prayer, Psalter and Psalms, " The Dignity of the Scriptures," " The second course of the hunter at the Romish fox," " Life and selected Orations of Demosthenes," some French books—one a Bible, another a grammar and dictionary—and a few in Italian, including " A comment on the four Evangelists " and " A treatise of the Resurrection of the Dead." [1]

Lady Hoby never failed to begin the day with private prayer and reading of the Scriptures, nor to end it in similar fashion. During the day, too, she spent much time in her chamber, meditating, praying, or reading religious works and making notes thereon. Both in her household and in the imaginary one that Googe describes in his " Foure Bookes of Husbandry " a chaplain was kept who conducted public prayers every day, and talked with his employers of spiritual things. One of the interlocutors in Googe's dialogue commiserates with the country gentleman upon his distance from the church : " Neither can you hear the Sermons nor be present with your wife and your household at service." His friend soon shows him his error, however. " I have service every day at certain appointed hours," he explains, " where preacheth to me

---

[1] See Burgon : " Life and Times of Sir Thomas Gresham," II, 415-16.

daily the Prophets, the Apostles, Basil, Chrysostom, Nazianzen, Cyril, Cyprian, Ambrose, Austin, and other excellent preachers, whom I am sure I hear with greater profit than if I should hear your Sir John Lack-Latins and foolish fellows in your churches. My wife also, being given to reading, readeth the Bible and certain Psalms translated into our own tongue : if there be anything too hard or dark for her, I make her to understand it : besides, she hath private prayers of her own that she useth." His chaplain on holy-days reads the Gospel, teaches the Catechism, and ministers the sacraments ; and his household always " serve God before their going to work, and at their coming to meals." Lady Hoby's chaplain read aloud while she and her maids worked ; and she herself frequently instructed her servants and the poor of the neighbourhood in the " sound principles of religion." Between them, the diary and the dialogue give us an extraordinarily clear insight into the devotional life of an ordinary household of more or less Puritan persuasions, and reveal what a tremendously vital part preachings, prayers, and theo-logical exercises, reading and disputation played in the lives of the normal Elizabethan man or woman.

Having thus isolated and stressed this particular aspect of the Elizabethan day, however, it is time to leave matters to Breton and the rest and see what duties and pleasures each hour brought in its train. Round about three o'clock on a summer morning people in the country would begin to be stirring : the milkmaids would be off to the dairy, the ploughman harnessing his horses, and the por-ridge pot simmering for the servants' breakfast. At four the porridge would be served out, and the shepherd with his dog would be starting off to the fold. Beggars, at this hour, so Breton tells us, " rouse them out of the hedges and begin their morning craft " ; and at the inns travellers would be preparing for their day's journey. Anthony Munday and John Norden, whom we left overnight in their hostelry in Chapter V, would be astir and calling for their horses.

At " five of the clock " Breton calls fie upon all sluggards who are still in bed : " The bells ring to prayer, and the streets are full of people, and the highways are stored with travellers ; the scholars are up and going to school, and the rods are ready for the truants' correction." Not only is the morning's business well under weigh, but " the blind fiddler is up with his dance and his song, and the ale-house door is unlocked for good fellows."

At six even the city comes fully to life : " The shops begin to show their wares, and the market people have taken their places." The Eton boy goes to his morning prayers : and elsewhere " the scholars now have their forms, and whosoever cannot say his lesson must presently look for absolution." In the country falconers and huntsmen are about their sport, and the hounds have already roused a hare. Even the idlest cannot for shame linger in bed after six ; " The sun at every window calls the sleepers from their beds ; and the marigold begins to open her leaves, and the dew on the ground doth sweeten the air."

By eight it is time for breakfast ; the market people have sold their goods, and are packing up ; the thresher takes a well-earned rest, and eats his frugal meal. By eight even the beggar, with luck, will have wheedled the price of " a pot of the best " out of someone. The traveller takes his first rest on his journey and waters his horse. And so the business of the day is in full swing. " Oh ! " cries Breton, " 'tis a world to see how life leaps about the limbs of the healthful : none but finds something to do ! " In another of his books Breton, contrasting the habits of town and country, makes the countryman say : " We rise with the lark and go to bed with the lamb, so that we have the break of day and the brightness of the sun to cheer our spirits in our going to our labours, which many of you bar yourselves of by making day of the night and night of the day."

But even in the city the virtue of early rising went not unmarked. Erondell's " French Garden " has a most improving dialogue on the subject. The mistress calls out to the chambermaid to know why she has not roused her, and the maid replies that she did not like to wake her out of such a sound sleep. When the lady hears it is half-past seven she is horrified. " I went to bed yesternight so timely," she laments, " at the farthest at six o'clock : now I verify in me the grave speeches of that great Philosopher, the Emperor Marcus Aurelius speaking of the unsatiableness of mankind, when he said (among other things) the more I sleep the more I would sleep. Go to, go to, draw the window curtains : call my page, let him bring some wood to my chamber door ; make a fire quickly that I may rise." When her smock is warmed she calls for all her finery and, leaving the maid behind to tidy up the chamber, at last sallies forth to see to her family and the ordering of her household. Your gallant who revels it all night may lie abed till noon, but ordinary folk, whether rich or poor, country-bred or city-bred, will be about their business by eight o'clock. Realizing acutely, as we read their literature, that in losing the dawn hours we have lost something fresh and beautiful, it is comforting to our modern self-respect to find also that the late riser flourished then as now, in spite of the national habit. Schoolboys were as loath to leave their beds as the gallants, and could be seen rushing out of the house at eight o'clock. Tutors complained to parents that " Guy is somewhat slow to rise in the morning, for one must call him three or four times before he come out of his bed," whereupon the mother of Guy would explain more or less forcefully that the best cure for the disease of sluggishness was to anoint the limbs of the victim " with the juice of Birch, which is excellent for such a cure if you apply it but twice or thrice " ! [1] The satirists have many a fling at the city dames for rising at ten or eleven or noon ; and maidservants and waiting gentlewomen found it difficult to be ready even on the morning when their lady overslept herself until half-past seven. " Mistress Joly ! " calls the chambermaid, " my lady called you in great haste." " Good Lord ! What shall I do ? " flutters Mistress Joly, " she will chide me. I pray thee, sweetheart, help me a little to put on my gown, give me that rebato as it is, I will pin it anon, I have not

[1] Erondell : " French Garden."

leisure to do it now. I cannot find my kirtle nor my apron."

In all ranks of life men had their affairs and women their households to see to in the morning. A typical entry in Lady Hoby's diary is : " *Monday.* After private prayer I saw a man's leg dressed, took order for things in the house, and wrought till dinner time." Preserving and distilling were two important duties which even great ladies did not despise ; they prided themselves, rather, upon their skill in such matters, keeping the shelves of their still-rooms covered with waters and cordials of every description from rose-water to usquebaugh. " Went about my stilling : stilled aqua vitae," Lady Hoby records. At their proper seasons there were fruits to be dried, or preserved, quince or damson marmalade to be prepared, cucumbers to be pickled, jellies and jams to be made from all the fruits the gardens and orchards could yield, rose-leaves to be dried for pot-pourri, syrups to be made from roses or violets, and candied flowers and comfits of all kinds to be provided for a sweetmeat-loving generation that was prepared to ruin and blacken its teeth rather than give up its sugar stuff. Delicacies, such as almond butter, marchpane,[1] gingerbread, and all kinds of puff paste many a lady would prepare in person for her table, or at least supervise at their making. Skill, too, in the use of medicinal herbs and dressings was considered a proper part of every woman's education : " Looked upon a poor man's leg," " Gave a poor woman a salve for her arm," are typical entries for Lady Hoby. If a maid fell downstairs or a man injured himself in the fields it was to the lady of the house they were brought for treatment. She it was who applied cloths wrung out in hot water for bruises, or for aches and pains produced some of her herbs

---

[1] Marchpane was a favourite sweetmeat. Sir Hugh Platt's recipe is as follows : 2 lbs. of blanched and dried almonds, beaten in a stone mortar and mixed with 2 lbs. of sugar, add 2 or 3 spoonfuls of rose water ; roll paste flat, lay it on wafers, bake, and ice with rose water and sugar ; put in the oven until icing dries, and then " garnish with pretty conceits and birds and beasts being cast out of standing moulds. Stick long comfits upright in it, cast biscuit and carroways in it, and so serve it ; gild it before you serve it."—" Delightes for Ladies," 1602.

or lotions, grown in her own herb-garden, gathered, dried, and prepared by her own hands. In ways such as these Lady Hoby's morning was fully occupied, " taking order for things in the house," and in town and country alike all good housewives spent at least some of their mornings each week busy with domestic duties of this kind.

While their mother was thus engaged in her kitchen or her still-room or her dairy her daughters would either be at their lessons or else would be learning from her example how to manage a household for themselves. The daughters of the house in Erondell's " French Garden " have their French lesson between seven and eight o'clock in the morning. The dancing master, Charlotte tells us, " commeth about nine o'clock, our singing master and he that teacheth us to play on the virginals at ten : he that teacheth us on the lute and the Viol de Gambo at four o'clock in the afternoon." When not occupied with such lessons, or with domestic duties, they would sit with their governess or their gentlewomen " pricking of clouts," as Harington calls it—embroidering cushions with gold and silver thread, making crewel-work for hangings or coverlets, or spending infinite pains upon the lovely and elaborate " cut work " lace, so popular for ruffs and collars and cuffs. Charlotte and Fleurimond in the " French Garden " are summoned to wait upon their mother in the long gallery in order that she may criticize their needle-work. Fleurimond's cut work is allowed to be " reasonably well made," and Charlotte displays some tapestry cushions, demanding more material in order to finish the last of the set. " I lack silk, I know not what is become of the cushion canvas, my gold and silver is done, I want more black yarn, I have not enough of blue crewel." A very frequent entry in Lady Hoby's diary is : " Sat and wrought with my maids."

A simple country gentleman such as Barnabe Googe describes in his " Foure Bookes of Husbandry " spent his morning peacefully yet busily. Having set his servants to work, he tells us, " I get me into my closet to serve God, and to read the holy Scriptures : (for this order I always keep, to appoint myself every day my task, in reading some part either of the Old Testament or of the New :) that done, I write or read such things as I think most needful, or dispatch what business soever I have in my house, or with suitors abroad. A little before dinner I walk abroad if it be fair, either in my garden or in the fields ; if it be foul, in my gallery : when I come in I find an egg, a chick, a piece of kid, a piece of veal, fish, butter and such like, as my folds, my yard, or my dairy and fish ponds will yield, sometimes a sallet, or such fruits as the garden or orchard doth bear : which victuals without any charges my wife provideth me, wherewith I content myself as well as if I had the daintiest dish in Europe." Meanwhile his wife's occupations were probably those of Lady Hoby, who has many entries such as : " After breakfast I was busy to dye wool " ; " Wound yarn " ; " I did busy myself about making of oil in my closet " ; " Bought a little spinning wheel and span of that."

If we follow Nicholas Breton into the kitchen about ten o'clock he introduces us to a busy scene. Preparations for the midday dinner are in full swing : " the trenchers must be scraped and the napkins folded, the salt covered, and the knives scoured and the cloth laid, the stools set ready and all for the table : there must be haste in the kitchen for the boiled and the roast, provision in the cellar for wine, ale and beer ; the pantler and the butler must be ready in their office, and the usher of the hall must marshal the serving men . . . the cook is cutting sops for broth, and the butler is chipping of loaves for the table."

Hollyband in his " French Schoolemaister " gives us a lively picture of the way in which his good citizen spends a morning. Apparently the day is a holy-day, when shops were required to be shut until morning prayer was over, as the citizen and his gossip are able to go off in company to see a wedding and then to listen to the sermon at Paul's Cross. In the Cathedral they admire the voices of the choir, and then they hasten to take their places amongst the crowd that is already thronging the benches in the churchyard around the Cross. The congregation sings a psalm as the preacher mounts into the pulpit, and then, after the sermon is over, one whispers to the other : " Now the sermon is about ended : let us rise to get out first : let us not tarry for the press " ; so with much elbowing of their way and " By your leave ; let me go by I pray you," they push their way quickly through the throng, and return home to a noonday dinner.

In London some ladies will call their coaches and do their shopping before dinner-time. Erondell's Lady Ri-Mellaine sets out for the Exchange shortly after ten-thirty, accompanied by two friends and a gentleman to escort them. If she takes her two little sons with her she is careful to see that they "wear their clothes gentlemen like " before they start. She inquires whether they have taken clean shirts that morning, orders one boy to button up his doublet tidily, points out to the other that his collar is dirty. The pageboy is sent to fetch their silver-hatched daggers, gets into trouble for not having brushed his young master's breeches overnight, is sent for a brush and made to brush them as they stand in front of their mother. " Lord God how dusty they are ! " she exclaims. " Put on your garters embroidered with silver. . . . Have you clean handkerchers ? Take your perfumed gloves . . . and take your cloaks lined with taffeta and your rapiers with silver hilts."

As they pass through the streets about eleven o'clock they see, newly dismissed from morning school, little groups of schoolboys hastening home for their midday dinner or loitering with their companions. Fashionable people find eleven an early hour for dining, but in the country " the porridge is set a cooling for the plough folk, and the great loaf and the cheese are set ready on the table " ; in Oxford and Cambridge, too, " colleges and halls ring to dinner, and a scholar's commons is soon digested." Even in town the streets and the shops, Paul's Walk and the Exchange begin to empty : the gallants repair to an ordinary at about half-past eleven—the fashionable hour, so Dekker assures his gull. " Ride thither upon your Galloway nag or your Spanish jennet," he advises him : " and being arrived in the room salute not any but those of your acquaintance : walk up and down by the rest as scornfully, and as carelessly as a gentleman usher : select some friend, having first thrown off your cloak, to walk up and down the room with you : . . . discourse as loud as you can, no matter to what purpose : if you make but a noise and laugh in fashion, and have a good sour face to promise quarrelling you shall be much observed." While he waits for the meat to come smoking to the board he should take out his tobacco box and show off his several tricks, such as the whiff and the ring ; and when finally set down to his meal he will eat " as impudently as he can," and twice as quickly as his neighbours. " When your knight is upon his stewed mutton, be you presently . . . in the bosom of your goose ; and when your justice of the peace is knuckle-deep in goose, you may . . . fall very manfully to your wood-cocks." [1]

After his dinner is over the gallant in the ordinary will sit dicing and quarrelling, drinking and playing cards, unless, indeed, he prefers to spend the whole of the time between eleven-thirty and two o'clock sitting over his viands. Googe's country gentleman, however, does not waste his time in this fashion. " I never lightly sit above one hour at my meat," he explains to his friend : " after dinner I pass the time with talking with my wife and servants, or if I have any, with my guests." Then he takes a turn about his grounds, to view the workmen, the pastures the meadows, the corn, and the cattle. " Returning home I go to writing or reading, or such other business as I have : but with study or invention I never meddle in three hours after I have dined. I sup with a small pittance, and after supper I either seldom or never write or read, but rather pass the time is seeing my sheep come home from the field, and my oxen dragging home the plough with weary necks, in beholding the pleasant pastures sweetly smelling about my house, or my herds of cattle lowing hard by me."

Googe, however, has hurried us on too quickly to the

[1] " Gull's Hornbook," Chap. V.

end of the day, for Breton has more to say of twelve o'clock,
and Lady Hoby has some pleasant entries in her diary.
At noon " Duke Humphrey's servants make their walks
in Paul's : the shopmen keep their shops and their servants
go to dinner : the traveller begins to call for a reckoning
and goes into the stable to see his horse eat his provender :
the ploughman now is at the bottom of his dish, and the
labourer draws out his dinner out of his bag : the beasts
of the field take rest after their feed, and the birds of the
air are at juke in the bushes : the lamb lies sucking while
the ewe chews the cud, and the rabbit will scarce peep out
of her burrow : the hare sits close asleep in her muse,
while the dogs sit waiting for a bone from the trencher."
While rich folks are starting upon the second course of
their banquets and beginning to call for wine, the working
man is taking his after-dinner nap. He will be back at his
job long before they have finished the sweetmeats and the
fruit and cheese.

By two o'clock most people have finished their dinner,
and the taverns and ordinaries are emptying fast. The
thoughts of the gallants turn towards the playhouse ;
they consult the first playbill they can find, prominently
displayed upon a post. If the announcement of one of the
Bankside theatres pleases them they will hail a sculler
—or preferably a pair of oars—and be taken across to
Paris Garden stairs. It is a busy hour for the watermen,
one of the best in the day ; their trade suffers badly in
plague time, when the theatres are shut. The play is
due to begin at three o'clock, but the audience gathers
half an hour beforehand or even longer ; by the time the
gallants arrive the pit is full of a noisy crowd, beguiling
the tedium of waiting by jests and friendly scuffles, much
eating of nuts and oranges, and the passing of remarks
upon the costume and appearance of their betters. Some
fashionably dressed youths make their way on to the stage,
where they are accommodated with stools by one of the
boys. One of them spreads his crimson cloak across the
knees of the group, and they engage in a game of cards
till three o'clock strikes. Then the trumpet is blown

to announce the beginning of the play ; the cards are put aside, or thrown about the stage by losers, the pit gradually quietens down, late comers are cursed for treading on other folks' toes, and as the prologue speaks his part or the players begin the scene, the audience turns its attention to the matter in hand.

If the day happens to be a Thursday, however, there will probably be a bull- or a bear-baiting instead of a play. This " royal game " still appealed to all classes—gallants and citizens flocked to it alike, and foreign ambassadors were frequently entertained by the Queen with a special baiting held at Whitehall. Paris Garden itself, on the Bankside, where the public baitings were given, was even at times honoured by the presence of the Queen or of distinguished personages. " It was a sport very pleasant," writes Laneham of the bear-baiting at Kenilworth, " to see the bear with his pink eyes leering after his enemies' approach, the nimbleness and wait of the dog to take his advantage, and the force and experience of the bear again to avoid the assaults. If he were bitten in one place, how he would pinch in another to get free : that if he were taken once, then what shift, with biting, with clawing, with roaring, tossing and tumbling he would work to wind himself from them : and when he was loose to shake his ears twice or thrice with the blood and the slaver about his phisiognomy was a matter of goodly relief."

And while the London gallants applaud the play or the bear-baiting, Lady Hoby up in Yorkshire is as busy as she was in the morning. For a short while after dinner she may perhaps read her " Herbal," or walk in the fields conversing with " Mr. Hoby "—as her husband is always denominated in the diary. But before long she will be up and doing again. " After dinner, " she writes, " I was busy, weighing of wool till almost night." Another time she was " busy about wax lights " : " I did see lights made almost all the afternoon." Sometimes she worked in her garden, especially in the spring. Another entry shows her with her hives : " I went to take my bees and saw my honey ordered." If it is a Sunday we find such entries as, " After

I dined I talked and read to some good wives," or " I went
to talk to my old women."   At other times she and Mr.
Hoby, like Googe's gentleman, survey their estates in
person.   "Took horse and rode to Harwoodall to see our
farm we bought," is one entry ; on another day, " I walked
with Mr. Hoby about the town to spy out the best places
where cottages might be builded."

Erondell's Lady Ri-Mellaine passes a much less energetic
afternoon.   It is three o'clock before she and her guests
rise from the table.   They then walk through the pleasant
gardens, indulging in polite conversation and admiring
the flowers.   One of the ladies expresses a desire for a rod
and line, which a gentleman at once procures for her,
and she finally lands her fish to the plaudits of the rest
of the party.   Even the indefatigable Lady Hoby, however,
occasionally relaxed from her strenuous ways : she, too,
went fishing with her friends.   Another time she records,
" I exercised my body at bowls," and once, at Scarborough,
she actually went on the sea in a boat with some friends.
More frequently she takes her coach and drives to visit
some of her relatives, or else simply drives in the fields to
take the air.   Sometimes, too, there were guests to be
entertained—guests not always so welcome as they might
have been.   " I was visited by a kinswoman," she writes
upon one such occasion, "which was some trouble at the
first, but considering all Crosses ought thankfully to be
borne."

So the afternoon passes away.   The children are let
out of school at five o'clock, and run home for supper.
In the winter time it is already dark, and most of them carry
lanterns to light the way.   They pass workers and labourers
whose day ends at dusk, but in the summer these are at
work until seven or eight o'clock, and the schoolboys meet
only the gallants and the citizens returning from the
play, or the more sober sort returning from evening prayer.
After supper the children are dismissed to bed, but their
elders will not retire for an hour or two in any but the
poorest homes where all must be up and working at dawn.
Googe's country gentleman, especially in winter, likes to

listen in his chaplain reading from the Holy Scriptures
or telling some pleasant story, " so that it be honest and
godly and such as may edify."   Lady Hoby, too, spends the
evening quietly, nor is the business of the estate forgotten
even then.   " After supper," she writes, " I talked a good
time with Mr. Hoby of husbandry and household matters."
Family prayers, in the Hoby household, as in all others
of a similarly devout nature, concluded the day, after which
every one retired to bed.   At Court they might revel it
till midnight or morning when a masque or dancing or a
play was toward, but after a friendly game of cards or an
old wife's tale ordinary people were ready for their night's
rest.

The last scene in Erondell's book " treateth of the
going to bed."   All is bustle in my Lady Ri-Mellaine's
chamber.   " Now maidens," exhorts the children's governess, " is all my lady's night gear ready ? . . . take out of
the way this pewter candlestick which is so foul : make
ready the silver candlesticks with the wax candles, for you
know she cannot endure the smell of tallow, because it doth
most often stink.   Where be the snuffers ?   Where is the
warming pan ? . . ."   When the lady arrives she inquires
the time, and the governess informs her that it is almost
eleven.   " We have been busy at supper," is my lady's
reply, " then afterward we have had dancing . . . then
came a masque which made a fair show.   They played at
cards, at cent, at primero . . . the maidens did play at
purposes . . . so that we could not come sooner.   But
it is all one, we will sleep the longer to-morrow for amends.
Go to, take off my clothes. . . .   Joly help me to put off
my gown, pull off my shoes, give me my pantofles and my
night-gown for fear I catch cold. . . .   Where is the white
hair lace to bind my hairs ? . . . .   Go to, kneel you
down . . . let us say evening prayers."

These said, the children ask their mother's blessing,
which she gives, and then bid her " good night and good
rest."   The maids echo them, " God give you good night
and wholesome rest, Madame," and the lady dismisses
them all with, " I pray God that so it be with you all :

God be with you." All is quiet, within doors and without.
If the lady turns on her pillow an hour or two later, half
awake perhaps for a moment, it will only be to hear the
watchman's "drowsy charm":

> Give ear to the clock, beware your lock,
> Your fire and your light, and God give you goodnight,
> One a clock!

Note.—For a delightful family sketch of Lady Hoby's in-laws, and
especially her mother-in-law, Lady Elizabeth Russell, one of the learned
daughters of Sir Anthony Cooke, sister of Lady Burghley and Lady Bacon,
see *Bisham and the Hobys* in A. L. Rowse's *The English Past* (1951). For
a sketch of Lady Bacon, see the present writer's *The Mother of Francis
Bacon* in *Blackwood's Magazine* (Dec. 1934). For extracts from the
journal of Grace Sherrington, daughter and co-heiress of Sir Henry
Sherrington of Laycock Abbey, Wilts., and wife of Sir Anthony Mildmay
of Apethorpe, Northants., written in her old age and giving a picture of
her childhood and life as a young married woman, see Rachel Weigall,
*An Elizabethan Gentlewoman. The Journal of Lady Mildmay, c. 1570–
1617 : Quarterly Review*, July 1911.

APPENDIX I

THE GOVERNMENT OF LONDON

THE government of the city has always been unique, and as it is difficult to find any brief account of its distinctive features the following summary may prove useful.

For purposes of government London was divided up into twenty-six districts known as Wards. These were not the same as the parishes ; only in two cases did the ward and the parish coincide. Each of these districts had its own Court of Wardmote—a local assembly which managed the affairs of the Ward and which elected its own officials and servants such as the clerk and the constable.

Besides these local tribunals, however, the city as a whole possessed amongst its various courts two that were of prime importance, namely, the Court of Common Council and the Court of Alderman. The latter, consisting of the Lord Mayor and the Aldermen, was the supreme authority ; in it each Ward was represented by its own Alderman, elected previously by the vote of the inhabitants. The former was a larger assembly, composed of the Lord Mayor and Aldermen, and some two hundred citizens, elected annually.

The function of the Court of Common Council was to assist the Lord Mayor and Aldermen, and in practice it gradually became almost entirely concerned with by-laws and such matters as the regulations dealing with the streets ; it passed such orders as that of 1599, which instructed householders to hang out candles to light the ways between the first of October and the first of March. The Court of Aldermen, on the other hand, was the real administrative authority ; it governed the prisons, controlled the finances of the city, appointed the city's chief official, the Recorder, and was the body which either confirmed or annulled the election of anyone aspiring to a city office or dignity. The records of the proceedings of both courts are preserved at the Guildhall in the " Journals " of the Court of Common Council, and the " Repertories " of the Court of Aldermen.

The Aldermen were the direct representatives of the twenty-six wards, elected for life by the inhabitants ; and from their number one was elected annually as Lord Mayor, the chief officer of the city, who, within its bounds, took precedence then as now of all save the King.   The Sheriff, " the eyes of the Mayor," was his chief executive officer, but delegated the actual work to an under-sheriff.   The Recorder was the representative and the legal adviser of the Court of Aldermen ; he was the mouthpiece of the Corporation, and in Elizabethan times was the chief medium of communication between the city and the Privy Council.

W. Herbert's *History of the Twelve Great Livery Companies of London* (1837), and George Unwin's *Gilds and Companies of London* (1908) are the standard works of reference for this subject.   The histories of the individual companies, mostly compiled last century, provide on the whole very little material for this period.   The most outstanding and the most useful to the Elizabethan student are the following:—

C. M. Clode: *Memorials of the Guild of Merchant Taylors.* 1875.

Bower Marsh: *Records of the Worshipful Company of Carpenters:* (see vols. 2–4 for this period). 1913–16.

A. H. Johnson: *History of the Worshipful Company of Drapers:* (see vols. 1 and 2 for this period). 1914–22.

C. Welch: *History of the Cutlers' Company.* 1916–23.

For histories of the Grocers, Barber Surgeons, and Skinners see, respectively, J. B. Heath, S. Young, and J. F. Wadmore. For a complete list of such works reference should be made to Conyers Read's *Bibliography of Tudor History* (1933) and the British Museum's latest *Subject Index.*

APPENDIX II

THE LONDON STREET CRIES

As the music of the cries is not well known the tunes of five of them, together with the Sweep's song and the Cooper's song, are given below. For the music I am indebted to Miss Hilda Andrews, who very kindly transcribed it for me from the manuscript part-books in which the cries have been preserved.

The tunes of a considerable number of the cries, together with an account of the delightful " Fancyes " into which they were elaborated by such musicians as Gibbons, Weelkes, and Deering, can be found in Sir Frederick Bridge's " Old Cryes of London " (1921). The cries of the above three writers have also been published as part-songs by Messrs. Novello (" The Cryes of London," Part-Song Book, 2nd series : Weelkes, No. 1343 ; Gibbons, No. 1345 ; Deering, No. 1346).

20

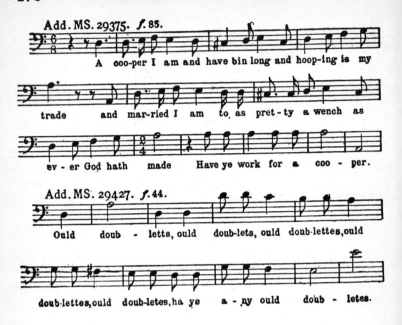

Add. MS. 29375. f. 85.

A coo-per I am and have bin long and hoop-ing is my trade and mar-ried I am to as pret-ty a wench as ev - er God hath made Have ye work for a coo - per.

Add. MS. 29427. f. 44.

Ould doub - letts, ould doub-lets, ould doub-lettes, ould doub-lettes, ould doub-letes, ha ye a - ny ould doub - letes.

APPENDIX III

MONEY AND PRICES

IT is always difficult to relate Elizabethan and modern money values. In 1916 the general view in *Shakespeare's England* was that we had to multiply by five or six to find the modern equivalent. In 1925 R. H. Tawney gave the figure as at least six (Introduction to Wilson's *Discourse of Usury*). In *An Elizabethan Garland*, 1953, A. L. Rowse suggests that we must now multiply by twenty or even twenty-five. But without relevant tables of incomes, wages and prices, and understanding of the Elizabethan social structure, these equivalents have little meaning.

It is interesting, however, to compare Elizabethan values *inter se*, and for this reason the following examples of prices paid have been appended, to supplement those already given in several of the preceding chapters.

1. *Charities, Tips, etc. :*
   To prisoners at Huntingdon, 1s. 8d. Newgate prisoners, 1s. To the Collectors for the repair of Paul's Steeple, 6s. 8d. To the London Waits, 5s. To a boy who presented a posy, 4d. To " one who played a hobby horse " before master and lady of the house, 6s. 8d. " Given at a house where her Grace dried her in the way," 1s. (*Ancaster MSS.*, 1560–62.)

2. *Clothing and Materials :*
   Shoes for children, 7d. a pair. Crimson satin, 3s. a yard. Peach-coloured beaver hat, edged with silver, and with band of cypress, £2. Yellow kersey, 4s. 7d. the ell. Silk points, 6d. a doz. Pair of Valencia gloves, 10d. 8 prs. knitted hose for children, 3s. 4d.
   (*Ancaster MSS.*)

   2 yards Spanish lace, 1s. 2d. Pair of Spanish leather pumps, 1s. 6d. ' Ready made ' shirt with cutwork band, 1s. 1 yd. ' Drake's colour ' velvet, 34s.
   (*Rutland MSS.*)

3. *Food, etc.* .

   A pig, 6d. 420 eggs, 5s. 10d. 400 oranges, 3s. 10d.
   White herrings at 23s. 4d. per barrel. 1 lb. mace, 14s.
   1 lb. cloves, 11s. 1 lb. cinnamon, 10s. 6d. 1 lb. ginger,
   3s. 8d. Hogshead of claret, 50s. Barrel of small
   beer, 4s. 4d. ; of double beer, 7s. (*Ancaster MSS.*)

   1585 : 120 oranges, 2s. 4d. 42 lemons, 7s.
                                          (*Rutland MSS.*)

4. *Miscellaneous :*

   " To a shipman which brought her Grace a canary
   bird," 20s. Pair of scissors, 6d. 1 doz. silver plate
   trenchers, £26. (*Ancaster MSS.*)

   New coach (in London) £38 13s. 2d. (1587–88).
   5 Venice glasses, with covers, 2 without, and 1 for oil
   and vinegar, 39s. Starch, 3d. per lb. A " port man-
   teaw," 4s. 6d. Tobacco, 12s. to 64s. per lb.,
   according to quality. (*Rutland MSS.*)

5. According to Roger's " History of Agriculture and
   Prices " the average prices of the following commodities
   from 1583 to 1603 fluctuated as below :

   Eggs per 100, from 2s. to 6s. 4d.
   Butter per doz. lbs., from 3s. 1¾d. to 5s. 4¼d.
   Cream per gallon, from 10d. to 1s. 10d.
   Sheep, from 6s. 3¼d. to 11s. 6¼d.   (*Vol. 5.*)

The Ancaster accounts refer to the early sixties, and the
Rutland to the eighties and nineties. It must always be
remembered, when dealing with the cost of goods, that money
fell in value throughout the whole Tudor period. In Elizabeth's reign the process would have been to some extent
arrested by her restoration of the coinage debased by her
father, had not the influx into Europe of gold and silver from
the mines of America sent prices up still further. In consequence, although wages rose, their purchasing power diminished.

For everything concerning wages and prices, reference will
eventually have to be made to Sir William Beveridge's exhaustive work on the subject—*Prices and Wages in England from
the Twelfth to the Nineteenth Century*. So far only the first
volume (1939) is available. It contains Elizabethan material.

APPENDIX IV

THE STRUCTURE OF THE THEATRE

AT the moment, with Dr. Leslie Hotson's new book, *The First Night of Twelfth Night*, promised for this year, anything may happen to our ideas about the Elizabethan theatre. Consequently, this sketch remains what it always was—a generalized concept, based on the material and ideas generally accepted. The one thing which can be said with confidence is, that there was no one Elizabethan theatre, and that conditions postulated for e.g. The Globe did not necessarily apply at any other playhouse, nor did they necessarily remain unchanged at the same playhouse. The basic fact about the Elizabethan public stage is that it was an open platform surrounded by an auditorium which, on three sides and sometimes on all sides, brought the whole of a large audience into much closer contact with the actors than is possible in a modern playhouse.

Conjectural reconstructions are based usually upon the following material : (*a*) The builder's contract for the Fortune Theatre (see p. 228 : ed. Greg, *Henslowe Papers*) ; (*b*) The Swan Theatre drawing by A. van Buchell after J. de Witt (University Library, Utrecht) ; (*c*) information derived from texts and stage directions of contemporary plays, and references and descriptions in contemporary writers ; (*d*) the stages represented in the frontispieces of *Messalina* (N. Richards, 1640), *Roxana* (W. Alabaster, 1632), *The Wits* (F. Kirkman, 1672) ; (*e*) the London pictorial maps showing the exteriors of the Globe and other theatres. To this Kernodle, Hodges and R. Southern would now add the street and fairground platforms of the continent, the Rederijker stages of Holland, and the triumphal arches erected both here and abroad for ceremonial occasions (see Hodges, *The Globe Restored*). The most comprehensive and detailed account is *The Globe Playhouse*, by J. C. Adams, but a number of his findings are disputed by Hodges, G. F. Reynolds and other scholars. Information about the functioning of the playhouses, prices of admission, hours of performance, etc., is surveyed in its entirety in E. K. Chambers' *Elizabethan Stage* (vols. II and III). We possess very few facts, much remains conjectural and controversial, and there is still scope for further research ; but the points over which scholars differ do not affect the fundamental fact—that the Shakespearian actor played, literally, in the midst of his audience, and that this intimacy makes a big difference to his performance and our response to it.

Before any theatres were built the players gave their public performances in the courtyards of the inns, their private ones in noblemen's banqueting halls ; naturally, therefore, the design of these buildings, especially when offering any particular conveniences, would influence the ideas of the builders of the permanent playhouses. These inn yards and halls are probably familiar to most people : the one with its balcony running round all four sides of the courtyard beneath the first floor windows ; the other with its minstrels' gallery at one end. In both the natural advantages of the gallery are obvious ; from it the players could hang curtains which would create at the back of their improvised stage a recess which they could utilize either as a dressing-room or for any such specially localized scene as a shop, or a cave, or a bedroom, the curtains being opened or drawn across according to the use to which the recess was being put. Further, the balcony itself offered such obvious opportunities for realistic presentation as many an amateur producer to-day would thankfully grasp. If a scene was supposed to take place upon the walls of a city, the top of a tower, or the balcony of a lady's bedroom, there were these most difficult of all stage properties already in position, and of reliably solid construction. Hence it is easy enough to see why, when they came to designing permanent theatres, the Elizabethans did not invent our modern picture frame stage, but built one made up of two parts —a main stage in the form of an open platform projecting into the part of the yard or hall where the audience stood, and a smaller rear stage with a balcony over it. Given this curtained recess under their gallery at the back of their open platform the absence of a proscenium curtain between them and their audience mattered to the players not at all. Scenes but vaguely localized as " a street " or " a house " could be performed upon the open platform, the players walking off and leaving the stage empty when the scene was over. When, however, the playwright demanded a realistic effort to convince the audience that the scene was the inside of an apothecary's shop, someone's study, or a bedroom in which someone lay dying, it was only necessary to " set " the scene with all the available properties behind the curtains of the rear stage, and at the right moment the apothecary could be discovered compounding his poisons, or the invalid could be revealed in his bed, just as they would be were the curtain to rise upon the same scenes in the modern theatre. Behind and around this inner stage were the rooms used by the actors, known as the tiring-house.

It is generally thought that the earlier theatres were circular in shape, reflecting the structural influence of the bull- and bear-baiting rings shown in the pictorial maps. It was not till the end of the century that the rectangular Fortune Theatre was built. The Globe is usually described as octagonal, and this is the view taken by Adams.

By 1600, with its architectural resources fully developed, the theatre had, above the inner stage, a balcony projecting a few feet from the scenic wall which could be curtained off when necessary. If not used during a performance it could accommodate the musicians or even spectators. The " chamber " over the inner stage, so Adams believes, was divided from the balcony or " tarras " (terrace) only by curtains ; and at each end of the tarras, above the stage-doors, was a bay-window, which could accommodate several actors at a time. Supporting his argument by the structural logic of the three-galleried auditorium, plus the indications given by plays, Adams also makes a good case for yet another gallery, used for the musicians, above the tarras. The " hut " he places above this top gallery, projecting forwards over the canopy. The hut housed the machinery for raising and lowering properties or actors, and these ascents and descents could only have been properly effective if they took place over the main stage. From the turret on top of the hut floated the company's flag on the days when performances were to take place.

The stage was partially protected from the weather by a canopy—" the heavens "—which was supported in front by two pillars, fixed about two-thirds of the distance from the inner stage opening. The surrounding galleries of the auditorium were also roofed, but the central open space, where the " groundlings " stood around the front and the two sides of the stage, was open to the sky. Here, in the " yard "—another obvious relic of the inn-yard days—there were no seats : the " gods " of the Elizabethan theatre may have been noisy, turbulent, captious, but the passion for theatrical performances which kept them standing throughout the play was no mean asset to the drama. Seats were provided only in the galleries, divided-up sections of which bore, like the yard, the trace of their origin in their name of the " rooms ". All paid alike for admission to the building, as a rule the sum of one penny ; then the better sort would make their way to the rooms and the galleries, their payments varying from sixpence to a shilling. For sixpence the gallant who wished to display his new clothes would be accommodated with a stool on the stage. At a " first night " prices seem sometimes to have been doubled. They varied from year to year, and the private theatres charged more than the public playhouses.

Entrance to the stage was provided for by doors leading from the tiring-house, one on either side of the recess. The rear stage was also provided with a door or doors ; it has been suggested that when the curtains were drawn across it was practically a corridor behind the main stage. Access to the gallery was obtained by a stair or stairs within the tiring-house. For purposes of sudden appearances and disappearances the floors of both stage and gallery were provided with trap-doors, by means of which, for example, the witches' cauldron in *Macbeth* would appear and vanish.

To us perhaps, if we really succeed in visualizing it, the most surprising thing about the stage of the Globe or the Fortune will be its size. From the facts and measurements given in the Fortune contract W. H. Godfrey reconstructs a rectangular platform 43 ft. wide, 27 ft. deep, without the inner stage, and projecting some 15 ft. into a " yard " 42 ft. in length and 55 ft. in width (see drawing, *Companion to Shakespeare Studies*). J. C. Adams works out for the Globe a stage 43 ft. across at its widest point and 29 ft. in depth from the front to the curtains of the inner stage. He believes—partly on the evidence of the *Roxana* and *Messalina* pictures —that it tapered from its widest point towards both front and rear ; and suggests a width of 24 ft. for the front of the platform, with 23 ft. for the width of the inner stage, which he takes to be about 7 to 8 ft. deep. He believes the platform to have been about 4 to 5 ft. high, and points out that the height of the inner stage is determined by the height of the first gallery, namely 12 ft. To realise the spaciousness of these stages consider the measurements of some modern theatres. The proscenium opening of Drury Lane is 42 ft. across, of His Majesty's 34 ft., and of the Comedy or the Ambassador's 24 ft., disregarding odd inches. A good indoor set in an ordinary modern production will not as a rule use a depth of more than 16 to 20 ft., out of a total available run-back of anything from 25 to 45 ft. An excellent idea of the possibilities offered by this large Elizabethan stage can be gained from the Harrow School annual performances, directed by Ronald Watkins, whose book *On Producing Shakespeare* gives a most stimulating account of what he has learnt from the practical experience of using it for a decade.

APPENDIX V

HISTORICAL FICTION AND THE ELIZABETHAN PERIOD

IN 1925 it was a comparatively simple matter to list in this Appendix a number of works of fiction which gave the reader a picture of the Elizabethan age in the course of telling a good story. The term " historical novel " was allowed to cover anything not avowedly a " juvenile " ; and contemporary productions in the kind were so few that it was hardly necessary to comment on the fact that " historical fiction " described them more accurately, and that the books it included were not much read by the educated adult. They were, on the whole, the books of one's schooldays, and if they were not read early enough the opportunity for maximum enjoyment was lost.

To-day the situation is very different. When the library of one of our older universities removes Margaret Irwin's " historical novels " from the fiction class, and honours them by entry in the general catalogue, am I to apologize to Miss Irwin for recommending her *Gay Galliard* under this heading? During these intervening twenty years, as a direct result of the publication of Lytton Strachey's *Eminent Victorians* and *Elizabeth and Essex*, biography has steadily encroached upon the domain of the novel—reaching a culminating point, apparently, in Francis Hackett's *Henry VIII*. The novel, however, has retorted with an even more significant raid into biographical territory. Helen Waddell's *Peter Abelard*, Virginia Woolf's *Orlando*, the work of Naomi Mitchison and Margaret Irwin, Rose Macaulay's *They were Defeated*, Robert Graves' *Claudius* volumes, Helen Simpson's *Saraband for Dead Lovers*, Jane Oliver's *Mine is the Kingdom*—to mention only those which I myself find the most outstanding —have brought the historical novel to a triumphant maturity. These are novels—among the most distinguished of our time. Nor are they " sports " ; they stand out against the solid background of a whole group of writers producing good work in the same kind.

The biographical affinities and affiliations which mark our best modern historical fiction now make it easy for us to separate the historical novel proper from the tale of adventure, juvenile or adult. And it must be admitted that while stories set in the Elizabethan age abound—many of them first-rate—Elizabeth the Queen and Elizabeth's England have yet to find their novelist of outstanding quality. Until such appears, Kingsley's *Westward Ho!* will remain our best rendering, in fiction, of the spirit of the time. Within the restricted scope of the short story there is nothing to touch Kipling's *Gloriana* (in *Rewards and Fairies*) for communicating to us, as only an artist can, the feeling for Elizabeth which dominated the mood of her contemporaries. Both are accurate in the use they make of historical scenes, personages, and facts. Kingsley's few chronological slips belong to the careers of his fictitious characters. He was steeped in the literature of the age, and his picture is not only vivid, but substantially true. Partly by temperament, partly by scholarship, he was able so to identify his own attitude of mind with that of his characters, that the book might almost have been written by a passionately Protestant Devon sea-captain. It breathes the very spirit of national loyalty and the intolerance of Spain and the Inquisition that brought the country safely through the Armada crisis.

It is only fair, both to Kingsley and Scott, to rid ourselves of the prevalent idea that *Kenilworth* is the best " novel " about the Elizabethan age. Its author himself called it a " romance " ; and it cannot for a moment be compared with *Westward Ho!* It is liable to prejudice young readers against Scott for the rest of their lives ; and its former popularity is no reason for blinding ourselves to the fact that it is one of his weakest books. Its reputation is largely due to the circumstance that, apart from *Westward Ho!* it was for nearly a century the only work by a great novelist which dealt with the age on an ambitious scale. The " historical " portraits, though reasonably well documented, are stiff and unconvincing ; and the background of the story is tiresomely misleading, because a full but irresponsible use is made of actual events and facts. While insisting on the years in which the story takes place, beginning in " the 18th of Elizabeth ", he makes use of material gathered from any date. Characters refer in 1576 to the Globe and Fortune theatres (cf. p. 228), and quote from *The Tempest, Midsummer Night's Dream* and *Winters' Tale;* while Shakespeare—then a youth of eleven—is referred to as the author of *Venus and Adonis* and a successful player and playwright. *The Fortunes of*

Nigel is a very much better book, and although set in the
reign of James I can be read in connexion with the Elizabethan
period for its pictures of London prentice life and of Alsatia,
the rogue-quarter.

Although only two of them are concerned with the Elizabethan period, R. H. Benson's four Tudor novels should
be read in chronological order. *The King's Achievement*
centres upon Henry's dissolution of the monasteries:
The Queen's Tragedy is a good study of Mary I; and *By
What Authority?* and *Come Rack! Come Rope!* tell in very
human terms the story of the struggle between the old faith
and the new religious compromise in Elizabeth's reign. Benson
knew the Tudor idiom, and there is a quiet authenticity about
his dialogue. Background and detail are good; though his
settings tend to be a trifle too comfortable and over-furnished,
and he is too fond of making men travel by coach when they
would, in fact, have ridden, either a gelding or a mule.

There are at least three good studies of Elizabeth of England :
Judge Parry's *England's Elizabeth;* H. C. Bailey's *The
Lonely Queen;* and Elswyth Thane's *The Tudor Wench.* Book
for book, however, Mary of Scotland still has the advantage,
with Maurice Hewlett's *The Queen's Quair*, Maurice Baring's
In my End is my Beginning, and Margaret Irwin's *Gay Galliard*.
Charlotte M. Yonge's *Unknown to History* will give the young
reader something of the fascination of the Mary Queen of
Scots legend.

Among recent novels three in particular stand out : Jane
Oliver's *Mine is the Kingdom*, centring round the life of
James I before he came to the English throne; John Brophy's
Gentleman of Stratford, a well-written, well-documented
novel about Shakespeare; and Elizabeth Jenkins' *The
Phoenix Nest*, also well-written and well-informed, depicting
the Henslowe–Alleyn–Marlowe theatre group and its doings
(cf. Chap. XIV). In this last connexion, mention should be
made of *Shakespeare's Christmas*, a short story by Quiller
Couch, which includes a lively rendering of the story of the
removal of The Theatre in 1599 (c.f p. 227). *The Ladder of
Swords*, by Gilbert Parker, deals with Elizabeth's connexion
with the Huguenots, and has good portraits of the Queen and
Leicester: *Where England sets her Feet*, by Bernard Capes,
is the story of a base-born son of Leicester, the historical
detail not overdone, but accurate and pleasing. *The Tudor
Rose* by Jesse Berridge, deals throughout with historical

substance, and reveals considerable familiarity with the period ; and it contains, among other good things, a charming and lively description of the rehearsal of a Miracle play. Hugh Walpole's *The Bright Pavilions* will not sustain comparison with his best work; but A. E. W. Mason's *Fire Over England* and *The Three Gentlemen* are stirring tales, told with all the accustomed skill of a master-craftsman.

Out of the many " juveniles " set in the Tudor period there are a few which deserve mention. Popular about forty to sixty years ago they are now almost forgotten, largely because they do not cater for the taste fostered by Harrison Ainsworth, or the more modern boys' adventure story, for thrills, bloodshed and excitement. The interest of these Victorian books lies in the fact that the best of them are, as a rule, founded upon genuine and sometimes out-of-the-way historical and even manuscript material. The ladies who wrote them were enthusiasts, like their contemporary Miss Strickland. Religious prejudice—Protestant, of course—is apt to colour their views ; but as in *Westward Ho!* it helps to lend verisimilitude to the writing. 'Juvenile' these books may be, in that Mr. Bowdler himself could find in them " no offence i' the world "; but they were written by educated gentlewomen, who knew both the literature and the history of the age, and could write the English language—with decorum and taste, if not with inspiration. Their dialogue does not make the reader wince, as some of the more modern and ambitious attempts still do ; and their detail and background is better informed and more accurate than in the modern historical film. Prominent amongst them are the books of Emily Sarah Holt, which build up an amazingly detailed picture of domestic life. Three of these, *Iseult Barry of Wynscote*, *Robin Tremayne* and *Clare Avery*, take the reader from the reign of Henry VIII up to the time of the Armada. She had the right instinct to avoid sequels, and, instead, to anticipate the modern habit of building up a complete world in which old friends out of one book could appear with propriety in the next. With these should be mentioned two of Emma Marshall's stories: *A True Gentlewoman* (1895), in which considerable use is made of Lady Margaret Hoby's M.S. diary (cf. footnote p. 256); and *Penshurst Castle in the time of Sir Philip Sidney*. The detail and dialogue of both are good—in spite of the intrusion of a Victorian family breakfast which would have shocked the more civilized Sidneys. Another story of the

Sidney family is Eliza Pollard's *A Gentleman of England*. The stories of these three writers, and of E. E. Green, can be recommended to the few juveniles who do not insist upon tortures and trapdoors, and prefer a quieter, more domestic note.

Postscript : 1954.—Since this revised appendix was written in 1944 the Tudor period as a whole seems to have become steadily more popular in fiction, with the background of actual historical events interestingly and often carefully handled. Authors have obviously been attracted to the first half of the century, not merely because it has been less exploited than the Elizabethan age but because their interest and that of their readers is now much less dependent upon the tremendous literary associations of that great age and derives greater stimulus from our increasing knowledge and appreciation of social history in general. In many cases, too, where the historian or the biographer finds the documentation too slight for anything more than a brief sketch of a character, the novelists find it a real advantage to have just enough but not too much for the creative imagination to work on without offending against their own sense of fact and its value. It is significant that the two outstanding achievements of the decade belong the one wholly and the other almost entirely to the pre-Elizabethan period. They are, of course, H. F. M. Prescott's two-volume novel *The Man on a Donkey* (1952), and Margaret Irwin's trilogy—*Young Bess* (1944), *Elizabeth, Captive Princess* (1948) and *Elizabeth and the Prince of Spain* (1953), taking the story of Elizabeth's life up to the time of her coronation. Both are conceived on the grand scale, and have taken their place as literature.

Among the recent Elizabethan novels known to the present writer *Crown Imperial* (1949) by J. Delves-Broughton deserves special mention as an unusually intuitive and well-informed character study and life-story of Elizabeth. Ursula Bloom in *The First Elizabeth* tells the story of England in her reign, and in *How Dark my Lady !* handles the private life of Shakespeare ; as do Ruth Holland in *One Crown with a Sun* and Gerald Bullett in *The Alderman's Son*, an imaginary account of the poet's childhood. E. D'Oyley tells the story of Amy Robsart in *Lord Robert's Wife*, and Barbara Willard the story of Sidney's life in *Portrait of Philip*. Jane Lane deals with the Regent Moray in *Parcel of Rogues*, and Jane Oliver with James VI and I in *Crown for a Prisoner*.

BIBLIOGRAPHY

THIS is not a list either of the books consulted by the present writer or of all the books mentioned in the text and footnotes. It is intended to serve as a guide to the general reader who wishes to pursue further some of the particular lines of study suggested by the various chapters. It is of course selective ; and the selection, as far as possible, has been governed by considerations of accessibility. The more advanced student, who wants an exhaustive and annotated bibliography, should always refer to Conyers Read's *Bibliography of Tudor History* (1933) ; also F. W. Bateson's *The Cambridge Bibliography of English Literature*, I (1940), British Museum and London Library latest *Subject Indexes*, and *The British National Bibliography* for 1950 and after. The progress of Elizabethan studies, literary and historical, can best be followed from year to year by reference to such periodicals as *The Review of English Studies*, *Modern Language Review*, *Publications of the Modern Language Association of America*, *The English Historical Review*, *History*, *Bulletin of the Institute of Historical Research* ; also the weekly *Times Literary Supplement*, the English Association's annual *Year's Work in English Studies*, *Shakespeare Survey* (1948, annually), and the Historical Association's *Annual Bulletin of Historical Literature*.

I. GENERAL

(i) CONTEMPORARY MATERIAL :

William Harrison : *Description of England* (1587) ; ed. Furnivall, *New Shakespeare Soc.* (selections from : *Elizabethan England* ; ed. L. Withington ; Scott Library).

Philip Stubbes : *Anatomy of Abuses* (1583) ; ed. Furnivall, *N.S.S.*

John Stow : *Annales of England* (1601).

Statutes of the Realm. 1810–28.

Calendars of Elizabethan State Papers (*Domestic*) : (abstracts of documents preserved in the Public Record Office).

A. Collins : *Letters & Memorials of State* : (" Sydney Papers "): 1746.

Thos. Birch : *Memoirs of the Reign of Queen Elizabeth* : 1754.

Sir John Harington : *Nugae Antiquae* : ed. 1779.

Acts of the Privy Council : ed. J. R. Dasent : 1890–1907.

Original Letters illustrative of English History : ed. Sir Henry Ellis : 1824–46.

Queen Elizabeth & her Times : ed. Thos. Wright : 1838. (Original letters of distinguished persons.)

Illustrations of British History ; ed. E. Lodge : 1838. (Contemporary correspondence.)

Progresses of Queen Elizabeth : ed. John Nichols : 1788–1821. (Rare pamphlets, poems, letters, accounts, etc.)

Letters of Royal & Illustrious Ladies : ed. M. A. E. Wood : (Mrs. Green). 1846.

England as seen by Foreigners : ed. W. B. Rye : 1865. (Contemporary accounts and opinions and references.)

Platter's Travels in England, 1599 : translated by Clare Williams : 1937.

Diary of Henry Machyn : 1555–63 : ed. J. G. Nichols ; Camden Soc. 1844.

Diary of Dr. John Dee : Camden Soc. 1842.

John Chamberlain's Letters : Camden Soc. 1861.

Life in Shakespeare's England : ed. J. Dover Wilson : 1911. (Contemporary literature and documents.)

Tudor Economic Documents : ed. R. H. Tawney and E. Power. 1925.

England in Shakespeare's Day : ed. G. B. Harrison. 1928. (Literary source book.)

Life and Work of the English People (Vol. 1) : ed. D. Hartley and M. M. Elliot. (Pictorial record from contemporary sources.)

The Elizabethan Home : ed. M. St. C Byrne : 3rd ed. revised and expanded : 1949. (The *Dialogues* of Claudius Hollyband and Peter Erondell.)

Elizabethan England : 1533–88 : 9 vols., ed. E. M. Tenison. 1933–53. (Notable for its rare illustrations.)

For *letters, accounts, inventories,* and similar material see the *Transactions* and *Publications* of the various county historical and archæological societies ; as, e.g. *Sussex Archæological Collections* (cf. p. 31), *Berkshire Ashmolean Society* (cf. p. 26) ; also some of the volumes of the *Historical MSS. Commission.*

(ii) MODERN WORKS :

A. F. Pollard : *History of England, 1537–1603* : 1910. (Vol. 6 of Hunt and Poole's *Political History of England.*)

A. D. Innes : *England under the Tudors* : 1905. (Oman's *History of England*.)

E. P. Cheyney : *A History of England from the Defeat of the Armada to the death of Elizabeth* : 2 vols. 1914–26.

J. B. Black : *The Reign of Elizabeth.* 1936.

Shakespeare's England : 2 vols. Oxford Univ. Press : 1916.

Hubert Hall : *Society in the Elizabethan Age.* 1901.

H. T. Stephenson : *Elizabethan People.* 1910.

H. and M. Quennell : *History of Everyday Things in England* : Vol. 2 ; 1919.

G. B. Harrison : *An Elizabethan Journal* : 3 vols. 1928–33.

A Companion to Shakespeare Studies : ed. Granville Barker and G. B. Harrison. 1934.

L. B. Wright : *Middle Class Culture in Elizabethan England.* 1935.

A. L. Rowse : *Tudor Cornwall.* 1941.

M. Campbell : *The English Yeoman under Elizabeth and the Early Stuarts:* 1944.

J. N. Figgis : *Theory of the Divine Right of Kings :* 1914.

J. W. Allen : *History of Political Thought in the 16th Century* : (pt. ii) 1928.

H. O. Taylor : *Thought and Expression in the 16th Century* : Vol. 2 : 1920.

Lewis Einstein : *Tudor Ideals:* 1921.

Social and Political Ideas of the Renaissance and Reformation : 1925 : *Social and Political Ideas of the 16th and 17th Centuries* : 1926. ed. F. J. C. Hearnshaw.

II. SPECIAL SUBJECTS

ARCHITECTURE AND FURNITURE (all illustrated).

J. A. Gotch : *The Growth of the English House.* 1909. *Architecture of the Renaissance in England.* 1894. *Early Renaissance Architecture in England.* 1914. *Architecture* : (*Shakespeare's England* : II 17 § 3).

J. Nash : *Mansions of England in the Olden Time* : ed. C. Holme. 1906.

T. Garner and A. Stratton : *Domestic Architecture.* 1908.

H. Avray Tipping : *English Homes.* 1922–24.

Aymer Vallance : *Art in England during the Elizabethan and Stuart Period.* 1908.

A. Stratton : *The English Interior.* 1920.

P. MacQuoid : *History of English Furniture.* 1904–8.

MacQuoid and Edwards : *Dictionary of English Furniture.* 1924.

M. Jourdain : *English Decoration and Furniture of the Early Renaissance,* 1500–1650. 1924.

Costume :

P. MacQuoid : *Costume* : (*Shakespeare's England* : II 19.)

H. Norris : *Costume and Fashion* : *The Tudor Period* : 2 vols. 1938.

F. M. Kelly : *Shakespearian Costume for Stage and Screen.* 1938.

M. C. Linthicum : *Costume in the Drama of Shakespeare and his Contemporaries.* 1936.

F. M. Morse : *Elizabethan Pageantry.* 1934.

M. Stone : *The Bankside Costume Book.* 1913. (Useful for schools for Shakespearian plays : inexpensive.)

Education :

Roger Ascham : *The Scole Master* : (1573) : Arber's *English Reprints.* 1895.

Richard Mulcaster : *Positions.* 1581.
The First Part of the Elementarie. 1582.

John Brinsley : *Ludus Literarius* : (1612). ed. E. T. Campagnac : 1917.

Foster Watson : *Tudor Schoolboy Life.* 1908.
English Grammar Schools to 1660. 1908.
Beginnings of the Teaching of Modern Subjects in England. 1909.
Old Grammar Schools. 1916.

C. Mallett : *History of the University of Oxford.* 1925.

J. B. Mullinger : *The University of Cambridge.* 1873–1911.

J. W. Adamson : *The Extent of Literacy in England in the 15th and 16th Centuries. The Library* : X : 1929.

J. H. Brown : *Elizabethan Schooldays.* 1933.

N. Wood : *The Reformation and English Education.* 1931.

T. W. Baldwin : *William Shakespeare's Petty School.* 1943.
William Shakspere's Small Latine and Lesse Greeke. 1944.

The Land (see Chapters V–VIII).

John Leland : *Itinerary* : ed. L. Toulmin Smith. 1906–10.

W. Camden : *Britania* : translated by Holland. 1610.

J. A. R. Marriott : *English Land System.* 1914.

A. H. Johnson : *Disappearance of the Small Landowner.* 1909.

R. H. Tawney : *Agrarian Problem in the 16th Century.* 1912. *Religion and the Rise of Capitalism.* 1926.

G. Slater : *Inclosure of the Common Fields considered geographically* : *Geographical Journal* : January, 1907.

E. M. Leonard : *Inclosure of the Common Fields in the 17th Century* : *Trans. R. Historical Soc. XIX.*

The Victoria County Histories.

The Countryman's Jewel : *Days in the Life of a 16th Century Squire* : ed. M. M. Woodward. (An informative account of country life, compiled from the writings of Leonard Mascall by W. A. Woodward.)

For *Gardens* see *Shakespeare's England* : I, 12. ; also

R. Blomfield : *The Formal Garden in England* : 3rd ed. 1936.

E. Sinclair Rohde : *Shakespeare's Wild Flowers, Fairy Lore, Gardens, Herbs, etc.* 1935.

LONDON :

Stow : *Survey of London,* 1598, 1603 : ed. C. L. Kingsford. 1908.

T. F. Ordish : *Shakespeare's London.* 1904.

H. B. Wheatley : *The Story of London.* 1904.

H. T. Stephenson : *Shakespeare's London.* 1903.

M. C. Salaman : *London Past and Present.* 1916.

G. E. Mitton : *Maps of Old London.* (Contains Agas', Wyngaerde's, Hoefnagel's and Norden's.)

MUSIC :

W. Barclay Squire : *Music* : (*Shakespeare's England,* II, 17 §2).

W. H. Hadow : *Music.* 1924. (Home University Library.)

E. Walker : *History of Music in England* : (Chs. III, IV). 1907.

G. H. Cowling : *Music on the Shakespearian Stage.* 1913.

F. W. Galpin : *Old English Instruments of Music.* 1910.

E. J. Dent : *Shakespeare and Music* : (*Companion to Sh. Stud.*) 1934.

RELIGION :

See Pollard, Innes, and *Shakespeare's England, ut supra.*

Henry Gee : *The Reformation Period* : 1909. (Brief general survey, mainly concerned with earlier Tudor reigns.)
Elizabethan Clergy and the Settlement of Religion : 1898.

H. N. Birt : *The Elizabethan Religious Settlement.* 1907. (The Catholic view-point : should be read to offset Gee, *supra*.)

J. H. Pollen : *The English Catholics in the Reign of Elizabeth.* 1920.

A. F. S. Pearson : *Thomas Cartwright and Elizabethan Puritanism.* 1925.
Church and State : *Political Aspects of 16th Century Puritanism.* 1928. (A more general study, deriving from the preceding.)

SOCIAL CONDITIONS, POOR LAWS, ETC. :

J. Thorold Rogers : *History of Agriculture and Prices* : Vols. 3–6. 1882–7.
Six Centuries of Work and Wages. 1890.

S. L. Ware : *The Elizabethan Parish.* 1882. (Johns Hopkins Univ. Studies, Hist. and Political Science.)

C. A. Beard : *The Office of Justice of the Peace in England.* 1904. (Columbia Studies in Hist., Econ., and Public Law.)

E. P. Cheyney : *Social Changes in England in the 16th Century.* 1891. (Pennsylvania Univ. Publications.)

W. J. Ashley : *Economic History* : Vol. 2. 1893.

E. M. Leonard : *Early History of English Poor Relief.* 1900.

W. Cunningham : *Growth of English Industry* : Vol. 2. 1903.

G. Unwin : *Industrial Organizations.* 1904.

S. and B. Webb : *English Local Government.* 1906–8.

F. Aydelotte : *Elizabethan Rogues and Vagabonds.* 1913.

E. Trotter : *17th Century Life in a Country Parish.* 1919.

F. P. Wilson : *Plague Pamphlets of Thomas Dekker.* 1925.
The Plague in Shakespeare's London. 1927.

Tudor Economic Documents : Tawney and Power : *ut supra.*

Campbell : *English Yeoman* : *ut supra.*

SPORT AND AMUSEMENTS :

D. H. Madden : *The Diary of Master William Silence.* 1897.

H. T. Stephenson : *Elizabethan People* : *ut supra.*

Shakespeare's England : II, 27. (Deals with every kind of outdoor sport, games, dancing and indoor games.)

THE THEATRE :

E. K. Chambers : *The Elizabethan Stage* : 4 vols. 1924.
William Shakespeare : 2 vols. 1930.

B. M. White : *Index to " Elizabethan Stage " and " William Shakespeare "*. 1934.

W. W. Greg : *Henslowe's Diary* and *Henslowe Papers*. 1904–8.
Two Elizabethan Stage Abridgements. 1922.
Dramatic Documents from the Elizabethan Playhouses. 1931.

V. E. Albright : *The Shakespearian Stage*. 1909.

A. H. Thorndike : *Shakespeare's Theatre*. 1916.

W. J. Lawrence : *The Elizabethan Playhouse*. 1912–13.
Pre-Restoration Stage Studies. 1927.
Shakespeare's Workshop. 1928.
Those Nut-cracking Elizabethans. 1935.

H. Granville Barker: *Prefaces to Shakespeare*: 5 vols. 1927-47.

Shakespeare and the Theatre : Papers by members of the Shakespeare Association. 1927.

C. J. Sisson : *The Theatres and the Companies* : (*Comp. to Sh. Stud.*) 1934.

V. C. Gildersleeve : *Government Regulation of the Elizabethan Drama*. 1908.

T. W. Baldwin : *Organization and Personnel of the Shake-spearian Company*. 1927.

A. Harbage : *Shakespeare's Audience*. 1941.

J. C. Adams : *The Globe Playhouse*. 1942.

Greening Lamborn and G. B. Harrison : *Shakespeare the Man and his Stage*. 1923. (Brief, accurate, inexpensive ; useful for schools.)

Shakespeare's England : II, 24, 25.

M. C. Bradbrook : *Elizabethan Stage Conditions*. 1932.

G. F. Reynolds : *The Staging of Elizabethan Plays at the Red Bull Theatre*. 1940.

G. R. Kernodle : *From Art to Theatre*. 1944.

Shakespeare Survey : ed. Allardyce Nicoll. 1948 (annually).

See also *articles* in

Joseph Quincy Adams : *Memorial Studies*, 1948. " The Original Staging of King Lear ": J. C. Adams. " Troilus and Cressida on the Elizabethan Stage ": G. F. Reynolds.

Theatre Notebook, Vol. 1, No. 8, 1947. " The Globe Play-house : Some Notes on a New Reconstruction." C. Walter Hodges.

III. BIOGRAPHY

Since the original publication of this book in 1925 Tudor biography has become increasingly valuable to the student of sixteenth-century life. A list of some of the more outstanding volumes and of those of the most general interest has therefore been added to this present edition.

For the first half of the century A. F. Pollard's *Henry VIII* (1913 ed.) and *England under the Protector Somerset* (1900) are indispensable ; and there are two good recent biographies of Queen Mary by Beatrice White and H. F. M. Prescott. *Great Tudors* (ed. K. Garvin, 1935) is a useful collection of brief lives, covering the whole country. G. Scott Thomson's *Two Centuries of Family History : a Study in Social Development :* (1930) is an admirable example of the way in which biographical writing can illuminate our understanding of the life of the period. Agnes Strickland's *Elizabeth,* in her *Lives of the Queens of England* should be read. The modern authoritative life is J. Neale's *Queen Elizabeth* (1934). One of the best of the short lives is C. Williams's *Queen Elizabeth* (1936) ; and Milton Waldman's *Elizabeth, Queen of England* (1933) is a sympathetic and interesting study but unfortunately ends with the Armada year. The titles that follow are not of equal value, *inter se,* historically ; but they have been selected to cover as wide a range of interest as possible.

Conyers Read : *Mr. Secretary Walsingham and the Policy of Queen Elizabeth.* 1925.
   The Tudors. 1936.
C. Goff : *A Woman of the Tudor Age.* 1930. (Life of Katharine Willoughby.)
E. Waugh : *Edmund Campion.* 1935.
E. K. Chambers : *Sir Henry Lee.* 1936.
D. Coke : *The Last Elizabethan : Sir John Coke* 1563-1644. 1937.
G. B. Harrison : *The Life and Death of Robert Devereux, Earl of Essex.* 1937.
A. L. Rowse : *Sir Richard Grenville of the " Revenge ".* 1937.
M. W. Wallace : *Life of Sir Philip Sidney.* 1915.
C. H. Warren : *Sir Philip Sidney.* 1936.

Milton Waldman : *Sir Walter Raleigh.* 1928.
    Elizabeth and Leicester. 1944.
Edward Thompson : *Sir Walter Raleigh.* 1935.
R. M. Sargent : *At the Court of Queen Elizabeth.* 1935. (Sir
    Edward Dyer.)
Philip Henderson : *Morning in his Eyes.* 1937. (Marlowe.)
J. Bakeless : *Christopher Marlowe.* 1938.
F. S. Boas : *Christopher Marlowe.* 1940.
F. A. Yates : *John Florio.* 1934.
Edith Sitwell : *Fanfare for Elizabeth.* 1946.
For Nashe see *Works*, ed. R. B. McKerrow (1904–10) ; for
    Webster see *Works*, ed. F. L. Lucas (1927) ; for minor
    writers, ref. Bateson's *Cambridge Bibliographies* (vol. I).
For Shakespeare see under *Theatre, supra.*

IV. LITERARY CRITICISM
(Recent developments)

For perhaps the last forty years the main trend of Elizabethan literary criticism has been directed away from purely
aesthetic appreciation. Three tendencies can be distinguished.
First in point of time, and largely responsible for this general
direction, is the bibliographical work initiated by A. W.
Pollard, W. W. Greg and R. B. McKerrow, dealing with all
problems concerning the texts and their transmission—in other
words, the attempt to determine what Elizabethan authors
actually wrote. Secondly, comes the type of criticism which
seeks to relate the text to its historical, political and social
background ; and which may or may not proceed to literary
evaluation. Thirdly, there is the attempt to outline the
general scheme of things, religious and philosophical, against
which Elizabethan literature as a whole must be viewed. As
these two latter are concerned with the way of life and the
background of thought shared to a greater or less extent by
all men, and are therefore relevant to this present study, a
short list of such books is given. T. S. Eliot's *The Sacred
Wood* and L. C. Knights' *How many children had Lady
Macbeth ?* provide a good introduction to the modern approach,
on the more purely literary side.

L. Winstanley : *Hamlet and the Scottish Succession.* 1921.
    Macbeth, King Lear, and Contemporary History. 1922.

E. G. Clark: *Elizabethan Fustian* (vol. I: general study of social, political and topical reference in drama): 1937.

W. L. Renwick: *Edmund Spenser.* 1925.

B. E. C. Davis: *Edmund Spenser.* 1933.

J. Dover Wilson: *What happens in Hamlet.* 1935. *The Fortunes of Falstaff.* 1943.

C. E. F. Spurgeon: *Shakespeare's Imagery: and what it tells us.* 1935.

Hardin Craig: *The Enchanted Glass. The Elizabethan Mind in Literature.* 1936. English edn. 1950. (Good bibliography.)

Theodore Spencer: *Shakespeare and the Nature of Man.* 1942.

E. M. Tillyard: *The Elizabethan World Picture.* 1943.

L. B. Campbell: *Shakespeare's "Histories", Mirrors of Elizabethan Policy.* 1947.

Edwin Muir: *The Politics of King Lear.* 1947.

Paul H. Kocher: *Christopher Marlowe. A Study of his Thought, Learning, and Character.* Chapel Hill. Univ. N. Carolina Press. 1946.

V. LITERARY MATERIAL

The references throughout the text indicate the kind of work upon which the present writer has drawn. Much information can be gleaned from *plays*, especially, perhaps, Shakespeare, Jonson, Dekker, Thomas Heywood and Middleton. The *satirical work* of Sir John Davies, Joseph Hall, Samuel Rowlands, Guilpin, etc., yields vivid scenes and character sketches, but must naturally be interpreted with some caution. The *pamphlets* of Greene, Nashe, Dekker and Lodge are particularly useful for *London Life* in its more sensational aspects. For *ordinary daily life* there is nothing to compare with the *dialogues* of Claudius Hollyband and Peter Erondell, drawn upon freely for this book. (Extracts accessible to modern readers in *The Elizabethan Home*, edited by the present writer.) For lively dialogues depicting *contemporary scenes and manners*, see John Eliot's *Ortho-epia Gallica* (1593). In *Shakespeare Survey 6* J. W. Lever argues very convincingly that this book was well-known to Shakespeare, and that passages in *Henry V* derive from and are explained by Eliot's work ("Shakespeare's French Fruits", pp. 79-90). Extracts from Eliot are available in *The Parlement of Prattlers*, ed. Jack Lindsay: 1928. Deloney's tales (*Works*, ed. F.-O. Mann) gives pleasant incidental pictures of *daily life* and festivities. The prose and verse of Churchyard and

Breton (*Works*, ed. Grosart) should be explored, and Tusser's *Five Hundreth Points of Good Husbandry* gives much interesting information about *country life*.

For a useful series of modern facsimile reprints, see *The Bodley Head Quartos*, ed. G. B. Harrison. A. V. Judges' *Elizabethan Underworld* is a good collection of " rogue " tracts and ballads.

SUPPLEMENTARY LIST 1954

(See also Notes on pp. 16, 101, 122, 175, 255 for additional titles and special chapter references.)

GENERAL

S. T. Bindoff : *Tudor England*. (Vol. 5 of Pelican 8-vol. history of development of English Society.) 1951.

J. E. Neale : *The Elizabethan Age*. (Creighton Lecture in History.) 1951.

A. L. Rowse : *The England of Elizabeth*. (Vol. I.) 1950.

G. M. Trevelyan : *Illustrated English Social History*. (Vol. 2.) 1950.

SPECIAL SUBJECTS

John Summerson : *Architecture in Britain 1530–1830*. (Part I.) (Pelican History of Art.) 1953.

Margaret Whinney : *Renaissance Architecture in England*. 1952.

Graham Reynolds : *Elizabethan and Jacobean 1558–1625*. Vol. III, Pt. 3 of *Costume of the Western World*, ed. J. Laver. 1951.

C. W. & P. Cunnington : *The History of Underclothes*. (Ch. II.) 1951.
  Handbook of English Costume in the 16th Century. 1954.

(See also for costume, C. De Banke, *Shakespearian Stage Production* (*infra*).

J. E. Neale : *The Elizabethan House of Commons*. 1949.
  Queen Elizabeth I and her Parliaments 1559–81. 1953.

J. C. Drummond & A. Wilbraham : *The Englishman's Food*. (Pts. I and II). 1939.

G. E. Fussell : *The English Rural Labourer*. (Pt. I.) 1949.

Christina Hole : *English Sports and Pastimes*. 1949.

C. de Banke : *Shakespearian Stage Production Then and Now*. 1953.

C. W. Hodges : *The Globe Restored*. 1953.

R. Watkins : *On Producing Shakespeare*. 1950.

INDEX

London—*contd.*
  countrified aspect of, 56, 57
  gardens, 57, 58
  lighting of, 52
  Lord Mayor and Aldermen, 52,
    62, 143, 144, 226, 235–237
  Lord Mayor's Show, 216
  maps of, 46
  overcrowding, 50, 51
  Royal Exchange, 50, 69–73
  St. Paul's, 49, 64–66
  shop signs, 63
  street cries, 60–62, 74, 78
  streets, 52–54
  suburbs, 54, 55
  taverns, 74 ff.
  the Bridge, 48
  the watch, 78, 79, 270
  underworld of, 76 ff.
  Whitehall, 50, 73
Lupton, Donald, 127
Lyly, John, 12, 58, 249

Machyn, Henry, 62, 63, 76
Manners, 30, 194
  at table, 180
  books on, 178, 194
Manorial System, 113 ff.
Manuscripts :
  in Bodleian Library—
    Ashmole, 4
  in British Museum—
    Additional, 56, 60, 62
    Egerton, 256
    Harleian, 12, 93, 94
    Lansdowne, 153
  private, printed by Historical
    MSS. Commission—
    Ancaster, 25, 29, 41–43,
      131, 137, 220–222
    Rutland, 25–27, 29, 42
Market days, 95
Marlowe, Christopher, 200, 238,
  239, 254
Marvels, 246, 247, 248. *See also*
  Beast-lore
Mary, Queen of Scots, 159, 170
Masques, 219
Mayne, Cuthbert, 168
Meals, 30 ff.
  breakfast, 30, 35
  dinner, 30, 32, 34
  drinking vessels, 30
  forks, 31, 33

Meals—*contd.*
  knives, 30
  salt cellars, 30
  spoons, 31
  supper, 34
  tablecloths, 30
  table napkins, 30. *See also* Food
Middlesex, 96 ff., 112, 113
" Mockbeggar Hall " (ballad), 103
Monasteries, suppression of, 102,
  117
Montague, Anthony Viscount, 31
  ff., 141
Moon-men, 151
More, Sir Thomas, 179, 180
Moreton Old Hall, 20, 21
Morton, Cardinal, 179
Moryson, Fynes, 49, 85
Mulcaster, Richard, 182, 184,
  191, 192, 210
Munday, Anthony, 95, 216, 258
Music, 192, 221–223

Nashe, Thomas, 63, 64
Nichol's " Progresses," 30, 31,
  38, 42, 206, 221
Nonconformists, 171 ff.
Norden, John, 47, 82, 92–101,
  111, 113, 258
Norfolk, 108, 112
Northamptonshire, 20, 93, 100,
  110, 111
Northamptonshire, Earl of, 42
Northumberland, 93
Nottingham, Earl of, 236

Omens, 248, 249
Ortelius, 254
Overbury, Sir Thomas, 124, 125,
  137, 207
Oxford, carriers to, 86. *See also*
  Universities
Oxford, Earl of, 200
Oxfordshire, 20, 110, 111

Painted cloths, 23
Palliards, 87, 88
Paris Garden, 48, 226, 267
Parish clerk, 119, 121
  the, 117 ff.
Parsons, Robert, 168, 169, 170
Pedlars, 136, 137
Pembroke, Earl of, 48